CARDIFF
SPORTING GREATS

CARDIFF
SPORTING GREATS

EDITED BY ANDREW HIGNELL
AND GWYN PRESCOTT

Learning Resources
Centre

12961647

First published 2007

STADIA is an imprint of
Tempus Publishing
Cirencester Road, Chalford
Stroud, Gloucestershire, GL6 8PE
www.npi-mediagroup.com

British Library Cataloguing in Publication Data.
A catalogue record for this book is available from the British Library.

ISBN 978 0 7524 4286 0

Typesetting and origination by NPI Media Group
Printed in Great Britain

INTRODUCTION

Cardiff is a city with a vibrant sporting community, and is the home to many professional clubs, as well as amateur sporting organisations. It also boasts a diverse range of teams and clubs offering opportunities for healthy recreation and entertainment for the many people of all ages who live in the Cardiff region.

The city's sporting stadia – both past and present – have been integral parts of the urban landscape, and it is a measure of Cardiff's standing in world sport that people know about the Welsh capital by having watched games – either in person or on television – at the Arms Park or Millennium Stadium.

Cardiff's sporting facilities are soon to be further enhanced by the creation of a new home for both the city's football and regional rugby team at Leckwith, incorporating a state-of-the-art base for the professional sportsmen, as well as world-class facilities for the city's athletes. The next couple of years will also see the opening of an international sports village in Cardiff Bay, and the redevelopment of Sophia Gardens – the headquarters of Glamorgan Cricket – that will result in the creation of a Test match ground that, in 2009, will host an Ashes encounter between England and Australia.

It is also a city with a rich and proud sporting heritage, with some of the world's greatest sporting names having appeared at the Arms Park, Ninian Park, Roath Park, Sophia Gardens, or at some of the city's past sporting venues such as Ely Racecourse, Maindy Stadium or the Empire Pool. Cardiff also has a long tradition of hosting national and international sporting events, and a richly deserved reputation for successfully staging these contests.

This book celebrates the achievements of many of the city's greatest sportsmen and women, and some of the most famous Cardiffians. We have included the sons and daughters of the city, its suburbs and its immediate hinterland who have achieved fame and fortune in the world of sport – both amateur and professional – as well as others who were born elsewhere but have moved to the Welsh capital, representing the city with distinction or becoming key figures in the administration and promotion of sport.

Just like selecting any sports team or squad, there were many candidates who deserved inclusion in our final line-up. Expert advice was sought from many quarters and, in some cases, there was plenty of debate before making our eventual choices. No doubt discussions will occur over the merits of those who were not included.

Our thanks to Rob Sharman and his colleagues at Tempus Publishing for inviting us in the first place to compile this book, and then subsequently giving us their advice and support during the production process. We are very grateful as well for the support of CC4, the Cardiff-based multimedia company. Our thanks also to our wives for their patient understanding as we spent many hours collating material and undertaking research, and many thank also to Anna Smith and her assistant, Victoria Rogers, at Cardiff's Old Library, who have co-ordinated an exhibition about the city's sporting greats at which this book was formally launched.

The men and women in this volume, as well as Cardiff's sporting stars of the future, fully deserve to have their feats and achievements celebrated on a permanent basis and, if there is the creation of a permanent exhibition at the planned Cardiff Local History Museum, we hope that this book will have assisted in the selection process.

Andrew Hignell
Gwyn Prescott
March 2007

ACKNOWLEDGEMENTS

The editors would like to thank all of the contributors for their excellent profiles. In addition, they would like to thank the following for their help with biographical research and the provision of photographs and other images: Katrina Coopey and the staff of the Local Studies Department at Cardiff Central Library, Cardiff City Council, Elizabeth Mobey-Gilbert, Tony Woolway, Susan Edwards and the staff at the Glamorgan County Record Office, John Loosemore, Suzy Braddick, Stewart Williams, Cardiff City FC, Howard Evans, Bryn Jones, Josie Rolls, Hills Welsh Press, Eric Hodge, David Edwards, Don Skene, David Herbert, Pearl Riches, Enid Wooller, Rob Cole, Monkton House School, *Western Mail* and *South Wales Echo*, UWIC, Glamorgan Record Office, Simon Turnbull, Downside School and Abbey, the late Haydn Wilkins, Phil Judd, Phil Blanche, Peter Jackson, Paul Rees, Simon Thomas, Lawrence Hourahane, Tim Auty, Mike Fatkin, Huw John, Wayne Thomas, Dave Cobner, Ron Jones, Glynne Clay, Onllwyn Brace, Dylan Jones, John Williams-Davies, Chris Mann, Siân Prescott, Richard Murray, Mrs J. Washer, Ian Dixon, Alan Evans, Neil Robinson, Glenys Williams, Adam Chadwick and the MCC Library, Duncan Gardiner, Martin Johnnes, Huw Owen and Welsh Athletics.

Cardiff Arms Park – the city's theatre of sporting dreams, as seen in June 1930.

CARDIFF SPORTING GREATS

An alphabetical index can be found at the back of the book.

ADDITIONAL FEATURES

GARETH EDWARDS AND BARRY JOHN

'Wales' greatest melody-makers'
by John Billot

As a partnership, they were the Richard Rodgers and Oscar Hammerstein of rugby. Melody and rhythm proved abundantly evident in everything they did. Gareth Edwards and Barry John were the supreme half-backs, together on 23 occasions for Wales and for Cardiff between 1967 and 1972. Gareth made his debut at scrum half for Cardiff in September 1966 when aged only nineteen, and he immediately impressed the selectors. A year later Barry joined and the two were soon regarded as the greatest half-back pairing in the club's long and distinguished history.

They were also the pair who launched the unforgettable decade of success for Welsh rugby in the 1970s. Barry enjoyed the uncanny power of persuading opponents he could pop up in two places simultaneously. They called him 'The King' for his exploits in New Zealand during 1971, when the British Lions won the Test series for the first time, a feat still to be equalled. Inside him, Gareth was no less a dominating force in the no.9 shirt. A natural gymnast and a former British junior record holder in the hurdles, Gareth was an amazing mixture of muscle and reflexes. Give him a sniff of an opportunity and no player grasped it with more alacrity. Fittingly, he was chosen as the greatest Welsh rugby player of all time by the Welsh Rugby Former Players Association in 2002.

Most of Gareth's 20 tries for Wales were breathtaking. Who will ever forget his break down the touchline against Scotland at the National Stadium in 1972? His kick-on and chase to score from almost ninety metres in the red mud in the south corner shocked Scotland like it was Culloden all over again.

That was a great solo try, but what about his great team try, again at the Arms Park, in January 1973 for the Barbarians against New Zealand? It was part of a blistering combined attack that left the All Blacks in complete disarray, and swept the length of the field after Phil Bennett had launched it under the shadows of the posts at the Barbarians end. His colleagues then counter-attacked with verve, and who was at the end of the series of deft passes that opened up the defence like a can of worms? Gareth, of course! His swift and elusive running brought to mind the words of that popular American song, 'The Runaway Train'. 'Number 9 came roaring down the track,' as Gareth built up an impressive head of steam to be there at the climax. It was one of the most spectacular tries of all time, and was the catalyst in the 23-11 victory over the Kiwis.

To have witnessed Gareth and Barry in action together was to have feasted at the table of the gods. Those who were fortunate to do so, either for Cardiff or Wales, can go to their maker content and eager to regale the angels with tales of the devastating duo. Barry floated rather than ran; everything he did appeared almost in slow motion compared with the more dynamic urgency of Cliff Morgan, David Watkins and Phil Bennett. Such was Barry's supernatural perception that he knew when a gap would open up before it had. Most outside halves create openings. Barry seemed to will them to appear; a personal invitation to explore and exploit unguarded space. He was, in this respect, the original space invader.

Alas, he was for too short a time the brilliant comet streaking across the rugby cosmos. After representing Wales in only 25 matches, he quit the game at the age of twenty-seven, overwhelmed by the hero worship and hype of being a superstar. Barry confessed he felt uncomfortable and wanted a quieter life as a media pundit. A lovely man, he deserves to enjoy life as he wished. I first saw him playing – then in his days with Llanelli – for Carmarthenshire in the Welsh Counties Championship. Barry dropped two goals; one with his right foot and then one with his left – not a bad trick. There was an innate sense of destiny in everything he did. This youngster – then learning the ropes with the big boys at Stradey Park – was something special.

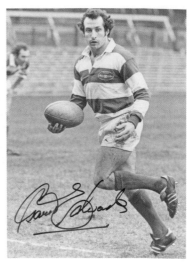

Above left: Gareth Edwards and Barry John.

Above right: Gareth the Great.

Gareth was no great shakes at first with his service from the set-piece when he broke into the Cardiff side from the Cardiff College of Education (now UWIC). But the youngster from Gwaun-cae-Gurwen worked on it and, lo and behold, there blossomed a scrum-half who perfected the ultra-long spin-pass. Everything after that was a bonus. And what bonuses he brought to the Welsh team with some heart-stopping breaks and 20 tries. He chipped calculatingly and rolled the ball into corners with faultless precision. Such has grown the legend of this astonishing player, there are some who insist Gareth could never miss a touch-finder if he tried! Ah, that life could be so idyllic. He launched his international career in 1967, but was on the winning side just twice in his first seven games – that was soon to change.

No captain could have been more blessed than John Dawes to have such half-back talent at his command with the 1971 British Lions in New Zealand. Dawes was a leader with the acumen of a Marius, Sulla, Pompey, Caesar and Scipio Africanus, and to have Gareth at no.9, and Barry at no.10, plus Gerald Davies and J.P.R. Williams was a luxury of gargantuan proportions. With that kind of material, there would have been no bridge too far at Arnhem!

When Barry joined Cardiff from Llanelli, his wing forward brothers, Alan and Clive, relished their duty of tracking him down whenever the two teams clashed. Barry's renowned glide to slice defences left bemused New Zealanders chuntering with rage. 'Pin him down like a butterfly,' was the All Blacks' order of the day. Some hope! He was never a member of the Suicide Runners Club; Barry sought the unfettered acres to congested midfield traffic, though even from tight corners he could materialise as if ejected from a pantomime trapdoor.

Barry made his Welsh debut in 1966 against Australia, partnering Abertillery's smooth-serving Allan Lewis. It was a game that saw the Wallabies win for the first time in Wales 14-11. Then, when Scotland won the opening fixture of the 1967 Five Nations 11-5 at Murrayfield, David Watkins was back in the hot seat. But at the end of the year, it was Barry and Gareth together for the first time when New Zealand arrived for their short visit and triumphed at the Arms Park. In fact, Barry was on the winning side in just one of his first seven appearances, and that success came 5-0 over Scotland at the National Stadium after Keith Jarrett converted Keri Jones' try.

Gareth's debut in a Welsh jersey had come in Paris in 1967 – it too ended in defeat for Wales as France won 20-14, with Guy Camberabero drop-kicking two goals, whilst notching up fourteen points for the home side. Gareth was no slouch either when it came to drop-shots, but when he kicked the ball at the Lansdowne Road posts in 1968 and referee Mike Titcombe awarded a goal there was a near riot. Irate Irish fans swarmed onto the pitch to hurl orange peel, apple cores and even some bottles to express their displeasure, as the ball had swung at least a foot outside the post. Fortunately for the home supporters, Mr Titcombe made a second error to give Ireland a 9-6 victory when he signalled that Mike Gibson's drop-kick had found the target – in fact, it should have been disallowed because the ball was touched in flight.

Gareth and Barry scored tries in the 17-3 victory over Scotland at Murrayfield in 1969 – a match that also saw the first appearance of two London Welsh players who were to shortly join Welsh rugby's catalogue of greats – full-back extraordinaire J.P.R. Williams and no.8 Merv 'The Swerve' Davies. The year 1969 also saw Gareth score a scintillating try in Paris as he dodged, twirled and bounced off would-be tacklers as France were thankful to draw 8-8, whilst the same season saw Barry snap up a try and drop a goal in a 30-9 victory over England – a match that also saw Maurice Richards, the Cardiff winger, swoop for a record-equalling four tries.

During the 1970s, Wales played a total of 46 full-cap games, winning 32, drawing three, and losing 11. Only New Zealand (twice) won in Cardiff, whilst seven defeats in ten years in the Five Nations were all away from home. Between France's victory at Cardiff in 1968 and Scotland's success in 1982, no Five Nations team won at the Arms Park – in all, 27 championship matches with only a 1972 draw with France as a brief hiccup.

Wales' trail of triumph during that glittering decade opened with a 6-6 draw with South Africa in the rain and mud at a soggy National Stadium. Gareth slithered across in the corner for a last-minute try and three points that brought the scores level. Earlier in the match, he had also slotted over a penalty goal – his only kick during an illustrious career for Wales, which saw the Cardiff scrum-half score 20 rip-roaring tries for his country. In 1968 against Scotland, Gareth also entered the record books by becoming the youngest man to captain Wales. At

Gareth in the no.9 Welsh jersey awaits the ball to emerge from a maul in the Five Nations encounter against France at the Arms Park in 1976. (*Western Daily Mail and Echo*)

Left: Gareth in action on the 1974 British Lions tour.

Below: Gareth tackles Jacko Page, the English scrum-half, in the Five Nations encounter at the Arms Park in 1971, with Barry poised to launch the attack. (*Western Daily Mail and Echo*)

twenty years and seven months, he took over from Llanelli hooker Norman Gale – it was just his fifth international appearance, but he led a winning team 5-0. In all, he captained Wales thirteen times.

The Lions tour of New Zealand in 1971 established Barry and Gareth as superstars. The Cardiff half-backs were together in all four New Zealand Tests. The Lions won the first, before losing the second and then winning the third to set up a desperate fourth and final chance for the All Blacks to save the series. It ended up as a 14-14 draw, as Barry kicked two penalty goals and converted Peter Dixon's try, before J.P.R. dropped a famous goal. Barry completed a record Lions aggregate of 188 points in 17 appearances. For a time too he was the most prolific scorer for Wales as, when he announced his retirement in May 1972, the twenty-seven year-old had accumulated a best-ever tally of 90 points, including five tries and a record eight dropped goals.

In all, Gareth took part in three Lions tours and played in ten Tests. In South Africa in 1974, he produced some of the finest football of his career to help the Lions to an undefeated Test series win. He continued to play for Cardiff and Wales until his retirement in 1978. His final international appearance was in the 16-7 Grand Slam victory over France. Incredibly, this was his fifty-third consecutive match for Wales. During his time as the ever-present scrum-half, Wales won three Grand Slams, five Championships and five Triple Crowns. It was no great surprise to many, then, when in 2003 he was voted the Greatest Player of All Time in a global poll organised by *Rugby World* magazine. Further recognition came recently with the award of a CBE. in the 2007 New Year's Honours list.

When Barry – who hailed from Cefneithen, the same village as legendary Llanelli and Lions coach Carwyn James – quit the game, Wales continued to dominate because Llanelli's flamboyant Phil Bennett, another star of the invincible Lions tour to South Africa, donned the no.10 jersey to partner Gareth in 26 full-cap fixtures. What a man to succeed 'The King'! The seventies ended. Barry, Gareth and Phil were gone. Will Welsh rugby ever be the same again?

MAURICE TURNBULL

'Cardiff's first Test cricketer and one of Wales' greatest all-round sportsmen'
by Andrew Hignell

Maurice Turnbull was perhaps the most gifted and complete sportsman born in Cardiff. Not only did he make a significant contribution to the city's sporting life, he was a leading figure in Cardiff's commercial and spiritual affairs, and all in a life spanning a mere thirty-eight years, tragically cut short whilst he was serving with the Welsh Guards in Normandy in June 1944.

Born in East Grove in the fashionable inner suburb of Tredegarville on 16 March 1906, Maurice was the third son of Bernard Turnbull, a Yorkshire-born shipowner who had built up a successful and sizeable fleet from Penarth Docks. His father was also a leading member of the city's Catholic community, and together with his seven brothers, young Maurice was educated at Downside School, the famous public school run by Benedictine monks to the south of Bath.

Despite a thin and small frame, Maurice showed outstanding ability at a number of sports, including cricket, rugby, hockey, boxing and squash. It was during his illustrious school career that the eighteen-year-old made his Glamorgan debut, against Lancashire – one of the country's strongest teams – at Swansea in 1924. The schoolboy, however, was not overawed, and he proceeded to be his side's top scorer as they recorded a famous victory.

In 1926 Maurice went up to Trinity College, Cambridge, where he won three cricket Blues and led the university side in 1929. He also played rugby for the Light Blues. During his summer vacations, he continued to be a prolific batsman with Glamorgan and, after their

Left: M.J.L. Turnbull of Cardiff, Glamorgan, Cambridge University and Wales.

Opposite: Maurice leads out the Glamorgan team from the Arms Park pavilion to play Kent in their County Championship fixture in 1936.

modest success in the 1920s, it was no surprise that in August 1929 he was appointed as the county's new leader, with the county hierarchy believing that Turnbull would be the man to transform the club's affairs.

They were not wrong, but not before Turnbull had made his England debut during the MCC winter tour to Australia and New Zealand. Anyone who, in the course of the past few years, had seen the right-handed batsman in full flow was left in no doubt that Turnbull was destined for higher honours, and he duly won the first of nine English caps in January 1930, as he became Cardiff's first Test cricketer by appearing in the match against New Zealand at Christchurch.

On his return to Cardiff, Turnbull set about transforming a downtrodden team of almost habitual losers, and a club with a sizeable overdraft, into one that combined success on the field with a healthy bank balance. He achieved this latter goal after many long hours on the road throughout South Wales, attending a host of fundraising events and ensuring, with his great friend Johnnie Clay, that the poverty-stricken county would survive. Turnbull was never afraid of using his business and social contacts to swell the coffers of the cash-strapped club. Their actions ensured that Glamorgan avoided being wound up and, during the winter of 1932/33, it was claimed that Turnbull danced and twirled more miles at fundraising balls and dances than he had scored runs the previous summer – an impressive feat considering that he had passed the 1,300-run mark.

On the field, he helped to transform a ragbag collection of cast offs from other counties, inexperienced professionals, and a motley assortment of amateurs into an effective and successful playing unit. Having cut his teeth as a captain at both Downside and Cambridge, Turnbull became a gifted county leader, always getting the best out of the resources at his disposal, and putting great faith in the young Welsh players – both amateur and professional – thereby helping to establish a club with a clear Welsh identity.

As befitted a man who lived life to the full, he was a leader of great energy, always playing hard but fair, ensuring that the game was played in the right spirit. Even in his off-field attire – pin-striped suit and brown felt hat – he always gave the impression of neatness and everything being in order. On the field, he held great store by the virtues of going out and playing a positive and attractive game of cricket. On a couple of occasions, he got into hot water with the MCC authorities by declaring early in rain-affected games in an attempt to entertain the final-day crowd with a run chase, whilst on others, he shamed opposing batsmen who opted for dour and negative tactics by encouraging Johnnie Clay to bowl slow, underarm lobs.

As far as his batting was concerned, his finest innings was undoubtedly in 1932 when Nottinghamshire visited the Arms Park with their two England bowlers Harold Larwood and Bill Voce eager to experiment with what became known as 'bodyline' bowling on their winter tour to Australia. Had the men in baggy green caps treated the bowling with the same disdain as Turnbull – proudly wearing his daffodil sweater and blue cap – did that afternoon at the Arms Park, then no furore would have broken out in the winter, straining even diplomatic relations between England and Australia.

Turnbull proceeded to score a double hundred, time and again hooking and pulling the short balls from Larwood and Voce with such ferocity that the crowd thronging the boundary ropes were put in danger as ball after ball disappeared into the enclosures. Together with Dai Davies, Turnbull added 220 for the third wicket as Glamorgan ended the day on 354-4, much to the glee of the thousands of home supporters who idolised Turnbull.

His diplomatic skills were also at the fore a few hours later when a few of the disgruntled Nottinghamshire bowlers – after a good session in the bars and alehouses in the Welsh capital – popped back into the Arms Park to show their contempt for the surface. Their nocturnal visit did not go unnoticed as groundsman Trevor Preece heard the commotion when the visitors removed the covers and 'watered' the wicket. He duly rang Turnbull who, in traditional amateur fashion, had been dining out with his opposite number in the Grand Hotel. Despite the late hour, Maurice returned to the ground and was shown by the perturbed groundsman several rust-coloured stains on the wicket. No doubt aware of the bad publicity the reporting of the antics would bring, he calmly told Preece to quietly do whatever was needed to repair the surface, and not to say a word to any journalists. A few of the hacks had been aware of the visitors' late-night return to the ground, but thanks to Preece's skill and craft, the offending marks had been long removed by the time the covers were rolled away the next morning.

Despite his duties as secretary and captain of Glamorgan, his fundraising activities, and his work in the insurance world, Maurice also found time to become the first-choice scrum-half for Cardiff RFC. He was a brave and fearless figure at the base of the scrum, and revelled in making swift and decisive breaks or long dive passes out to his fly-half partners Harry Bowcott and Royston Gabe-Jones. He developed a great rapport with his outside halves and, despite missing a couple of seasons when on tour with the England cricketers, he was chosen to play in final Welsh Trials, before winning selection for the Welsh side against England at Twickenham on 21 January 1933.

Maurice and his characteristic dive pass. (*Western Daily Mail and Echo*)

Almost seventy-five years on from that famous afternoon in Welsh sporting history, it is quite apt to reflect on how one of Wales' true sporting heroes made his debut in a red jersey, when Wales won for the first ever time at Twickenham. He had a fine game, twice being tackled just short of the line after making some sniping bursts through the English defence and, in the second half, his swift service out from a loose maul to Bowcott led to an attack by the Welsh centres Wilf Wooller and Claude Davey, which resulted in Ronnie Boon – the Welsh amateur sprint champion from Barry – racing in to score a match-winning try.

As Maurice and the team made their way from the pitch they were mobbed by a delirious band of supporters who had travelled up from Wales, more out of a sense of duty than in any expectation of a win. A long evening of hearty celebrations then took place for the jubilant Welshmen – both players and fans – as they literally attempted to paint the town red. But Maurice was unable to join them at first as, in bravely defending in the closing minutes, he had sustained a badly bruised jaw and right shoulder. After a quick visit to the X-ray department of a local hospital, the Cardiff scrum-half was given the all clear, but his injuries forced him to withdraw from the Welsh side for their next match, against Scotland at Swansea. The following month he returned to the side for the visit to Ireland, but the game at a blustery Ravenhill in Belfast saw Maurice savour the other side of international rugby, as the rampant Irish pack dominated both the set pieces and the loose, winning the game 10-5.

This was to be Maurice's final appearance in a Welsh jersey, as a wrist injury sustained the following season forced him to retire from rugby. It did not end his sporting activities during the winter months, though, as hockey and squash became his favoured recreations, and it was testament of his all-round abilities that he won international honours in both. With support from his business friends, he also created a limited company that bought land and an old farmhouse in Ryder Street, Canton so that Cardiff Squash Rackets Club could be formed. It was here in the winter months that Maurice kept fit, playing many of his friends from the local sporting community, including Haydn Davies, the Glamorgan wicketkeeper, whom Maurice had installed as the squash club's professional and coach.

The 'Prince of Wales' meets the Prince of Wales! Maurice shakes hands shortly before the start of the famous international rugby match at Twickenham in January 1933. (Tim Auty)

Maurice had taken over the Glamorgan captaincy in 1930 when the club was at one of the lowest ebbs in its history. By the end of the decade, the daffodil county was in a far healthier state, with new talent, like fresh buds and shoots, having been nurtured and cultivated by the influential Turnbull who, by the late 1930s, was held in such high regard amongst the higher echelons at Lord's that he was invited to act as an England Test selector – the first person from the Welsh club to hold high office.

By 1939 the dark clouds that had been hanging over Glamorgan CCC earlier in the decade had completely dissipated, but there was gloom and uncertainty hanging over the nation as a whole with the onset of the Second World War. Maurice signed off in Glamorgan colours with a majestic century in his final innings of the season, against Leicestershire at Aylestone Road, and then he did his bit for the country by joining the Welsh Guards. But, before swapping his cricket whites for his military uniform, there was another important deed to be undertaken, as he married his fiancée Elizabeth Brooke, the daughter of a north-eastern industrialist, in September 1939.

The years of the so-called Phoney War saw Maurice, typically and swiftly, rise up to the rank of major, in addition to becoming a father following the birth of the first of three children in August 1940. But his joy of fatherhood and a growing family was tempered by his military duties and, in the spring and early summer of 1944, he was amongst the many thousands of brave men and women encamped at secret locations along the South Coast awaiting the start of Operation Overlord. He eventually crossed the channel on D-Day Plus Eleven, and soon after arriving at Arromanches, he saw the horrors that war and the Normandy Invasion had brought along the golden sandy beaches and previously picturesque countryside.

But this was no time to get sentimental, for there was a job to be done and, in typical fashion, Major Turnbull led from the fore as his battalion headed inland, towards the strategic town of Caen, as part of Operation Goodwood. July and early August saw Major Turnbull and his battalion snuff out pockets of resistance amongst the retreating German troops, many of whom were frightened fresh-faced youngsters, barely out of their teens, and only too happy to

Above left: Maurice and Elizabeth Turnbull.

Above right: Maurice in the cricket nets at Fenners.

give themselves up after the ferocious Allied attack. But, by the time they approached the quiet village of Montchamp in early August, there was greater hostility, with the Nazis mounting a counter-attack after Turnbull and his unit had secured the centre of the village.

Observing the approaching line of Panzer tanks, Maurice led a party of troops into a field adjoining the sunken lane and, together with his men, they crouched up against the hedges, ready to disable the oncoming vehicles. As the lead tank passed them, Maurice's men sprang into action, but the turret swung round sharply towards the hedge, and opened fire. Tragically, Maurice was shot through the head and killed instantly.

His selfless actions thwarted the counter-attack and allowed the Guards to continue their headway through northern France. Maurice's body was taken back to brigade headquarters, before being laid to rest at Bayeux amongst the simple white-stoned graves in the British War Cemetery.

Other great names in Welsh sport have had grand memorials erected in their memory, but for Maurice Joseph Lawson Turnbull, his final resting place is in northern France with the nation's other true heroes who gave their lives for king and country. That life and sport should carry on as normal from 1945 is Maurice's greatest legacy, and something for which all of Cardiff's sportsmen and women since then should be eternally grateful.

FRED KEENOR

'The Bluebirds' home-grown FA Cup-winning captain'
by Richard Shepherd

It is eighty years since Cardiff City won the FA Cup in 1927, but ask most Bluebirds fans who it was that led City to victory on that famous occasion and the chances are that they will know the name of Fred Keenor. And if only for the fact that it was Cardiff-born Keenor leading his home-town club to victory over Arsenal in that final to take the trophy out of England for

Maurice batting for England against India in a Test match match in 1933. (MCC library, Lord's)

the only time to date since the competition began in 1872, then Fred's name is assured of its place in Bluebirds' history as long as the club exists.

But what background is known of the man himself? Frederick Charles Keenor, one of nine children of a Cardiff bricklayer, was a heavy chain smoker who trained in his old army boots to strengthen his leg muscles, and he was one of those players that you would prefer to have on your side rather than playing against you! He made 507 appearances for the Bluebirds in the Southern League, Football League and various cup competitions between 1913 and 1931, and his name was synonymous with Cardiff City during the twenties when the Bluebirds were one of the leading clubs in the country.

A Welsh international in two Victory games in 1919 and in 32 peace-time appearances, at a time when Wales played just three matches per season in the old Home International Championship, Keenor was not so much a great footballer, but a great leader in terms of his competitive spirit and will to win. In 1928, he was described in the following terms:

> A leader in every sense of the word, he commands the respect of his colleagues by his whole-hearted enthusiasm. He might not be a stylish player, but his doggedness and determination make him one of the most effective half-backs in the country.

Born in Roath on 21 July 1894, Fred attended Stacey Road School and played at outside-right in 1907 against England at Walsall in Wales' first ever schoolboy international. He then rose to prominence in local amateur football with Roath Wednesdays FC before joining Cardiff City as an amateur in the summer of 1912 and signing professional forms at the end of the following November.

His first-team debut came against Exeter City at Ninian Park during early December 1913 in a Southern League First Division match, and he went on to make a further two Southern League appearances in that 1913/14 season. He was establishing himself in the side in 1914/15 when the Great War, which broke out in August 1914, put a stop to competitive League football at the end of that season. Keenor had, in fact, joined the Army in early February 1915 but continued to play for the club during the remainder of the season whilst waiting to report to the services.

Fred Keenor and the FA Cup. (Richard
Shepherd)

He had enlisted in the 17th Battalion Middlesex Regiment (known as the 'Footballers
Battalion'), and he was eventually sent to France, taking part in the Battle of the Somme
during July and August 1916. He was twice wounded and so spent a period of convalescence
in a Dublin hospital. Fortunately, Fred's injuries did not have an effect on his football career
and, at the end of the war, he was stationed on the outskirts of west London, playing for
Brentford, whom he helped win the Championship of the London war-time Combination
League in 1918/19.

Fred returned to a Cardiff City side that did well enough in the Southern League First
Division as regards performances and support in 1919/20 to be elected direct into the Football
League's Second Division, while the rest of the Southern League formed the new Third
Division. Prior to that, in April 1919, Fred made his debut for Wales, playing in the home and
away 'Victory Internationals' against England.

During the 1920s, Fred was a major force for his club and country, his regular position
being at wing half (midfield in modern terms), though on occasion he did play at centre half,
a position which was to develop into a central-defensive role with the 1925 change in the
offside rule. Although Fred captained Wales from 1924 onwards, he did not become captain of
Cardiff City until the 1926/27 season, though he did lead the side on several occasions prior
to that in the absence of regular skipper Jimmy Blair.

One of Fred's most memorable moments took place in a Welsh shirt at Ninian Park during
February 1924 when Wales played Scotland – Fred skippered Wales, and his club captain
Jimmy Blair led Scotland. Fred was at centre half when City lost 1-0 to Sheffield United the
following year in the 1925 FA Cup final. The Bluebirds did not do themselves justice in that
match, and Fred stated his ambition to return to Wembley with City, and this time to win the
FA Cup. But although he did so as captain two years later in 1927, it very nearly didn't happen
for him. He had lost his place in City's line-up just after Christmas 1926, partly through injury
following a 5-0 defeat at Newcastle United. Apart from a mid-January appearance, he did not
regain his first-team place until early February. In the meantime, he asked for a transfer, but
he was back for the latter stages of City's successful FA Cup run, and the transfer request was
forgotten.

Fred introduces his players to the King at Wembley in 1927. (Richard Shepherd)

Fred was outstanding in the FA Cup final against Arsenal, whose captain Charlie Buchan later recalled, 'I can still remember Fred's great display on that occasion. He marshalled his men magnificently – his store of energy seemed inexhaustible.' Teammate Ernie Curtis, the youngest member of the FA Cup-winning Bluebirds team and who died in 1992 as the last survivor of the side, remembered Fred with affection: 'He liked his pint and his cigarettes, his language on the pitch was usually unprintable, and he could run all day. Mind you, he couldn't run with the ball!'

Such was Fred's versatility that when City played at Ninian Park seven days after the Wembley triumph, he was at centre forward and scored the only goal of the game against Everton. A do-it-yourself enthusiast who built his own detached house in Whitchurch, his hobbies included motoring in those days when comparatively few people had their own cars, and shooting rabbits!

There were many memorable moments in Fred's career, such as the occasion in October 1930 when Wales played Scotland at Ibrox Park, home of Glasgow Rangers. English clubs had refused to release their leading Welsh players because of League matches being played on the same day, and Wales had to select non-League players, amateurs, three from Cardiff City and one from Newport County, both clubs then struggling in their respective divisions. One of the Bluebirds' trio was Fred Keenor who captained the team that was labelled by the press as 'The Welsh Unknowns'. Fred said to them before the game, 'There's eleven of us, eleven of them, there's one ball – let's make sure it's ours!' And such was Fred's inspirational display that the Welsh no-hopers held a strong Scotland side to a 1-1 draw after taking an early lead!

But the good times for Fred at Ninian Park were long gone, and at the end of that 1930/31 season, with Cardiff City relegated to the Third Division (South) just four years after winning the cup as a First Division side, Fred was given a free transfer by his club, having been associated with City for almost twenty years. His final appearance, together with that of all-time Bluebirds record goal scorer Len Davies, was in a 0-0 home draw against Tottenham Hotspur on 6 April 1931 in front of a paltry 6,666 attendance – a far cry from the great days of the early-to-mid-twenties when any number from 30,000 to 50,000 would pack Ninian Park.

Fred and his Cardiff City colleagues celebrate their FA Cup success in the Wembley changing rooms after their historic victory over Arsenal in 1927. (Richard Shepherd)

The Cardiff City team that beat Arsenal in 1927. From left to right, back row: George Latham, Jimmy Nelson, Tom Farquharson, Tom Watson, George McLachlan. Middle row: Tom Sloan, Sam Irving, Fred Keenor (captain), Billy Hardy, Len Davies. Front row: Ernie Curtis, Hughie Ferguson. (Richard Shepherd)

In May 1931 Fred moved to Crewe Alexandra with whom he gained a further cap for Wales in 1932/33. He was an Alex regular for three seasons before joining Oswestry Town as player-manager in August 1934. He was there for season 1934/35, and then moved on in a similar role to Tunbridge Wells Rangers for 1935/36 whilst also running a newsagent and tobacconist shop. Fred then became a poultry farmer, but fell on hard times as a result of suffering from diabetes. Bluebirds fans held fundraising events for him as a token of their appreciation for all that he had done to help the club reach such heights in the 1920s.

Fred recovered well enough to find work as a builder's labourer, not such a difficult role for him, having built his own home in Cardiff years earlier, and he returned with his wife to live in the Welsh capital in 1958, working as a warehouse storeman until his retirement in his mid-sixties. He was still a welcome visitor to Ninian Park, where his son Graham was club secretary, and when City played at home to Arsenal in a January 1969 FA Cup match, Fred appeared on the pitch before the game for a television interview together with several of his 1927 teammates and opponents.

Fred Keenor died in a residential nursing home in November 1972 at the age of seventy-eight, an event that was officially recorded in the Cardiff City Directors' Minute Book. And in a fitting tribute to his memory, in the early part of the current decade, a reception room displaying photographs of Fred at various stages of his career was named 'The Fred Keenor Lounge'.

JIM DRISCOLL

'Peerless Jim – Cardiff's boxing champion'
by Gareth Jones

A world title is every boxer's goal. To turn down a shot at the belt is almost unthinkable. To do so because of a promise made to a group of nuns stretches credibility to the extreme. But Jim Driscoll, the greatest ring artist Cardiff ever produced, stunned the American fight business when he rejected a rematch with champion Abe Attell in order to return to his home city and box an exhibition in aid of the orphans of Nazareth House.

Driscoll, born in Ellen Street in the Irish colony of Newtown, had just handed Attell a boxing lesson over ten rounds in New York, a state where competitive contests were at the time illegal and so-called no-decision bouts were the norm. Fans relied on the ringside newspapermen to tell them who won – and on this occasion the local scribes were unanimous. 'The little Briton opened the eyes of the crowd and closed one of Abe's,' wrote one of their number, underlining the fact that Jim was now 'the premier featherweight boxer of the world'.

It was a performance which earned him his immortal nickname, gunfighter turned sports editor Bat Masterson dubbing him 'Peerless Jim'. The Welshman's display had brought the prospect of wealth and honours, with Attell said to be willing – for the right money – to face him again in a state where an official ruling could be given and the title would be at stake. But Driscoll was adamant.

'I promised I would box for Nazareth House and they are expecting me,' he said, before sailing for home. No wonder the nuns still make sure there are flowers on Jim's grave in Cathays Cemetery and were at the forefront of the campaign to raise a statue to one of the city's finest sons.

The young Driscoll, giving up a five-bob-a-week apprenticeship with the *Western Mail* printing works, earned three times as much taking on all-comers in the fairground booths. There he learned the defensive skills that took him to the top. His official record begins in 1901 and by the end of the year he had claimed the Welsh featherweight crown. By 1904 he had introduced himself to the toffs of the National Sporting Club, the effective governors of the sport in Britain, and two years later outpointed former world bantamweight ruler Joe Bowker to become British champion.

Jim added the Empire belt when New Zealander Charlie Griffin was thrown out for butting him and then headed off on the Mauretania to conquer the United States. There he had nine fights and won the lot, many via 'newspaper verdict', before his historic meeting with Attell.

Back in Britain, once his duty to the nuns had been fulfilled, Driscoll regained the domestic title by halting Seaman Arthur Hayes, receiving the first of the famous Lonsdale Belts to be awarded for the nine-stone division.

Geordie Spike Robson, a former claimant, was seen off before the Cardiffian headed back across the Atlantic. But a chest infection and injury in a road accident days earlier meant a below-par showing. This time the journalists voted for opponent Pal Moore. Instead of a hoped-for second showdown with Attell, Jim had to return home, but his consolation was a clash of the titans against Freddie Welsh, the Pontypridd product who, three years later, would become undisputed lightweight champion of the world.

Jim Driscoll as seen on two cigarette cards.

Giving away almost a stone, Jim was always up against it in front of a packed house at the American Skating Rink in Westgate Street. Welsh, a pupil of the gyms of Philadelphia, employed all the dirty tricks he learned there. Driscoll's Irish temper was roused and when he eventually responded with a flagrant butt, referee 'Peggy' Bettinson disqualified him. The fans rioted, while Jim's irate mother informed Bettinson, 'You're as false as the teeth in my head!'

By now Jim was weakened by the recurrent bronchial problems that were to bring his early death. But he was still capable of a repeat victory over Robson, making the Lonsdale Belt his own property, and added the vacant European title by knocking out Jean Poesy, afterwards lifting the Frenchman from the canvas and carrying him back to his corner.

Driscoll's wife, Edie, wanted her sick husband to call it a day and he vowed to do so after one last fight, against brilliant Brummie Owen Moran. The pair drew over twenty rounds and Jim – though it took him six months to get around to it – duly relinquished his championships.

On the outbreak of the First World War, he joined the Army, a gas attack at Ypres doing nothing to ease his breathing difficulties. But once peace had been restored, Driscoll, now thirty-eight, was unable to resist the temptation to lace up the gloves once more. A win over one-time bantamweight king Pedlar Palmer – who was actually older than the Welshman – convinced Jim he could still perform. He proved it by out-boxing young prospect Francis Rossi at Mountain Ash, even if the referee somehow saw it as a draw.

But it could not go on. In October 1919 Jim stepped into the ring at the National Sporting Club to face a young Frenchman, Charles Ledoux, in a bid for his old European title. For fourteen rounds the greying wizard gave a boxing lesson to the squat champion. But the next session saw youth take control and in the sixteenth the veteran's seconds hurled a towel through the ropes to rescue their man.

A post-fight collection by club members yielded £1,500 – the fund eventually reached £5,000 – with Ledoux contributing a fiver to 'my master in boxing'. This was invested to prevent Driscoll, a notorious gambler, from blowing it all on the horses. While Edie ran their pub, the Duke of Edinburgh, Jim spent his time teaching youngsters to box and, typically, organising charity events for, among others, the nuns of Nazareth House.

He caught a chill around New Year's Day, 1925, and died of pneumonia at the end of January, at home in the Duke, in Ellen Street, just a few doors from where it all began. Cardiff came to a standstill for his funeral, more than 100,000 lining the streets as his coffin, carried on a military gun carriage, paraded through the city, a mile-long column of mourners in its wake. And the procession was led by the children of Nazareth House, each carrying a wreath for the man who sacrificed his dreams on their behalf.

COLIN JACKSON

'The greatest Welsh athlete?'
by Andrew Hignell

Described as 'the greatest Welsh athlete' by First Minister Rhodri Morgan, Colin Jackson was the nation's most decorated athlete during his glittering hurdling career. He first shot to fame winning the 110-metre hurdles at the 1986 World Junior Championship, and in the course of the next eighteen years he won silver in the 1988 Olympics at Seoul, four successive gold medals in the European Championships between 1990 and 2002 and, just for good measure, gold medals in the Commonwealth Games at Auckland in 1990 and Victoria in 1994, as well as gold in the World Championships at Stuttgart in 1993 and Seville in 1999.

In the world's finest stadia and premier competitions, his races would always begin with an explosion of raw pace and machismo, before his gazelle-like ability took him nimbly, and gracefully, over the row of hurdles in front of him and then, as the winning line approached, with Jackson often in front, he would produce his trademark dip, leaning forward to advance the position of his shoulders, thereby improving times and, if need be, positions.

Born in Cardiff in February 1967, he grew up in the Llanedeyrn area and, at the age of twelve, young Colin joined the local junior athletics group. He was also a talented cricketer and, aged fourteen, he had the option to play in a junior county cricket match or to represent Cardiff in a track and field event. After tossing a coin, athletics won and he subsequently showed rich promise with the javelin as well as in the high jump and long jump, leading some to believe that he could become the next Daley Thompson. But with the guidance of coach Malcolm Arnold – the man who had guided John Akii-Bua to the Olympic 400-metre hurdles title in 1972 – Colin opted to focus on the high hurdles. He also turned down a chance to go to university in America, opting instead to stay in Cardiff, train as an apprentice electrician and to focus on his athletics career.

In June 1981 he had won the Welsh under-15 80-metre hurdles competition at the Morfa Stadium in Swansea with a championship best time of 11.9 seconds. Four years later he won the silver in the European Junior Championship, before winning the silver for Wales in the Commonwealth Games at Edinburgh. Colin followed that with a World Championship bronze in 1987 and another silver at the Seoul Olympics in 1988, before becoming crowned Commonwealth and European champion in 1990.

Jackson was tipped to get the gold medal at the 1992 Barcelona Olympics, but an injury saw him limp home in seventh place. After this disappointment, his American rival Tony Dees claimed that Jackson was a 'bottler', but Barcelona in 1992 proved to be a pivotal moment in his career as, in the course of the next few years, he proved himself to be more of a battler, winning his first world title at Stuttgart in August 1993 and breaking Roger Kingdom's world record with a time of 12.91 seconds in the 110 metres hurdles.

Colin was a very committed and focused athlete and, as he said in a magazine interview shortly before his retirement, 'to succeed, you have to be strong, aware and totally selfish. The mind can be a very powerful tool and it's this that separates your everyday medal contenders from actual winners. You need high levels of self-discipline to become a world beater.' At times, he led an almost monastic life, with his girlfriend coming in second place in his affections to hurdling. His diets also bordered on the anorexic and, when he smashed the world 110 metre hurdling record at Stuttgart in 1993, it followed a near starvation routine, with Colin going for days without a proper meal in order to become lighter and faster than his opponents.

He also did well to overcome the sudden death in 1999 of his best friend and hurdling prodigy Ross Baillie who died as a result of a nut allergy after eating a coronation chicken sandwich. Colin also overcame an acrimonious breakdown in his hitherto good relationship

Left: Colin Jackson at the Welsh Games in the 1990s. (Clive Williams)

Opposite left: Sally Hodge, typically leading from the front in a road race in 1988. (Eric Hodge)

Opposite right: Sally Hodge celebrates winning another national title. (Eric Hodge)

with star sprinter Linford Christie. Colin had never previously permitted anything to interfere with his running, but in 1992 the pair set up a sports management company called Nuff Respect. Things soon turned sour, with Colin reflecting later:

> We didn't work well together at all. I was more thoughtful than Linford, I had more direction, and I wasn't so backward-thinking as he was. Basically, he wasn't in touch with reality at all, and as far as I could see, the business to him was all about ego and becoming a superstar. I was not interested in that.

Colin retired in March 2003 after running in the World Indoor Championships in Birmingham and, by the time he hung up his spikes, he had no less than 25 international championship medals and 71 international vests to his name. Despite being amongst the world's best hurdlers, the Olympic gold medal proved elusive, with Colin finishing fifth in his final attempt at the Sydney Games in 2000. But when questioned by journalists about his failing again, he responded in typically positive manner:

> How can I possibly be disappointed with the career I have had? I am still the world record holder and I am still the world champion. The Olympic gold medal would have rounded it off, but I have had a great career with a lot of success, far more than a lot of British athletes and more than a lot of foreign athletes, so how can I be disappointed?

Colin received official recognition of his achievements in 1990 when he was awarded the MBE, upgraded in the 2003 Queen's Birthday Honours List to a CBE, whilst in November 2003 he and Tanni Grey-Thompson were given the Freedom of Cardiff. In recent years, Colin has developed his coaching and broadcasting career, in addition to being a member of the successful London 2012 Olympics bid team. Colin has also appeared in various celebrity competitions, including BBC television's *Strictly Come Dancing* in which he finished as runner-up to England cricketer Darren Gough in 2005, showing the characteristic lightness of foot that won him so many honours on the athletics track.

SALLY HODGE

'Cardiff's world champion cyclist'
by Gwyn Prescott

When Nicole Cooke was a youngster and beginning to take her sport seriously, she looked around for a suitable club to join. The future Tour de France winner and world number one-ranked rider chose Cardiff Ajax CC, inspired by the fact that the club had a world champion cyclist in Sally Hodge.

Sally's cycling record is indeed an inspiration to any ambitious athlete. Born in Cardiff in 1966, and educated at Cardiff High School, she was a precocious competitor. When aged only sixteen, she became the youngest ever British National Sprint Champion and, in recognition of this outstanding achievement, she was awarded the 1983 Carwyn James Award for the BBC Wales Young Sports Personality of the Year.

This was the first of many major competitions that the gifted Cardiff cyclist was to win. Over a twelve-year career, in a range of events, she won no fewer than thirteen British National titles and was placed runner-up on ten occasions. In 1984, when still a teenager, Sally broke the British record for both the 200 and 500 metres and she held on to the latter record for seven years. Remarkably, she is still the current British National Championship record holder for the 30 kilometres Points Race. Sally also won many Women's Cycle Racing Association and Welsh National titles.

Sally represented Wales and Great Britain on the road and track for many years in venues around the world. So that she could concentrate on competing on the world stage, whilst still remaining an amateur, it became necessary to look for support funding from sponsorship. This was achieved through the formation of a new club, Velo Club Ajax, with her father Eric acting as secretary. This remained Sally's club while she competed internationally over the next eleven years, after which she reverted to riding again for Cardiff Ajax, who then made her a life member.

This action soon produced beneficial results when the twenty-year-old took the gold medal in the 20 kilometres Points Race in the 1986 Goodwill Games in Moscow. This was followed by even greater success two years later with her stunning performance in the 30 kilometres Points Race in the 1988 UCI Track World Cycling Championships held in Ghent. In this event, Sally Hodge became the first Welsh woman to win a world cycling title and the first British woman since Beryl Burton, when she won her fifth world track title, in 1966. Sally dominated the race from start to finish, taking control in the early stages to gradually build up her lead to 12 points with only five sprints left. The title was never in doubt thereafter. Cardiff had its World Cycling Champion.

Sally was twice an Olympian, competing in the 50 kilometres on both occasions. She finished ninth in Seoul in 1988 and unfortunately crashed four years later in Barcelona. Her last major honours came in the Commonwealth Games held in Victoria, British Columbia, in 1994 when, in recognition of her outstanding sporting achievements, she was selected as the overall Welsh Ladies team captain. Here she capped her wonderful career by taking the bronze medal in the 25 kilometres Points Race.

Since retiring from competition, Sally, a qualified cycling coach, continues to inspire others, putting her experience, knowledge and enthusiasm to good use for the benefit of her sport. She has taken both a Maindy Track League Juvenile team to national competition and, as squad manager, the Welsh Ladies team to senior national races. A keen sportswoman, for some years she also played women's football for Dinas Powys, where she now lives. Throughout her sporting career, Sally Hodge has been a superb ambassador for Wales, Great Britain and the sport she has graced so well.

CLIFF JONES

'The first truly great fly-half'
by Alun Wyn Bevan

2 February 1935 – a date that was etched on my grandfather John Bevan's memory until his dying day. He and a group of friends were sat in the front row of the old North Stand at the Arms Park looking forward to the encounter between Wales and Scotland. Some six minutes into the game, the Welsh outside half Cliff Jones ghosted through the Scottish defence, initially running menacingly across the field before racing some forty metres for a truly spectacular try. In anticipation of what was about to take place, the front row of the stand rose as one, and my grandfather, overcome by the excitement of the moment, hurled his newly-acquired Saville Row hat into the air – that was the last time he ever saw it!

Followers of the game of rugby football from Hawick to Hamilton are familiar with the so-called 'outside half factory' that exists in the Welsh valleys. Most of these fans would argue that the production line swung into action during the early 1950s, and subsequently produced such household names as Cliff Morgan, David Watkins, Barry John, Phil Bennett, Jonathan Davies and latterly James Hook. But for the older generation this concept is an anathema, as the factory had been in action far earlier and, as far as they were concerned, they bore witness to the prototype against which all others were modelled.

Cliff Jones, a son of the Rhondda Valleys born in 1914, graced the rugby fields during the 1930s and, whilst still a pupil at Porth County School, his ball skills were evident for all to see. In those days, these skills were demonstrated on the football pitches, not the rugby fields, and he did not appear to show any interest in the oval ball. All this was to change when at fourteen the young lad from Porth was enrolled at Llandovery College. Sport was ranked equally alongside academic subjects, such as Latin, history and mathematics in the public school's curriculum, and during the annual encounter with Christ College, when Brecon loomed on the horizon, Virgil, Caesar and Pythagoras were consigned to the lower ranks.

Within days of his arrival at Llandovery, the college's games teacher T.P. 'Pope' Williams saw

Cliff Jones.

in Cliff Jones a star in the making – someone who with his style of play could hypnotise the opposition and onlookers alike. At the end of each coaching session, when the rest of the team had decamped to the refectory for their pie and chips, teacher and pupil could be seen out on the rugby field earnestly discussing various aspects of the game.

'TP' would present Cliff with a specific challenge to which the youngster would be expected to respond. In the young Cliff Jones, he recognised an individual with all the attributes required to make an outstanding rugby player. Although he was physically slight of body, he was very fleet of foot, ran with the artistry of an Olympic athlete and was blessed with a swerve and sidestep that could deceive any opponent.

For four years, five nights a week, the coach would mould his young charge into the world-class player that he would become. T.P. focused on getting the young outside half to run, thus creating space for his centre – a basic philosophy of the game but, given that Cliff had such innate talent, it made the coach's work relatively easy, and he was soon weaving his magic for the College's First XV. Cliff soon came to realise that it was the fly-half who controlled the course of any game, and in their post-match discussions, T.P. would stress to his pupil the need to create a degree of uncertainty amongst the opposition. Whilst his ball-handling skills were already in place, his self-belief and attitude needed some fine tuning, and what T.P. successfully achieved was to combine the instinct and resolution of the Rhondda, with the finesse developed at Llandovery.

Thus all the elements were finally in place by the time Cliff left Llandovery to grace the rugby fields of Cardiff, Cambridge, Wales and other more distant parts of the rugby-playing world. On leaving Llandovery he proceeded to Clare College, Cambridge where he developed a fine rugby partnership with the legendary Wilf Wooller, a strong-running and fearless centre. One move instigated and perfected at Grange Road, and again at the Arms Park, involved Jones running at speed into a gap, attempting to breach the defence, and then passing swiftly to Wooller who would be at his shoulder in an instant. Time and again, this move resulted in a try. He won three Blues at Cambridge between 1933 and 1935 and was first capped while at university.

Cliff in action.

He had played club rugby for Pontypridd and Cardiff before he was eighteen, and had survived, largely because of the fine grounding he had received at Llandovery and the fact that the College played mainly against adult teams. Injuries – both serious and small – were to blight his club and international career, as he played in only 22 matches for Cardiff between 1932/33 and 1939/40. He fractured four bones before he was twenty, missed the Five Nations games in 1936/37 through a broken collarbone, temporarily retired during 1938/39 in order to study (and successfully pass) his law finals, before finally making a comeback and injuring his elbow in September 1939 in Cardiff's opening game of the season.

Cliff's international career was, therefore, a relatively short one, as he won thirteen caps between 1934 and 1938, taking on the captaincy in his last season. The pinnacle of his international career was undoubtedly reached on 21 December 1935 in a Herculean contest at the Arms Park between Wales and New Zealand. With ten minutes left for play, the score stood at Wales 10 New Zealand 12. Nelson Ball had scored two tries for the All Blacks, with Geoffrey Rees-Jones and Claude Davey replying for Wales. Things looked bleak for the home team when Don Tarr, the Welsh hooker, was carried off having sustained a broken neck, but undaunted the Welsh team fought back.

From a scrum fifty metres out from the Kiwi try line, Haydn Tanner threw a bullet-like pass to Cliff Jones, who in turn ran across field briefly replicating the oft-repeated move at Cambridge, before racing for the gap and linking up with Wooller, who kicked over the heads of the All Black defence who seemed temporarily paralysed by the Welsh counter-attack. Wooller set off in pursuit of the ball, and nine times out of ten it would have bounced back into his hands. But on this occasion, the hard surface of the Cardiff ground resulted in the ball flying up over Wooller's head, but thankfully, very kindly, into the hands of the chasing Rees-Jones. Wooller landed up in a heap in the straw near the try-line, but he picked himself up and saw his teammate score the decisive and winning try. The 50,000 present were jubilant and hailed Cliff as the hero of the hour.

In post-war years, he served Welsh rugby equally well as an influential administrator. A strong advocate of coaching, he was a national selector for twenty-two years and was WRU President during the 1980/81 centenary season. He died aged seventy-six in Bonvilston in 1990.

An aerial view of the Arms Park, taken in the 1920s, showing the straightened River Taff, the cricket and rugby grounds, Cardiff Castle and the city centre, and the railway line, built in the 1840s, which first prompted the creation of the city's sporting epicentre.

CARDIFF ARMS PARK
by Andrew Hignell and Gwyn Prescott

Cardiff Arms Park – to many the vibrant heart and visible epicentre of all things sporting in Cardiff, if not in Wales as a whole. Yet many generations of Cardiffians have to thank Isambard Kingdom Brunel, the famous engineer and perhaps the greatest Briton in Victorian times, as well as the Marquess of Bute, the aristocratic landowner based at Cardiff Castle, for the 'creation' of the Park in the first place, and its subsequent metamorphosis into Cardiff's premier sporting venue.

Brunel's involvement coincided with the construction of the South Wales Railway during the mid-nineteenth century, and the difficulties over a suitable site for the new railway station, free from the danger of flooding by the Taff, which at the time looped in a huge meander, close to Quay Street and many other properties in St Mary Street. Brunel's solution was to divert the river away to the west, thereby creating a larger and safer site to the south where the railway station could be built.

The straightening of the river also extended the area of meadowland at the rear of the Cardiff Arms, an impressive seventeenth-century townhouse, which had been built for a wealthy family close to the West Gate and the Castle. In 1787 the house and its garden was sold and the property was converted into an inn, known variously as the Cardiff Arms Hotel or Cardiff Arms Inn – the name 'Arms' being derived from a shield containing the red and yellow chevron crest of Cardiff which hung above the doorway – and the garden at the rear soon became known as the Cardiff Arms Park.

In 1803 the Cardiff Arms and the Park became the property of the Marquess of Bute, who readily allowed it to be used for recreation as well as for civic events, such as the town's celebrations in 1837 for the accession of Queen Victoria. Until the 1840s, the Park was poorly drained and prone to flooding, but Brunel's scheme ended these difficulties, in addition to enlarging the Park to some eighteen acres. With its improved drainage, the Park was used from 1848 by members of Cardiff Cricket Club and, with the full agreement of the Marquess, the club established their permanent home in the northern part of the Park in 1867.

Two years later, Cardiff Arms Park hosted its first 'county' cricket match as the newly formed Glamorganshire Cricket Club played their inaugural match against Monmouthshire whilst, by the early 1870s, organised rugby was taking place in the southern part of the Park. Cardiff RFC was formed in 1876, and in April 1884 the Arms Park hosted its first international fixture, with the first Welsh try being scored by Tom Clapp of Newport, but made by a characteristic jinking run by Cardiff great Frank Hancock.

In June 1889 Glamorgan CCC played for the first time at the Arms Park – a friendly against Warwickshire – whilst in 1905 one of the greatest moments in Welsh sporting history came at the Arms Park as Wales defeated New Zealand, with several Cardiff men playing key roles in the famous victory over the mighty All Blacks.

By the time this famous rugby match took place, a number of ground improvements had taken place. The growing popularity of rugby in the late nineteenth century had prompted increasing demands for improved facilities for spectators, and with the numbers watching Cardiff RFC continuing to rise, there was constant pressure for new and improved accommodation such as grandstands, standing areas, temporary stands, press boxes, footboards, fencing and footpaths. The first substantial grandstand was erected in 1885 and two wings were added nine years later. In 1890, new standing areas were constructed along the entire length of the ground and these were enlarged in 1894. Additional stands were erected in 1896.

Following the Triple Crown decider against Ireland in 1899, Cardiff committeeman Bill Phillips claimed that only three other grounds in the country, 'Crystal Palace, Aston Villa and Everton,' could have accommodated the record crowd, which was estimated at 40,000 that day. In 1900, an agreement with the WRU was entered into to further increase the seating and standing accommodation, with the Union funding three-quarters of the cost. This important decision marked the beginning of the process which would eventually lead to the WRU taking over the ground in 1968.

Glamorgan's success as a Minor County team also prompted the erection of a grand, new pavilion in the south-west corner of the cricket field – paid for and used by both the rugby and cricket clubs from 1904. At the end of the 1911/12 rugby season, a new south stand and temporary stands on the north, east and west terraces were added, again partly funded by the WRU. They were officially opened by Lord Ninian Crichton-Stuart, who kicked off in the match between Cardiff and Newport in October 1912. The Arms Park had become the finest rugby ground in the country, with an official capacity of 43,000.

After the First World War, the Arms Park cricket ground also hosted regular County Championship matches, including Glamorgan's first-ever County Championship match

Cardiff Arms Park cricket ground, with the rugby ground in the rear in the early 1900s. To the right is the lavish pavilion, used by both the cricketers and rugby players.

A view from the Arms Park pavilion as the South Wales batsmen walk out to face the Australians in August 1905. This cricket match coincided with the lavish civic events to celebrate Cardiff becoming a city, and an enormous crowd turned up at the Arms Park to watch the famous cricketers from Australia.

in 1921 and, once again, several Cardiffians were to the fore, as Norman Riches – one of the finest cricketers produced by the city – led the county to success.

The inter-war period also witnessed further improvements to the rugby ground, with the WRU again financing the construction of the new double-decker North Stand – which seated 5,200 people – and which was opened when Wales played England in January 1934. The building was badly damaged by a landmine during the Second World War. In 1956 a new South Upper Stand was added – jointly financed by the Union and Cardiff Athletic Club – which brought the overall capacity of the Arms Park up to 60,000, of whom 12,800 were seated.

But the Arms Park staged more than just top-class rugby and cricket. The first association football international in South Wales was played there in 1896, while in the early twentieth century, Cardiff City used the ground a couple of times before moving to their permanent home at Ninian Park. In 1958 the Arms Park played host to the Empire Games, with the finest sportsmen and women from the Commonwealth taking part in the opening and closing ceremonies, as well as the athletics events being staged on a cinder track laid around the perimeter of the rugby pitch.

As well as seeing performances from human stars, the Arms Park also hosted canine ones, following the decision in the late 1920s by the Cardiff Greyhound Company to transfer their operations from the GKN Sports Ground in Sloper Road – known as the 'Welsh White City' – to a track around the circumference of the rugby stadium.

For over half a century, there were regular greyhound races on Mondays and Saturdays, with the calendar including the Welsh Greyhound Derby and the Welsh Greyhound Grand National. Many local people trained a succession of successful greyhounds, including John Hegarty – who subsequently became racing manager at the Arms Park – who trained Beef Cutlet for Sir Herbert Merritt, a legendary figure amongst the dockland business community, a great supporter of Cardiff sport and the chairman of Cardiff City FC during the inter-war period.

30 July 1977 saw the final greyhound race being run, ten years after county cricket had also ended at the Arms Park following the move by the cricket section of Cardiff Athletic Club and Glamorgan CCC to Sophia Gardens in 1967. The ending of cricket and greyhound racing was the result of the decision by the Welsh Rugby Union to develop a world-class rugby stadium in Cardiff, and the upshot was that the Arms Park became transformed and upgraded into the National Stadium. This also involved Cardiff RFC having to transfer their activities onto the former cricket ground, but in so doing this has ensured that Cardiff Arms Park still survives as the name of a proud sporting venue.

RYAN GIGGS

'He just floated over the ground like a cocker spaniel chasing a piece of silver paper in the wind'
by Grahame Lloyd

Of all the millions of words that have been written and spoken about the genius of Ryan Giggs, that single sentence from Sir Alex Ferguson seems to perfectly capture the Welshman's extraordinary talent. When asked to describe the first time he set eyes on the boy wonder from Cardiff, the Manchester United manager conjured up a fitting poetic image to describe a player who has personified poetry in motion since making his Old Trafford debut.

Over the last sixteen years, Ryan Giggs has developed into a rare model of consistency in the modern British game. In becoming the most decorated player in English football, the former Welsh skipper has continued to display his remarkable skills – fleetness of foot and thought, superb ball control and a keen eye for goal – at the highest level.

Although often referred to now as 'veteran' or 'evergreen', Ryan is still a key component in the latest United team being built by Ferguson. A yard of his searing pace may have been lost but by employing him in a central midfield role – the same position from where he until recently captained his country – the United manager has shrewdly enabled the former flying winger to extend his Premiership career.

In an era dominated by greed, hype and mega money, Ryan Giggs has shown a refreshingly unusual commitment to the old-fashioned concept of loyalty: to his mother, who brought him up in Cardiff and then Swinton, to his friends and family and to Manchester United. Of course, the rewards for staying at Old Trafford have been considerable but, while a move abroad would have made him even more wealthy, he has stayed true to his roots – both in Wales and in his adopted home of Manchester.

As he explained in his autobiography, Giggs is a fiercely proud Welshman. He was born in St David's Hospital in Cardiff on 29 November 1973 when both his parents, Lynne Giggs and the Cardiff and Newport rugby player Danny Wilson, were seventeen years old. Ryan reveals theirs was a 'fiery relationship which would occasionally spill over into real unpleasantness.' While his mother held down two jobs, the young Ryan was looked after by his two sets of grandparents in Pentrebane and at the age of seven he moved with his parents and younger brother Rhodri to Lancashire when his father turned professional.

'I didn't want to leave Cardiff and my mates,' recalls Ryan. 'I was only a kid and I couldn't understand why we had to move so far from home. I knew I was going to miss my grandparents badly, especially on my Mum's side. But we had no choice. Dad's mind was made up.' Links with Cardiff were maintained through regular trips south at weekends and during school holidays – he would even come down just for the day to sample his grandmother's Sunday roast – and despite playing for England Schoolboys because he attended an English school, he 'never felt English, always Welsh.'

After appearing as a substitute against Everton, Ryan made his full debut for United in a Manchester derby in May 1991, before becoming the then youngest player to represent Wales five months later. At the age of just seventeen years and 321 days, he replaced Eric Young for the last six minutes as Wales were trounced 4-1 by Germany in Nuremberg. It was the first of five appearances as substitute before he marked his full debut with his first goal in a 2-0 win in a World Cup qualifier against Belgium at the old Cardiff Arms Park in 1992:

> I volunteered to take a free-kick just outside the box on the right and bent it with my left foot over the wall. It's one of my favourite goals of all time and what made it better was that so many of my family were there.

Ryan Giggs, who announced his retirement from international football in June 2007. (Hills Welsh Press)

The profound disappointment of later missing out on a trip to the 1994 World Cup finals with Wales followed the euphoria of Manchester United lifting their first title for twenty-six years in the Premiership's inaugural season. 'The relief and the intensity of the celebration was on a scale we'll never see again,' recalls the 1993 Young Player of the Year.

As well as winning every major honour in English and European football, Ryan Giggs has scored his fair share of memorable goals – none more so than the winner in an FA Cup semi-final replay against Arsenal in 1999 as Manchester United made their way to a unique treble by winning the Champions League soon after completing the domestic double. The extra-time goal was the dramatic culmination of a run which began ten yards inside his own half and took him past Patrick Vieira, Martin Keown, Lee Dixon and Tony Adams before he beat David Seaman with a spectacular left-footed drive. 'It was the kind of amazing finish you dream about,' Ryan recalls. 'It was my best goal ever and the one I'd like to be remembered by.'

Personally, I have nothing but admiration for Ryan Giggs. Through covering Welsh football as a journalist over the last twenty-five years, I have always found him to be courteous and helpful and when I was writing Terry Yorath's autobiography in 2004, Ryan readily agreed to provide a foreword for the book.

Wisely protected from the media by Sir Alex Ferguson until he was twenty, the archetypal boy next door has matured into a thoughtful and responsible family man. Having avoided the pitfalls associated with being described as 'the new George Best', he has refused to let fame and fortune turn his head. When not flummoxing flailing defenders, his feet have remained very firmly on the ground and he is a credit to both his profession and his family.

After making his way from a council estate in Ely to the top of European football, Ryan Giggs ranks as one of Cardiff's greatest sporting heroes. Although his Old Trafford career

Above left and right: Ryan Giggs in action for Wales.

is far from over – he looks on course to break Sir Bobby Charlton's all-time record of 759 appearances – it is not inconceivable that he could return to play in the Welsh capital on a more permanent basis. His mother was an ardent Cardiff City supporter – once running on to the pitch at Ninian Park to give star striker John Toshack a birthday present – and Ryan has intriguingly hinted that he could end his playing days with the Bluebirds: 'Cardiff have always been my second team and they're the first team I look for when the results come out over the weekend. Who knows what will happen?'

BOB MAPLESTONE

'The first British athlete to run a four-minute mile indoors'
by Clive Williams

If ever the phrase 'Cardiff born and Cardiff bred' applied to anyone, it certainly applies to Bob Maplestone. Born in 1946, he lived in Ely, before moving to the United States in 1970. But he did very little running at Ely's Cyntwell School, and showed no promise as a runner until he joined the Territorial Army at Cardiff's Maindy Barracks in 1965. There he was cajoled into running in their cross-country championships by Norman John, the secretary of Roath Cardiff Harriers. Roath merged with Cardiff's other athletics club, Birchgrove Harriers in 1968 to form Cardiff AAC.

Little did Welsh athletics fans realise when he finished eighth in that first race on Cardiff's Blackweir playing fields, that he would become the first British athlete to run a mile in under four minutes indoors and finish third in the USA Championships, just missing the UK 1,500-metre record by a fraction of a second!

After taking up the sport seriously in 1966, he made the Welsh team for the 1970 Commonwealth Games in Edinburgh, but failed to reach the final of the 1,500 metres. Bitterly disappointed, and looking to pack in running, he had his first thoughts of moving to the USA after the Games. Bob takes up the story:

> After that disappointment, I was about to quit. But the late John Walsh convinced me to run in the AAA (UK Championships) just after the Games finished. I made the final of the 1,500m running a personal best 3:45 in the heats and finished 6th in the final in 3:47:01. After the 3:45, I decided I was either going to quit or get serious. At this time a number of UK athletes were being offered scholarships in the United States. I enquired and, with the help of a Stanford University athlete, Dave Deubner, who was doing graduate work in Cardiff, was offered a scholarship. Attending College in the USA offered an opportunity to earn a degree and, I hoped, provide more time to train and fulfil my potential.

So he packed his bags and arrived at Eastern Washington University, some 300 miles east of Seattle, where he now lives, on the last day of August 1970. He later went to Oregon State University to earn his Master's degree in industrial engineering.

His indoor triumph in San Diego in February 1972 came about by accident, as he only got his place in the event because some of the leading US athletes were boycotting the race. Despite not feeling well in training the previous week, he hit the front with a lap and a half to go. He recalls:

> The crowd of over 8,000 went wild. I can remember running down the finishing straight and wanting to look up at the clock to see how close I was. When I crossed the line someone came over and said 3:59… something. My first thought was that the official time would be over 4 minutes. But the official time was announced as 3:59.5 – the first time I had run under 4 minutes, indoors or out.

Such was his laid-back demeanour that he had no idea that it was a British record and that he was the first British athlete to break four minutes indoors!

He had high hopes of making Britain's team for the 1972 Munich Olympics, and made the long journey home to run in the trials. But he had a poor race and failed to qualify. However, that year was definitely his best as he won 23 of the 26 races he ran. One of his fondest memories that year was beating the world record holder Jim Ryun in the Drake Relays mile in Des Moines. Bob won the race in a meeting record of 4:00.4.

His best outdoor performance came in the USA Championships in June that year. Held at Seattle, he ran a 1,500-metre personal best of 3:42.6, following a last lap of 55 seconds to win his heat. In the final, two days later, he was one of the favourites and led through the three-quarter-mile mark in 2:57, before tiring in the home straight to finish third. His time was a personal best of three minutes 39.7 seconds, which was only three tenths of a second away from the British record set by Peter Stewart the previous week.

Despite his great exploits in the States, Bob never won a Welsh title. He had to settle for runner-up spots in the 1,500 metres in 1969 and the 800 metres in 1970. He was a member of the Cardiff AAC team that broke the UK clubs 4 x 1,500 metre relay record in 1970. He also returned home whenever he could to run in Cardiff's British League team, during the time that Cardiff was Britain's leading athletics club.

Now a US citizen – he is professor of mechanical engineering at Highline College – he still remains a Cardiffian at heart. When I visited him in Seattle a few years ago, I took him Frank Hennesey's CD 'Cardiff After Dark'. Carol, his partner, told me some weeks later that he played it non-stop for a fortnight!

The true test of Bob's ability can be gauged by the fact that his best times for the 1,500 metres and mile would still have ranked him the second fastest Welshman in 2006 – thirty-four years after his startling performances. Altogether, he bettered four minutes for the mile on four occasions. Not bad for an Ely boy!

Bob Maplestone (far right)
in action in a race in the
USA during the 1970s.
(Clive Williams)

BARRY JONES

'Cardiff's super-featherweight world champion'
by Gareth Jones

It should have been the time of his life. The youngster from Ely was still basking in the glow
of becoming a world champion. Then came the hammer blow which wrecked his career.

Born in 1974, Barry Jones had first laced on the gloves at ten in Ray Thorogood's Highfields
gym. An outstanding junior, he had claimed a European silver medal and competed in the
World Championships, while winning the Welsh senior title the same year. He was still only
eighteen when he turned pro in 1992, trained by Pat Thomas, the St Kitts-born Cardiffian
who was British champion at two different weights.

Barry's first twelve fights culminated in a British featherweight eliminator victory over
tough Justin Murphy from Brighton. But he never contested the domestic honour.

Personal problems meant a year off, working in Ireland. His comeback bout saw him harshly
awarded no more than a draw against fellow Cardiffian David Morris, but top promoter
Frank Warren still secured him a match with the IBF Inter-Continental super-featherweight
champion, a Yorkshire dustman called Peter Judson.

A points win was followed by a successful defence at Cardiff's STAR against French veteran
Affif Djelti, but Jones was eyeing a greater prize. Warren came up with the goods, a crack at the
vacant World Boxing Organisation Championship, with Colombian warrior Wilson Palacio in
the opposite corner at the London Arena days before Christmas 1997.

Barry, having worn the shirt of his beloved Cardiff City into the ring, paraded the WBO belt
as he left, having clearly outpointed the experienced South American. He enjoyed the holidays,
looking ahead to a lucrative defence against French hero Julien Lorcy. But fate had other plans.

A routine brain scan four months later revealed an anomaly: there was a tiny gap in the
membrane and nobody could tell whether it put the Welshman at greater risk than other
boxers. In the wake of the Michael Watson tragedy, the British Boxing Board of Control were
taking no chances. They suspended Jones while they investigated.

The arguments raged for seven months before the board, assured by specialist Peter Richards
that there was no undue cause for concern, restored his licence. But by then the WBO had

stripped Barry of his title, although they promised he would get another shot if and when he was allowed to return.

By the time the opportunity came around, the belt belonged to a fearsomely hard-hitting Brazilian, Acelino Freitas. They met at the Octagon in Doncaster in January 2000. Incredibly, the famously light-punching Jones floored the champion in the opening seconds. It was a brief period of supremacy. Freitas dumped Barry on the canvas six times before his corner pulled him out after eight rounds.

He never boxed again, moving to London, where he now teaches physical education in local schools. If that medical scare had not intervened, his story might have been longer. But nothing can take away the fact that he was a world champion.

VALERIE DAVIES

'Cardiff's medal-winning swimmer who revelled in the Taff Swim'
by Andrew Hignell

Valerie Davies (later Valerie Latham) was the star of Welsh swimming in the 1920s and 1930s, winning a clutch of Olympic, Empire and European medals, as well as starring in many domestic events and gleefully taking part in the Taff Swim, held at the time in Roath Park Lake. In all, she won eleven major medals.

Born on 29 June 1912, the daughter of a Cardiff shipping magnate, Elizabeth Valerie Davies learned to swim at the age of five. Within only a few years, she was competing successfully at Roath Park Lake and travelling regularly to London for expert coaching during the winter months.

By the age of fifteen, she had won fourteen championships in Wales and was showing so much promise that she was selected for the British team which competed in the first European Swimming Championships held in Bologna in 1927. There – in a remarkable performance for one so young – Valerie won gold as a member of the successful 4 x 100-metre relay team.

Possessing such outstanding ability, she was the youngest member of Wales' party for the inaugural Empire Games held in 1930 at Hamilton in Canada where Valerie carried the Welsh flag. She returned home with three medals in backstroke and freestyle events. Each race was won by England's Joyce Cooper with Valerie finishing in second place in the 100-yard backstroke and 440-yard freestyle to win the silver medals, before adding a bronze in the 100-yard freestyle, as Scotland's Ellen King pipped Valerie to the silver.

Two years later, Valerie was included in the British swimming team for the 1932 Olympics, held in Los Angeles in the midst of the Great Depression. At the time, it was Britain's smallest Olympic team since 1904, but they performed with credit, with Valerie winning two bronze medals in the sprint events. She was the only British swimmer to take an individual medal.

In the 100-metre backstroke Valerie clinched a bronze medal after finishing in third place, three seconds behind Eleanor Holm of the United States, and Australia's Bonnie Mealing. She then teamed up with Joyce Cooper – her nemesis from the Empire Games – as well as Edna Tildesley Hughes and Helen Varcoe to win a Bronze in the 4 x 100-metre freestyle relay, although the British ladies were soundly beaten by the Americans, who finished 14 seconds ahead of Valerie and her colleagues, with the Dutch team finishing in second place.

This was not the end of Valerie's medal-winning achievements, as the twenty-two-year-old then added another bronze to her tally in the 1934 Empire Games, when she was the Welsh team captain. This time Valerie did not have to travel too far to take part from her home in South Wales, as the Games were staged in London. In the 100-yard backstroke, Valerie won the bronze medal after finishing third, behind England's Phyllis Harding and Scotland's Margot Hamilton. As in 1930, she was Wales' only swimming medallist.

Left and below: Roath Park Lake, as seen in the years either side of the First World War.

Action from the Taff Swim in the 1920s prior to the event switching to Roath Park. (Local Studies Department, Cardiff Central Library)

Despite her fame and achievements, Valerie continued to train at Roath Park Lake as well as take part in the Taff Swim, alongside a host of fellow Cardiffians in this grand municipal event. Her participation also helped to swell the number of spectators who flocked to Roath Park to watch this annual challenge and, given her outstanding career and high standing in the affection of Cardiff's sporting community. Valerie – who died in Newport in 2001 at the age of eighty-nine – was subsequently inducted into the Welsh Sports Hall of Fame.

THE TAFF SWIM
by Dennis Morgan

'The Taff Swim' was an eagerly anticipated event each year in Cardiff for more than thirty years, attracting some of local swimming's most famous names, as well as others – as in today's half-marathons – who just enjoyed taking part.

It began in 1924 when the contestants entered the river near Cardiff Castle and swam as far as Clarence Bridge. However, it became impossible to use the River Taff when Cardiff Bridge was widened in 1930, and the swim was then transferred to Roath Park Lake – which had been opened in the late nineteenth century on Bute-owned land in the northern suburbs.

The Taff Swim continued to be a popular attraction until the 1960s, when pollution in the lake brought the event to an end.

JOSEPH BRAIN

'The "brains" behind the early development of Glamorgan CCC'
by Andrew Hignell

Joseph Brain was the first in a distinguished line of influential captains of Glamorgan CCC, but it was the Cardiff brewer who, more than most of the other leaders, left his mark on the club by overseeing their transformation from a third-class county into one ready for elevation into the first-class game.

Indeed, it was Joseph Henry Brain who was the person responsible for Glamorgan's elevation in 1897 into the Minor County Championship – a move which made clear the club's aspirations of one day becoming Wales' representative in the first-class world, and putting the club's affairs onto a more professional basis.

He also used his vast connections, within both the business and sporting world, to secure the services of decent professionals, and he even dipped into his own pocket so that some of these men could gain winter employment at his family's Old Brewery in St Mary Street.

The acquisition of these better players around the turn of the century not only raised playing standards, but helped the fledgling county, formed in July 1888, shed the tag of being yet another gentleman's cricket team based in south Wales – a millstone that had weighed heavily around the necks of those involved with the earlier South Wales CC (formed in 1859) and Glamorganshire CC (formed in 1869).

Both of the earlier organisations had relied too heavily on gentlemen cricketers, choosing teams sometimes more for social reasons than cricketing ones. Despite having the support of many leading figures in the economic and political world of South Wales, both had ceased to operate by the mid-1880s.

At that time, Brain was an undergraduate at Oxford. The Old Cliftonian had already made his county debut for his native Gloucestershire in 1883, and was in the University XI that

J.H. Brain.

defeated the Australians in 1884. Later that summer, he also scored 108 for the county against the tourists, and he was viewed as a young man who one day might step into the shoes of the legendary Dr W.G. Grace in leading Gloucestershire.

However, Brain's father wanted Joseph and his brother William – himself a fine wicketkeeper who also played for both Gloucestershire and Glamorgan – to follow in his footsteps and instead have a successful business career. Indeed, in the late 1880s Joseph acquired The Old Brewery in Cardiff and shortly afterwards was appointed as its manager.

Sporting enthusiasts throughout South Wales can therefore be grateful that the Brains transferred their allegiance across the Severn Estuary as Gloucestershire's loss was definitely Glamorgan's gain, as Brain, in his role as captain and secretary of Glamorgan between 1891 and 1908, transformed their affairs and helped them become joint Minor County champions in 1900.

Brain's outstanding batting also made him the mainstay of the side and, in all, he struck five centuries for his adopted county, hitting over 5,000 runs, besides keeping wicket on several occasions when others, including his brother, were unavailable.

On three subsequent occasions in the years leading up to the First World War, Glamorgan were runners-up in the Minor County competition, with Brain at the helm each time, leading the team in his gentle, paternal way. Like a master brewer, he successfully blended the talents of its hard-nosed and worldly-wise professionals with those of the talented amateurs, in their gaily-coloured blazers. Just like the good beers from The Old Brewery, Brain produced a successful product that attracted larger crowds to their fixtures, thereby swelling the coffers of the club, offsetting the costs of hiring the professionals, and allowing the club to secure lucrative fixtures with touring teams.

The early 1900s were a buoyant time, not just for the Glamorgan side, but for the economy and political standing of South Wales as a whole and, with the rise of national identity, Brain led a bid for Cardiff to be allocated a Test match against the 1905 Australians. He had already used his sporting and social contacts in the city to raise sufficient capital for the erection of a spacious pavilion at the Arms Park, and with their new facilities receiving much praise, Brain led the campaign to secure an Ashes Test.

Sadly, his bid failed by one vote as, in December 1904, the MCC authorities, by the narrowest margin possible, allocated a Test match instead to the Trent Bridge ground in

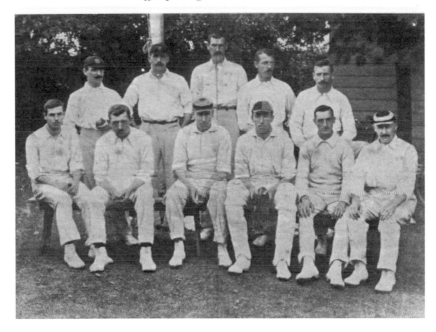

J.H. Brain (front row, third left), his brother William (front row, fourth left) and the rest of the Glamorgan team which played Devon at Exeter in 1901.

Nottingham. Brain though remained undeterred and, boosted by further achievement on the field, including a successful game between South Wales and the Australians in 1905, he became involved in the county's bid for first-class status.

Using his contacts once again across the region, and also within the Conservative Party in the Welsh capital, he helped to secure pledges of support from a host of influential figures. Indeed, without his painstaking efforts in the years leading up to the First World War, the club might not have so successfully overcome a tricky financial period. But, tragically, Brain never saw the fruits of his labours as he died after a short illness in June 1914.

MARK RING

'Cardiff's adventurous rugby and baseball international'
by Gwyn Prescott

When Mark Ring was in his prime, it was always disappointing for supporters to learn that he was not in the Cardiff line-up. His presence on the field invariably guaranteed that an entertaining afternoon was to be had. In some respects, he shared a similarity with Percy Bush, the Cardiff outside half and centre of an earlier generation, who also delighted in the role of crowd pleaser.

During the Ireland match in 1991, Mark fielded the ball when isolated deep in Welsh territory with the Irish tearing down on him. Then, with the same cheeky unpredictability for which Bush was famous, instead of kicking, he just stopped and stood still. So did the surprised opposition and this provided time for support to arrive. Mark then began a brilliant counter attack which resulted in a memorable try by Neil Jenkins.

Phil Davies, the current coach of Llanelli Scarlets, and a member of the Welsh team that day, has described him as the most mercurial of players, always looking to do the impossible and always believing he could win every game. Charismatic, adventurous, colourful, maverick, genius, outrageous and controversial are only some of the other epithets that have been used of this most gifted of players.

Born in Splott in 1962, Mark came to prominence through the usual channels of junior rugby, via St Albans and Lady Mary schools, Cardiff Schoolboys, Cardiff Youth and the Welsh Youth. Making a debut for Cardiff at only eighteen would be enough of an ordeal for anyone, but Ringo had to do it in the harsh environment of France against Côte Basque in April 1981. The talented youngster had arrived.

Less than two years later, and after only twelve First XV matches for Cardiff, Mark was drafted in to the Welsh side at centre as a replacement for the injured Rob Ackerman. The match against England was drawn but, despite his relative inexperience, Mark was already developing a critical view of the conservative tactics adopted.

By 1984/85 Cardiff had become the dominant side in Welsh rugby and Ringo was now a regular member of the Cardiff three-quarters, playing in the club's sixth successive victory over Australia. He represented Wales four times that season, playing particularly well against Scotland and France, being the only Welsh back in the latter game to create any penetration. Unfortunately, a severe knee injury in a club match not only kept him out of the final game against England but also out of most of the following season. Nevertheless, he was still named Welsh Player of the Year by the *Western Mail*. It took him nearly a year to recover but he returned to the game just in time help Cardiff to victory over Newport in the 1986 Welsh Cup final. He was also in the side which retained the cup against Swansea a year later.

Despite Mark's strong allegiance to Cardiff, he had two spells with Pontypool when he felt he was not being adequately appreciated by his home-town club. In 1987/88, he formed a brilliant half-back partnership with his close friend David Bishop and helped to take them to the Welsh Championship that season. Thus, it was as a Pontypool player that he represented Wales at centre in a Triple Crown year, which included their last victory at Twickenham in 1988. He rejoined Cardiff soon after but, five years later, he returned to captain the Gwent club.

Another serious injury playing for Cardiff in late 1988 removed the possibility of his selection for the Lions tour to Australia the following summer and the rugby public were therefore deprived of the mouth-watering prospect of a Mark Ring-Jeremy Guscott partnership.

He took part in two World Cups for Wales. In the first, held in 1987, he was a member of the Welsh XV which won the third-place play-off against Australia. After the 1991 competition, when he played in his favoured position at outside half, he decided to retire from international rugby, partly in despair at the state of the Welsh game. He had won 32 caps for his country.

Right: Mark Ring, just before his baseball debut for Wales against England at the Civil Service ground in 1984.

Opposite: Mark Ring (centre) in action for Wales against Scotland in 1990, as Allan Bateman (with ball) makes a break. (*Western Mail and Echo*)

But these weren't his only international appearances. Only four men have represented Wales at rugby and baseball and Mark Ring is one of them. Playing for Old Illtydians and then Grange Albion, he won four baseball caps between 1984 and 1991 and following his displays in the victory over England in 1986, he was named Man of the Match.

His last game for Cardiff was the European Cup final in 1996 which Stade Toulousain won in extra time. He had played 262 games for the club and scored 94 tries. He then went into coaching with West Hartlepool – then in the Premier Division of English rugby – Penzance & Newlyn and Caerphilly, whom he took to the final of the European Shield. He is still directly involved in the game and is currently coaching in Ireland.

WILLIAM GALE

'Cardiff's first great athlete'
by Clive Williams

Born in Cardiff in 1835, William Gale was one of the leading professional walkers – or pedestrians as they were called – of his time. They often covered prodigious distances, such as the 2,500 miles Gale attempted (but understandably failed) to walk in 1,000 hours at the then headquarters of British athletics, Lillie Bridge, in West Brompton, London in November 1880.

Gale was a diminutive man, weighing around 8st 4lbs and was only just over 5ft 3ins tall. Despite his size he was a formidable athlete and one of the leading lights in professional sport at the time. Such was his reputation that he became the first Cardiff sportsman to have a book written about him, when in 1877 J.A. Brooks published his *Life and Performances of William Gale, the Celebrated Cardiff Pedestrian*.

He gave clear indication of his potential at The Gnoll in Neath – the town's cricket ground – in September 1855 when he was just twenty. He walked seven miles and 230 yards in 59 minutes 29 seconds, which was a remarkable achievement, even by today's standards.

The contestants line up behind The Malsters in Llandaff in 1905 for a walking race to Cowbridge Road and back. In all, a journey of sixteen miles was covered in just two hours and twenty minutes by the winner Arthur James, standing third from the left in the front row of walkers. (Cardiff Central Library, Local Studies Department)

Brian Lee says in his book *Cardiff Remembered*, 'His first big walking exhibition took place in Canton Market in 1876 where he walked 1,000 miles in 1,000 hours or to be more precise 41 days.' His headquarters in Cardiff were at the Criterion pub, which used to stand opposite St John's Church in Church Street.

One of Gale's finest performances came in 1877, when he achieved the phenomenal deed of walking 1,500 miles in 1,000 hours. Also held at Lillie Bridge, it was accomplished by walking one and a half miles each hour. Once the distance had been covered, he would rest and commence walking again at the start of the next hour. The task took in excess of six weeks. It was hailed at the time by *The Illustrated London News* as: 'A great pedestrian feat… far superior to the exploits of Captain Barclay, who walked a 1,000 miles in 1,000 hours at Newmarket in 1809.'

One of his other fine performances was covering 1,000 quarters of a mile in consecutive intervals of ten minutes. This meant that he had walked a mile and a half per hour for a fortnight. During this period, he took no more than seven-minute rest periods at a time. Cardiff's first nationally famous sportsman had set a high standard for others to follow.

BILLY BOSTON

'A rugby league legend'
by Huw Richards

Billy Boston was the third of Cardiff's holy trinity of rugby league hall-of-famers, as emblematic of the game in the 1950s and 1960s as Jim Sullivan and Gus Risman (each Cardiff greats themselves) had been to the previous three decades. A memorable name helps, but he would have been a rugby hero even if called Dai Jones or Tom Davies.

Among exported Welsh heroes, perhaps only near-contemporary John Charles' adoption by Turin matches Boston's by Wigan. As Dave Hadfield has written, he is 'the only man whose name comes close to George Orwell in terms of being synonymous with Wigan,' and 'the most enduringly famous figure in the game.'

Half a century after he signed for Wigan, the anniversary was felt significant enough to be marked by a public function, music provided by Leigh-born jazz and blues legend Georgie

Fame, who confessed to deserting his home-town club as a boy in the 1950s because he could watch Boston at Wigan.

Boston epitomised Cardiff's ethnic diversity, growing up in a time when, Phil Melling has written, 'Tiger Bay, not Brixton or Bradford was the nerve centre of multiracial Britain.' He was born in 1934, the sixth of eleven children of a Sierra Leonian father and an Irish mother. The family lived on Angelina Street, and his Tiger Bay friends and contemporaries included boxer Joe Erskine and singer Shirley Bassey. Like Risman he attended South Church Street School.

Like Sullivan and Risman he left Cardiff while still in his teens. But his pace and power had already made an impact in union. He was capped for Welsh Boys Clubs, captained the District XV in its annual early-season match against Cardiff at the Arms Park, was a rumbustious presence in the teams of the cosmopolitan Cardiff International Athletic Club (CIAC) and played the occasional game for Neath.

National Service brought him to wider attention when he scored 126 tries in 30 matches for an all-conquering Royal Signals team including six, happily captured on still-extant film, in the Army Cup final against the Welsh Guards. In March 1953 he signed professional forms with Wigan, who were coached by Jim Sullivan. There was such excitement in the town, his debut for the second team against Barrow seven months later attracted a crowd of 8,500.

The anticipation was fully justified. He scored two tries in that second-team bow, then again on his senior debut three weeks later, going on to score twice in his second senior game, three times in his third and four times in his fourth. After six matches he was chosen for the Great Britain tour of Australia and New Zealand. There he scored twice on his test debut, a GB record-equalling four in one Test against New Zealand and 38 times in 18 matches in all.

While the two-tries-per-match tempo of his early career inevitably eased, his impact on the game did not. His career total of 571 tries, at just over a try per match, is a record for a British player, exceeded only by his prodigious Australian near-contemporary Brian Bevan. He played 31 times for Great Britain, scoring 24 tries including 10 in 11 against Australia.

It was typical that he should do so well against the supreme adversary. Like John Charles, he had little relish for slaughtering smaller and weaker opposition, but reserved his best for those more his own size and ability.

Ray French, an imposing international forward in both union and league, certainly felt no mercy when they played each other in Wigan-St Helens matches, later writing:

At fifteen stones he was a fearsome sight coming at you and, in facing a man who could sidestep, swerve and hand-off, we were often at a loss as to how to stop him. Very often he just powered his way through us, and seemed to delight in leaving bodies scattered in his wake.

His style of play changed over a career that lasted from 1953 to 1970. His biographer Jack Winstanley wrote that, 'When he first came into the game, he was thirteen stone with a nine-foot sidestep. When he left it he was fifteen stone with a nine-inch sidestep.' What did not change was the footballing ability that underlay his formidable physical qualities.

New Zealand half-back Cec Mountford said he would sign Boston before any other player in league because, 'he can do more things better than any other player in the game… I would have a man of so many trades that I would be certain to get my money's worth.'

He reckoned that, while there were players who were faster or heavier, 'no-one has a better speed-weight ratio than Boston,' who could 'play an excellent game on either wing, at centre or stand-off,' and in defence 'can have the shattering effect of a flying bomb'. He played every back division position except scrum-half for Wigan.

And for all his international feats, it was in the cherry and white of Wigan, often playing outside a comparable talent in the creative centre and outstanding leader Eric Ashton, that he entered league folklore – charging unstoppably across muddy surfaces to the delight of crowds at the club's legend-encrusted Central Park. A dozen games for Blackpool Borough, the last as a second row, were a mere coda to his 488 matches and 478 tries for Wigan.

He stayed in Wigan, becoming the licensee of the Griffin pub close to Central Park. When, aged sixty-two, he was struck by a hit-and-run driver in 1996 it was the car that was written off while the perpetrator was placed under a curfew to protect him from the reprisals of outraged Wiganers. He remains a genial, approachable figure on the rugby league circuit, at once proud Cardiffian and living northern legend.

HAYDN TANNER

'The schoolboy who helped to defeat the All Blacks'
by Alun Wyn Bevan

The random selection of genes that occurs during the reproductive process results in the creation of an individual who will have exceptional characteristics. These may manifest themselves in the form of physical, intellectual or spiritual traits as exemplified by such noteworthies as Aristotle, Samson, Einstein, Mozart, Helen of Troy, da Vinci and Mandela to name but a few.

It would be crass and inappropriate to add to this list someone who excels in the sporting arena. However, if one were to compile a list of such luminaries, the name Haydn Tanner would undoubtedly be an early entry. Born in Gowerton in 1917, he plied his craft on the sporting arenas of St Helen's, Swansea and the Arms Park at Cardiff during the 1930s and 1940s. His career at Swansea began while he was still a pupil at Gowerton Grammar School. Scouts for the All Whites had passed many a Saturday morning observing the half-back pairing of Haydn Tanner and W.T.H. (Willie) Davies as they engineered yet another victory for the school team.

Nevertheless, the announcement that these two schoolboys were to be included in the Swansea team to play New Zealand on 28 September 1935 at St Helen's was received with no small amount of shock and disbelief by the press and public alike. Imagine the scenario. The young scrum-half

Right: Haydn Tanner.

Opposite: Billy Boston (front row, second left) and the Cardiff International Athletic Club rugby team of 1951/52 – a season when the CIACs were unbeaten. (John Billot)

standing outside his headmaster's study – his hand shaking visibly as he knocks the door (due no doubt to a mixture of excitement and trepidation). Once inside he can barely utter the words, 'Please, sir, may I take the afternoon off next week? I'm playing against the All Blacks!'

There is no record of the headmaster's response, but the young Tanner's request was granted. Thus, on a wet and windy autumnal afternoon in front of a crowd of 30,000 partisan supporters, the young, inexperienced All Whites took to the field to face the might of Jack Manchester's All Blacks. Some said it was a scene reminiscent of the gladiatorial games in the Colosseum and, as one newspaper headlined, it was 'Lambs to the Slaughter'.

As the game progressed it became evident that the Swansea pack were able to hold their own against the much heavier opposition. Indeed, their performance enabled Tanner and Davies to dictate the course of the game – the latter managing to create two openings that enabled the giant Claude Davey to score two tries. Despite the conditions, St Helen's was a cauldron of aggression and passion for the duration of and following the end of the game. At the final whistle the scoreline read: Swansea 11 New Zealand 3. The post-match quote from the New Zealand captain is still music to the ears of every All Whites supporter some seventy years on: 'Please don't tell them back home that we were beaten by a pair of schoolboys!'

Some two months later, and still only eighteen years old, Haydn Tanner was selected to play for Wales against the All Blacks at the Arms Park. This time his partner was the mercurial Cliff Jones. In the tradition of the best folk stories, he was again influential as Wales beat New Zealand 13-12.

Tanner had now attained iconic status – the press and public idolised him in equal measure. What was the secret of his success? Unlike most scrum-halves, Tanner was a big man, physically robust and able to withstand the most bone-crunching tackle. He had a fast, accurate service which seemed to compel his partner to run at speed onto the ball. He could read any situation quickly and possessed a lateral vision which opened up several options for the team whether this be in an attacking or defensive situation.

In 1938, Haydn Tanner was selected for the British Lions tour to South Africa. This proved to be an unpleasant experience for the young man, as he spent virtually the whole tour on the sidelines following a catalogue of injuries, and consequently he played in only one test.

Haydn in action at a special photographic shoot.

At the end of the Second World War, Tanner joined Cardiff RFC. Here again he was a major contributor in one of the most successful periods in the club's history. In his second game against his old club, Swansea, he scored two outstanding tries that resulted in a 13-8 defeat for the All Whites. Under his captaincy, between 1947 and 1949, Cardiff lost only five of their 85 fixtures and in 1947/48 they enjoyed perhaps their most successful season ever, which included an 11-3 victory over Australia. In his book *Rugger My Life*, the prince of centres, Bleddyn Williams, heaps praise on the scrum-half: 'The great Haydn Tanner was a master of scrum-half play.' The late Clem Thomas in his much-praised volume *The History of the British Lions* agrees: 'I would have no hesitation in putting him forward as one of the very finest scrum-halves of all time.'

Tanner played 25 games in the Welsh jersey – twelve as a Cardiff player – and was pivotal in many of the team's victories. If there is one game that typifies his all-round talent, it was the match against France at Stade Colombes in 1947. The atmosphere was electric with no quarter given or taken. Wales were victorious thanks to a fifty-yard penalty kick from the boot of Cardiff's Bill Tamplin, but it was Tanner who had provided the inspiration for the win.

On this occasion, it was his defensive play that came to the fore in an often brutal encounter. He managed to nullify the threat posed by his French counterpart, Yves Bergougnan (himself revered as a god by his adoring French fans). Time and again Tanner would fall on the ball and time and again he would be tramped underfoot by the rampaging French forwards. Bergougnan left the field in tears, but again as Bleddyn Williams wrote in his book, 'there was never any disgrace in being beaten by Haydn Tanner. I never saw him outplayed.'

In 1948, and for the first time in the history of the game, Australia played their final tour match against the Barbarians, and Haydn was given the honour of leading an illustrious encounter in front of 50,000 fans at the Arms Park. The Barbarians won 9-6 and, to this day, the aficionados enjoy recalling the intricate moves that led to one score. Tanner broke menacingly from the base of the scrum that had formed near the left-hand touchline and fed his half-back partner, Tommy Kemp. He in turn kept the movement going by passing to Bleddyn Williams who penetrated the defence before releasing Billy Cleaver who, in turn,

Stevie Lyle. (Andrew Weltch)

passed back inside to Williams. The centre threw a long pass out to Martin Turner on the wing, who seemed in the clear, but for an impenetrable Wallabies defence. Just as he was about to score, Turner was tackled, but managed to pass inside to the waiting Haydn Tanner – a maestro who in his own field is up there with the best.

STEVIE LYLE

'The Cardiff Devils' star netminder'
by Andrew Weltch

Cardiff has been something of a 'factory' for high-quality ice hockey players, since the city's belated involvement with the sport in the 1980s, but none has made the impact of Stevie Lyle. His success has been all the more remarkable because his position, netminder, is regarded as the most difficult to master.

Lyle, born in Cardiff on 4 December 1979, made his debut for the Cardiff Devils' first team in a challenge match at Swindon in 1994 at the age of fourteen and went on to be named the club's Rookie of the Year. He backstopped the Devils in their sensational European Cup campaign that season, helping Cardiff to a shock victory in their quarter-final group, beating champion teams from the former Soviet republics of Ukraine and Kazakhstan, and earning himself the tournament's best netminder award.

Already a Great Britain international at under-16 and under-20 level, he made his debut for the full national team in the 1996 World Championships – at sixteen becoming the youngest player ever to be called up for GB duty and helping his country to victory over mighty Belarus on the way. His list of individual honours includes BBC Wales Young Sports Personality of the Year 1995/96, Superleague Player of the Year 1996/97, Cardiff Devils

Player of the Year 1996/97, and Best Netminder awards five times between 1998/99 and 2003/04.

In Cardiff, he helped the Devils to the inaugural Superleague title in 1996/97 and the play-off championships in 1999, but the ambitious youngster had his eye on a career in big-time hockey across the Atlantic, and ultimately a place in the National Hockey League (NHL). He made the trip to North America in 1997, drafted by Plymouth Whalers, of the Ontario Hockey League, a development team for the NHL's Detroit Red Wings. He played six games, but was released because of a rule restricting the number of European players.

He found a spot with Kindersley Klippers of the lower-level Saskatchewan Junior Hockey League, and was a big hit – finishing top of the netminder statistics at the end of the league season, and becoming joint winner of the team's Most Valuable Player award. But his hopes of progressing up the ranks in North America seemed slim: the second-level American Hockey League and International Hockey League (IHL) could not sign players until they were twenty, and by the summer of 1998, Lyle was still only seventeen.

He decided to return to Cardiff, where the Devils were playing in the Superleague – the short-lived all-professional UK competition. 'The Superleague standard is much better than Canadian junior and not far off the IHL,' he told *The Ice Hockey Annual* at the time. After a further three seasons with Cardiff, he was part of a mass exodus in the summer of 2001, when the Devils came close to folding and re-emerged as a low-budget team in dispute with their fans and struggling in the lower-level British National League (BNL).

Lyle was one of several Devils who headed north to Manchester Storm and he performed well as the team's only British player that season, which turned out to be Storm's last full campaign. Manchester's collapse, followed by that of the overambitious Superleague itself, saw Lyle return home to Cardiff, where his arrival sparked an upturn in fortunes, with the Welsh team reaching the BNL play-off final.

The next season, 2003/04, saw Lyle at Guildford Flames, and victory in the play-off final, before a single season with Bracknell Bees, where he was hailed as the club's most important signing and received the coach's award and Best Defensive Player award. A season in Italy with Appiano Pirates was followed in 2006/07 with a move to French side Morzine Penguins, and a return to the national set-up in 2006 saw him win acclaim at the World Championships in France, where he was named GB Player of the Tournament.

ICE HOCKEY IN CARDIFF
by Andrew Weltch

Cardiff was late to embrace ice hockey – the city's first ice rink opened in 1986, some fifty years after Britain won Olympic Gold in the sport for the only time. The grandly-titled Wales National Ice Rink in Hayes Bridge Road saw a near-2,500 sell-out for its opening game in November that year – a 32-0 demolition by Cardiff Devils of Ashfield Islanders.

As the Devils progressed rapidly through the ranks of the British game, so the city-centre rink underwent a series of improvements, including extra seating and plexi-glass to replace netting, with the team's entry into the short-lived Superleague in 1996. After a series of delays over a much-trailed move to a bigger venue in Cardiff Bay, the rink was demolished in September 2006 to make way for a shopping development. Its final game – between the 2005/06 Devils and a team of former Cardiff players – took place in April 2006.

While delays in constructing the 7,000-seat arena as part of a Sports Village – first mooted in the 1990s – stretched to several years, the Devils moved to a temporary home in the Bay in December 2006. The opening game was postponed at the last minute because the ice was not up to standard, and fans complained that the new venue offered poor sightlines and inadequate facilities. The rink was also criticised for being too cold – tarpaulin, which formed part of the structure, flapped furiously in the strong winds coming off the water. The decision in February 2007 to deny Cardiff a 'super casino' appears to mean a further delay for the main arena, and the Devils seem likely to remain in their 'temporary' home for some years to come.

TANNI GREY-THOMPSON

'Britain's greatest Paralympian'
by Andrew Hignell

Dame Tanni Grey-Thompson, born in Cardiff in July 1969, is one of Britain's most decorated Olympians. In most people's minds, she is also the country's greatest Paralympian with a string of titles and medals including eleven gold medals, three silvers and a bronze, and six London Marathon titles between 1992 and 2002. During her glittering career, she also set world records over distances ranging from 100 metres to 800 metres, and held British records over every distance from 100 metres to 10,000 metres. In 2002 Tanni proudly carried the flag for Wales at the opening ceremony of the Manchester Commonwealth Games, whilst in 2006 she was team captain of Wales at the Melbourne Commonwealth Games. No surprise, therefore, that she should be the first ever Paralympian to be voted onto the elite World Sports Academy Hall of Fame.

Her outstanding feats in both short- and long-distance events, plus her cheerful personality, have made her a household favourite back home in Wales, with Tanni winning, no less than three times, the BBC Wales Sports Personality of the Year title. She was also made an MBE in the 1992 Honours List, before securing an OBE in the Millennium New Year's Honours List, and then deservedly becoming a Dame in the 2004 New Year's Honours List – a most fitting honour in recognition of her wonderful services to sport and her tireless efforts in championing the cause of disabled sportsmen and women.

Right from the earliest days of her glittering career, Tanni has been an outstanding ambassador for Paralympic sports. Time and again, she has been asked the same disparaging questions about the participants, and each time Tanni has stressed how she and all the others taking part have always wanted to be considered as athletes, rather than disabled people who race. 'It's so important that the Games are seen as parallel Olympics,' she said in a recent newspaper interview. 'That's in fact where the name comes from – not para-lysed or para-plegic – just parallel, and that's all we want to be recognised as.' Indeed, when first crowned as Welsh Sports Personality of the Year, the twenty-three-year-old said, 'this award means more to me than others I have won because I have won it as an athlete and not as a disabled person.'

During Tanni's illustrious sporting career, she has witnessed many changes in the way that disabled athletes have been treated. When she made her Commonwealth Games debut at Auckland in 1990, she had to share kit with fellow wheelchair athlete Chris Hallam. As she later recalled, 'our races were only demonstration events, and there was just one vest between Chris and myself. Luckily, I was racing first, and his was the next day, so I had the evening to wash it – drying it with my hair dryer!'

In fact, Chris Hallam was one of Tanni's first sporting heroes, and the efforts in the London Marathon of the wheelchair athlete from Cwmbran – with his beach-blond hair and garish leopard-skin lycra – were an inspiration for young Tanni:

> I had a go at archery, basketball and swimming, but athletics became a big thing for me after watching on television the performances of Welsh athletes like Chris Hallam and John Harris in the London Marathon. To see them achieving so much got me thinking seriously about taking part in the Marathon myself.

Tanni Grey-Thompson in August 1990. (*Western Mail and Echo*)

As a young athlete, she gleefully embarked on a strict training and diet schedule, mixing road and track work which involved racing for up to fifteen miles each day on the roads around her family's home in the Heath, plus three sessions per week on the track at the Cardiff Athletic Stadium. As Tanni said in a magazine interview a few years ago:

> I preferred the independence of athletics to team sports. In a team you can have the best day of your life, but you do not achieve anything if the team is not playing well around you. In athletics, you are playing against yourself, constantly striving to be better than the last time. It's the need to be the best you can be.

Such determination and the will to win were her watchwords, as she began competing for Wales at the age of fifteen in the junior national championships. At the age of nineteen, she won her first Olympic medal – a bronze in the 400 metres – in the 1988 Games at Seoul, which were also the first Olympics in which the Paralympic competitors were allowed to wear the same kit as the other competitors.

Four years later, at the Barcelona Games, Tanni won gold in the 100 metres, 200 metres, 400 metres and 800 metres – the first of a string of Olympic events in which Tanni was so proud to hear the national anthem echoing around the stadium in recognition of her gold medal-winning feats. The earlier days of discrimination against wheelchair athletes, and the patronising comments from people who should have known better, must have seemed light years away.

In 2002 Tanni recalled some of these in her moving autobiography *Seize the Day*, recounting how she had winced at school when adults had looked at her in her wheelchair and said, 'you

Dame Tanni, as seen in June 1994. (*Western Mail and Echo*)

poor little thing.' Remarkably, such attitudes still existed in her early adulthood, such as the time when one international airline refused to allow her to travel without a companion. She vehemently protested, got her money back, and flew with British Airways instead – all alone.

Spina bifida has meant that Tanni has been wheelchair-bound since the age of seven – 'the year before I had my chair was probably the worst of my life,' she later recalled in a magazine interview. 'I was in so much pain, and walking was so painful. I never saw my wheelchair as a negative thing, and it was something that meant I could get moving again.'

Educated at Birchgrove Junior School and St Cyres Comprehensive in Penarth, she then read politics and social administration at Loughborough University. Tanni now lives in Redcar with her husband and fellow athlete Dr Ian Thompson, whom she married in May 1998, and their young daughter Carys, born in 2002. Despite the demands of family life, Tanni continues to be a wonderful ambassador, mixing work for various charities and for UK Athletics with her role as a motivational speaker, and as a broadcaster on radio and television.

In March 2007 she announced that she would be retiring after the Visa World Cup in Manchester in May. With tears welling up on a face that has become one of the most cherished – and instantly recognised – in British sport, Tanni said:

> I never thought there would be anything more important than athletics, but for me to go to Beijing for the 2008 Paralympics would mean I'd be away from home and my family for too long, and that is not what I want to do any more. I have always said I'd retire when I had done enough. I think, finally, I have.

Very few would disagree.

JIM ALFORD

'Cardiff's gold medal-winning athlete at the 1938 Empire Games'
by Brian Lee

Almost seventy years have passed since Jim Alford, who was born in Cardiff in 1913, won the blue riband event at the 1938 British Empire Games – the magic mile. A member of Roath (Cardiff) Harriers, he served his club and country well over many years. A most versatile athlete, he won no fewer than twelve Welsh titles between 1934 and 1948 at 440 yards, 880 yards, the mile, three miles and at cross-country running. He also represented Great Britain on five occasions. Jim was simply one of the greatest athletes ever produced in Wales.

A graduate of Cardiff and Bristol Universities, Jim won both the 800 and 1,500 metres in the 1937 World University Games in Paris. He was the sole Welsh athlete at the 1938 Empire Games held in Australia, when he was the favourite for the 880 yards. But suffering from humidity and lack of sleep, he finished a disappointing fourth after tying up in the closing stages of the race. However, he more than made up for this by producing, on a grass track at Sydney Cricket Ground, his finest ever performance in the mile, improving on his personal best by over five seconds. Recalling the event, many years ago now, he had this to say:

> The first two laps were very fast for those days – the half-mile stage was covered in two minutes and four seconds – and I had to stay well back and gradually work my way through the field. But the third lap slowed up so abruptly just before the bell that I found myself in the lead long before I wanted it. Then came my bad moment... I had only one thought, to hang on, then as I came round the last bend there was a roar from the Sydney crowd for the Australian runner Gerald Backhouse just behind me – but all was well.

The opening ceremony of the 1958 Empire Games, held at the Arms Park in July 1958.

In winning the gold medal, Jim set a new Games record with a time of 4:11.6 which beat the previous record set in London in 1934 of 4:12.8, held by the famed Jack Lovelock, the 1936 Olympic 1,500 metres champion. Like so many others of his era, his career was then curtailed by the war. Nevertheless, ten years after winning gold, Jim won the 1948 Welsh Senior Cross-Country Championship over nine miles at Caerleon Racecourse, proving just how versatile an athlete he really was. He then went on to become the first National Coach for Wales in 1948 and was subsequently responsible for coaching many medallists and other successful athletes.

THE EMPIRE AND COMMONWEALTH GAMES
by Brian Lee

From 18 to 26 July 1958, Cardiff hosted the sixth British Empire and Commonwealth Games. At the time they were considered the best ever, comprising nine sports – athletics, boxing, cycling, fencing, lawn bowls, rowing, swimming (and diving), weightlifting and wrestling.

A variety of venues were used, including some outside Cardiff. The only purpose-built facility was the Empire Pool for the swimming and diving. The cycling was held at Maindy Stadium, with the 120-mile road race taking place around a seven and a half mile circuit near the River Ogmore. The boxing and wrestling took place at Sophia Gardens Pavilion, whilst Cae'r Castell School in Llanrumney was used for the fencing. The Cardiff, Mackintosh and Penylan clubs all hosted the lawn bowls competition, the weightlifting was staged at the Barry Memorial Hall and the rowing at Lake Padarn in Snowdonia in North Wales.

The athletics were held at the Cardiff Arms Park and my outstanding memories are of the great Australian Herb Elliott winning the mile, and New Zealander Murray Halberg taking the three miles. Elliott – the greatest miler ever and never beaten over the distance – won by twenty yards in three minutes and 59 seconds. Halberg, who broke away from the field with three laps to go, won in 13 minutes and 15 seconds, then the third fastest time in the world.

And any Welshman or woman who was there could not forget the roar of the crowd when, on the last lap of the six miles, Wales' John Merriman sprinted after the pace-making Australian Dave Power. The more experienced Power held on to his lead to win by three yards before collapsing on the grass. Merriman, looking much fresher, waved to the crowd, delighted with his silver medal.

Power went on to win the marathon and when he entered the stadium ahead of South Africa's Jan Barnard the atmosphere was electric. He clocked two hours, 22 minutes and 45.6 seconds, establishing a new Games best performance. In fact, the first eight athletes home all beat the previous best performance. A total of 1,398 athletes took part in those games and I had a small, if insignificant, part to play in them. I was one of the escort runners to former Commonwealth Games runner Ken Harris, who carried the silver-gilt baton containing a message from the Queen which he passed on to former Welsh rugby international and sprinter Ken Jones who in turn passed it on to the Duke of Edinburgh to read out at the opening ceremony.

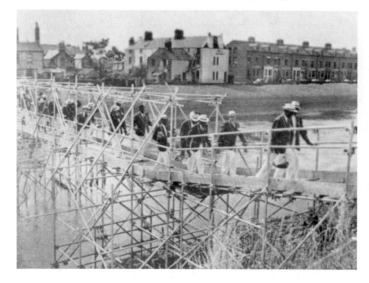

The special bridge erected for contestants and officials to cross over the River Taff.

The Great Western Hotel at the bottom of St Mary Street was the administrative centre for the 1958 Empire Games.

Ken Jones
hands over the
baton to HRH
The Duke of
Edinburgh at
the opening
ceremony.

The start of the
Empire Games
Marathon on
25 July 1958
as the runners
leave Cardiff
Arms Park and
head north up
Westgate Street

TED PETERSON

'A legend in Welsh baseball'
by Andrew Weltch

Ted Peterson's contribution to Welsh baseball was greater than any other player or administrator, earning him every honour in the game and even the MBE. Ted was a formidable bowler, with his international appearances for Wales stretching from the 1930s to the 1960s, and when his playing days were over, he devoted his energies to administration.

He was named 'unsung hero of sport' by the Welsh Sports Hall of Fame, and in 1996, at the age of eighty, he received the UK National Help the Aged Golden Award for contribution to sport. He died in December 2005, aged eighty-nine, still holding the post of president of the Welsh Baseball Union (WBU). A Wales team selector and member of the International Baseball Board, there is even a cup competition named in his honour. No wonder he was known as 'Mr Baseball'.

Born in Canton in 1916, Peterson got a taste of big-time baseball, when he was substitute for his school team, Roath Park, in a cup final, played as a curtain-raiser to the annual Wales-England international at the Welsh White City Stadium in 1928. When he left school, he played for local church teams before breaking into the Penylan side in 1934 – a club he would remain with throughout his career. He spent most of that first season with the second team, but in one first-team appearance, against Splott US (University Settlement), he recorded impressive figures of 8 for 24.

In 1935, he became a Penylan first-team regular, as support bowler to Wales international Bob Roper, and two years later received his own call-up to the national side. He took 6 for 33 in two spells against England in 1937 at Stanley Greyhound Stadium, Liverpool, and was also the top Welsh batsman, with 10 and 4, but it was not enough to help Wales avoid an innings defeat.

After missing the 1938 international through injury, he was back in the team for the 1939 trip to Liverpool, and another Welsh defeat in torrential rain. The Second World War saw him on active service with the Royal Engineers, and he was at both Dunkirk and Dieppe, before returning to civilian life and the Great Western Railway, where he was employed, mainly in the docks, for fifty-one years.

The first post-war international was the 1948 game in the grounds of Cardiff Castle. Peterson captained Wales and opened the bowling in front of a record 16,000 crowd. He got four England players out for ducks and steered his team to victory by 11 runs, thus ending England's five-game winning streak.

The following year at New Brighton, Peterson gained his fourth cap. As second bowler to Maurice Groves, he finished England's first innings with figures of 4 for 27. He also cemented his reputation as something of an all-rounder: his total of 14 equalled his best international score and took his Wales total to 40 in four games – the average of 10 runs per game being an outstanding figure for a bowler.

Back on home soil for the 1950 international, the game had to be replayed after torrential rain disrupted proceedings at Sophia Gardens. Peterson bowled superbly to take out eight Englishmen in the first innings and seven in the second. He also scored 9 in his only innings with the bat to help Wales to a comfortable win.

On the domestic scene, the Penylan hero effectively clinched the Welsh League title for Splott US, when he bowled out Splott's title rivals Grange Albion for a season-low total of 26, inflicting a defeat that secured the Dewar Shield for the University Settlement team.

He played in the 1951 and 1952 international wins and was picked as substitute, but not used, in the 1953 game. He captained a Welsh team against the English at Sophia Gardens in

Ted Peterson. (*Western Mail and Echo*)

1957, a special representative match – in addition to the annual international – staged to raise money for the Empire Games funds. His final appearance for Wales came in 1960, and he took 4 for 9 in the first England innings, as the Welsh won a thriller at Maindy Stadium.

In club competition, Peterson's Penylan scored the league and cup double in 1952, beating Splott US in the WBU Cup final by 79 runs, and there were further successes in both premier competitions through the late 1950s and into the 1960s. Indeed, in 1961, 1962 and 1963 Penylan won the treble of league title, WBU Cup and Welsh National Baseball League (WNBL) Cup.

In 1963, he became chairman of the WNBL, and in 1978 – at the age of sixty-two – finally hung up his baseball boots. In 1980 he was invited to City Hall to meet the Queen and Duke of Edinburgh, who were in the capital to mark Cardiff's seventy-fifth anniversary of achieving city status.

In 1985 he retired after twenty-two years as secretary of the Penylan club and, with the amalgamation of the WNBL and Welsh Baseball Union, he became chairman of the new WBU, which at that time administered seventy-two men's teams, thirty-two women's teams and 250 junior sides. Stepping down as chairman in 1996, he remained president until his death in 2005.

Regarded as a great sportsman, gentleman and family man, his phenomenal contribution to baseball is remembered in the Ted Peterson Cup, contested by Welsh clubs each summer.

PERCY BUSH

'Welsh rugby's Will o' the Wisp'
by Gwyn Prescott

Some accounts claim that Percy Bush hailed from the Rhondda but, in fact, he was born in Cardiff in 1879 into a local sporting family. His father, James, was a pioneer of cricket and rugby in Cardiff, who played in the earliest ever recorded 'football' match at the Arms Park in 1868. He was also involved with the Tredegarville (Roath) club which – it has recently been discovered – was playing rugby as early as 1870.

If rugby had become the people's theatre in Wales by the turn of the century, then Bush was one of its starring artistes. An irrepressible joker, trickster and leg-puller, he enlivened dressing-room, clubroom and football field alike. The 1908 match against England took place in heavy fog. Asked before the game in which direction Wales would play, he responded, 'with the fog'. At half-time, he was spotted in the crowd chatting to spectators. During the match, he and Rhys Gabe found themselves with a loose ball in the English half. They pretended to wrestle for it and then Bush ran off into the fog shouting, pulling the defence with him. Meanwhile, Gabe calmly went the other way and scored completely unopposed.

Percy was a product of the huge enthusiasm for rugby which swept through Cardiff in the wake of the enormous success of Frank Hancock's 1885/86 team. Educated at local private schools, where he first learned the game, he later joined Cardiff Romilly RFC, one of Cardiff's stronger 'district' clubs. In 1896, he entered University College and it was whilst playing for them at the Arms Park that he was spotted by a Penygraig scout, who promptly signed him up. This is the simple explanation for his connection with the Rhondda club which he later captained in the highly competitive and combative Glamorgan League.

Having served a demanding apprenticeship in district and valleys rugby, Percy played for Cardiff from 1899, though he did not command a regular place until 1903. Following some dazzling displays for the club that season, he was selected for the 1904 British Lions tour to Australia and New Zealand. Although still uncapped, he was the Lions' outside half in all four Tests and became the undoubted star of the tour, both on and off the field, being dubbed 'Will o' the Wisp' by the Australian press for his devastating displays. His box of tricks included an uncanny ability to elude tacklers at will, whether by sidestepping off either foot, or by dodging or swerving. Another knack of his was to stop dead as frustrated opponents swept past. He also possessed great kicking skills. Not surprisingly, with such an array of talents, he was a gifted cricketer and he played for Glamorgan for several seasons.

The Welsh selectors eventually decided to pick him at outside half for the historic contest against New Zealand in 1905. The reputation he had gained during the 1904 tour was to contribute to the winning try of that match. The All Blacks were keeping a close watch on Bush, when he executed a decoy run to the right, as Owen switched the ball to the left for Teddy Morgan eventually to score.

Surprisingly, however, Bush was never really favoured by the Welsh selectors and he only ever represented Wales on eight occasions. This is often explained by his inability to develop a successful understanding with the brilliant Swansea scrum-half, Dickie Owen: both men liked to control events and were therefore not compatible at half-back. There may be some truth in this, for Percy had what was unquestionably his finest game for Wales when he was partnered by his Cardiff teammate Dicky David. In what became known as 'Bush's Match', he helped create all six tries and dropped a goal in the stunning 29-0 victory over Ireland in 1907. Rarely has an international match been so dominated by one player.

Percy captained Cardiff for three seasons, including 1905/06 when only one fixture was lost. This 8-10 defeat came at the hands of New Zealand and it was a foolhardy error by Bush, who

Bush scores a try for Cardiff against Newport.

fatally delayed touching the ball down in goal, which cost Cardiff the game. This time his trickery let him down. However, he made amends the following season by captaining the club to victory over the South Africans by 17-0, the Springboks' largest ever defeat until the modern era.

Bush's lack of judgement in the New Zealand game was an example of an aspect of his play which some criticised as arrogance. One highly regarded journalist wrote that, at his best, he possessed amazing audacity and skill but that he was also variable, temperamental, erratic and too prone to making errors. But, the critic conceded, on his good days Bush was superlative.

In 1910, he resigned from his teaching post at Wood Street School and took up a business job in Nantes. He continued to play when in France, captaining the Stade Nantais club and famously scoring all 54 points in one match against Le Havre. After the Great War, he was appointed vice consul in Nantes. He retired in 1937 and returned home to Cardiff where he was celebrated as one of the most brilliant if mercurial sportsmen ever to come from the city. He died in 1955.

EDDIE AVOTH

'A Cardiff boxing great'
by Gareth Jones

Egypt is not renowned for producing boxers. But Eddie Avoth first clenched his tiny fists in a military hospital on the outskirts of Cairo in 1945. Father Jack – serving with the Royal Engineers at the end of the war – had met Josephine, the daughter of a NAAFI manager; within weeks they were married, and young Edward duly followed.

Jack had boxed in the Army, and passed his enthusiasm on to his sons: Dennis won the Welsh heavyweight title and Les was a useful welter, but Eddie was the Ely family's pride and joy. A Welsh amateur champion, he turned pro at eighteen with top manager Eddie Thomas, picking up 20 victories in 21 contests before his steady progress was brought to an abrupt halt. Rheumatic fever sidelined him for eight months and the effects never fully left him.

Eddie Avoth (centre) pictured
with his brothers Leslie and
Dennis. (*Western Mail and Echo*)

Six more wins earned him a shot at the Welsh light-heavyweight title. But the Cardiffian's stamina had yet to recover, and holder Derek Richards took a clear points decision. Despite the setback, Eddie stepped into the ring with a transplanted Dubliner, Young John McCormack, to contest the vacant British crown. A clash of heads left Avoth with a cut 'like a mackerel's mouth', as he himself put it, and the referee called a halt.

The Welshman had to wait nineteen months for a second chance; this time it was McCormack who was injured and the premature ending favoured Eddie. A third meeting would see the Irishman controversially disqualified. In between the last two McCormack fights, Avoth became the first Briton to contest a European title behind what was still a pretty heavy Iron Curtain, finding himself on the wrong end of a dubious decision against Yugoslav Yvan Prebeg in Zagreb.

Manager Thomas felt his man was now ready to challenge world champion Bob Foster, and the match was pencilled in for Liverpool Stadium. But a visit to Los Angeles brought a points loss to unbeaten teenager Mike Quarry and the Foster fight disappeared. However, the Commonwealth title was vacant and Avoth was paired with Australian Trevor Thornberry in Brisbane. The local man was in trouble throughout and his seconds pulled him out at the end of the sixth. Eddie was ordered to defend both his crowns against former Olympic champion Chris Finnegan. In the first British title fight on a Sunday for more than forty years, the southpaw challenger dominated and Avoth was rescued just forty-eight seconds before the final bell.

There followed a win and a loss in Johannesburg before he returned to Caerphilly for what proved his last contest, against former victim Bunny Johnson. A left hook out of nowhere nailed the Cardiffian at the start of the third and referee Adrian Morgan wisely called a halt.

Eddie was uncertain over whether to continue boxing, but the discovery of a problem with his right eye made the decision for him. He went into pub management, before taking over a restaurant on the Costa del Sol. He is now a successful businessman back in Wales.

Phil Dwyer. (Richard Shepherd)

PHIL DWYER

'Stalwart Bluebird with a record number of appearances for Cardiff City'
by Andrew Hignell

In February 1985 Phil Dwyer made his 573rd and final appearance for Cardiff City – a record for the club, having progressed from the youth and reserve teams to being ever-present for over a decade in City's line-up, either at full-back or in the centre of defence. In fact, Phil was 'present' for many more games as, back in the 1960s, the football-mad youngster, and his friends from near his home in Penarth Road, would sneak into Ninian Park, often by climbing along a railway sleeper which they had propped up against the wall of the ground.

Phil had already fallen in love with soccer by the time he left St Patrick's School in Grangetown and went to Bishop Mostyn in Ely. From here he progressed into the Cardiff Boys Under-15 team and a place at centre-half in the Welsh Schoolboys team. It was not long before he was invited by Harry Parsons – the Bluebird's kitman – to go training at Ninian Park, followed by a place on the City's groundstaff. In 1971 he was a member of the Cardiff side that lost to Arsenal in the final of the FA Youth Cup and, on his eighteenth birthday, he became a full-time professional.

It was another year before he made his first team debut in a League match but, once in the side, the tough-as-teak defender became an almost permanent fixture for the next thirteen years, always giving 120 per cent and marshalling City's defence. In fact, 'Joe' (as he was christened by 'keeper Fred Davies for his resemblance to Everton centre-forward Joe Royle) made 76 consecutive League appearances from his debut, until injury forced him onto the sidelines, albeit briefly.

He also overcame a nasty incident in the match at Gillingham in the 1975/76 season, which nearly had tragic consequences. As he was going to head the ball, an opponent struck Joe on the back of his head, causing him to collapse on the ground and swallow his tongue.

Fortunately, Ron Durham, the Cardiff City physiotherapist saw what happened, ran on the pitch and gave Phil the kiss of life. His quick actions saved Phil's life, and it was typical of the granite-like defender that he was back in action for his beloved City the following week.

In 1978 Phil won the first of ten caps for Wales in their international against Iran and, in the course of the next few years, he continued to be the rock at the centre of the City's back-line, and for the faithful on the Bob Bank, the heartbeat of the club. As Grahame Lloyd wrote in *C'mon City!*, Phil was not a typical footballer:

> With his splayed feet and lack of pace, he was blessed not so much with natural ability but the biggest of hearts. Pretty effective, but certainly not pretty, Phil was the unsung hero, always in tune with the public. They appreciated his reliable and unfussy approach to the game.

Joe was a great scrapper, almost sweating blood for the team and, despite at times being over-physical, he was utterly dependable, and often the first name down on the manager's team sheet. At times, when City were short of strikers, Joe would also give it a go upfront and, on several occasions, he revelled in his new position, typically giving his all, as 'Mr Cardiff City'.

Phil's career at Ninian Park ended shortly after Cardiff's 4-1 defeat against Notts County on 17 February 1985. It was his 471st League appearance and, like that of several of his teammates, it was far from being his best. Sensing that he no longer figured in the plans being drawn up by Alan Durham – the eighth manager under whom he played – he shortly afterwards agreed terms with Rochdale, for whom he subsequently made fifteen League appearances, before retiring and returning to his home city.

Phil has subsequently worked as a CID officer with the South Wales Police, in addition to helping manage the Cardiff Civil Service team in the Welsh League. Apart from his brief sojourn in Lancashire, Phil spent his entire professional career, as man and boy, with Cardiff City – an example of loyalty and attachment that is so rare in the modern world of player mobility and an ever-expanding transfer market.

SARAH LOOSEMORE

'Cardiff's teenage tennis star'
by Andrew Hignell

Sarah Loosemore, the Cardiff schoolgirl, was the rising star of British tennis in the late 1980s. At the tender age of sixteen, she played in the 1988 All England Championships at Wimbledon, and defeated Peanut Harper of the USA in the first round. The following year, the teenager became the youngest-ever winner of the Prudential National Tennis Championships – a victory that saw Sarah being hailed as someone who was poised to become Britain's finest ladies player since the 1977 Wimbledon winner Virginia Wade. But, within a handful of years, Sarah had swapped one court for another, as after graduating from Oxford University, she became a lawyer.

Born and raised in Dinas Powys, Sarah soon picked up a love of sport from her parents – Pam, a former Welsh tennis international and a professional coach and John, a leading solicitor in Cardiff and a keen cricketer with St Fagans CC. Indeed, her brothers, Mark and David, as well as sister Kim, also picked up the tennis bug, with all four young Loosemores representing Wales in an inter-regional competition in January 1985.

Young Sarah had initially shown a preference for swimming and gymnastics, but the pre- and post-school training sessions, especially the early morning routines in the swimming pool, soon nudged Sarah towards tennis. By the time she was a pupil at Bishop of Llandaff School, Sarah had already picked up a string of junior titles and was a member of the British junior squad, and it was not long before she was a regular on the international tournament circuit.

Sarah Loosemore in action in a tournament in Australia in the late 1980s.

With the help of coaches Ken Fletcher – the Australian who won doubles titles at Wimbledon in the 1960s – and later Andrew Jarrett – now a well-known tournament referee – Sarah made a smooth transition onto the ladies circuit, winning the Prudential Championships and defeating Hana Mandlikova in the 1988 Hopman Cup in Australia. Not bad for someone who was also taking her A-levels at New College in Cardiff!

In 1989 Sarah left school and for the next three years appeared on the professional circuit, playing with such success that she became the British number one with a place as high as the mid-sixties in the world rankings. In June 1990 she also became the first British singles player for four years to defeat a seed at Wimbledon, as she beat the world number sixteen, Barbara Paulus of Austria, 6-2, 3-6, 6-4 in a first-round tie. Sarah's victory was well deserved and, like her shots, was also very well timed, as her father had brought to the All-England Club a coach party of over fifty to celebrate the twenty-fifth anniversary of his law firm.

A couple of years later, Sarah opted to cut back on her professional commitments as she secured a place at Oxford to read experimental psychology. It marked the start of the end of her professional tennis career as, whilst up at St Hilda's College, she met and fell in love with the Oxford rugby captain, Chad Lion-Cachet, the South African Under-21 international. The pair married in 1998 – the year when Sarah also qualified as a solicitor, specialising in commercial litigation with Herbert Smith, the leading City of London firm.

Sarah now lives in Oxford, and mixes her duties as the mother of three strapping young boys with training young advocates. As she recently revealed in a newspaper interview, Sarah has no regrets about swapping a career as a professional tennis player for a legal career in the City of London: 'I just wanted a more normal lifestyle. As a tennis player, you travel twelve months of the year, and it's very hard to have friendships and relationships. It can be very hard and lonely.'

CARDIFF LAWN TENNIS CLUB
by Andrew Hignell

Cardiff Racquet and Lawn Tennis Club was formed in 1888 and, in the late Victorian era, gentlemen could become members of the club in Westgate Street, adjacent to the Arms Park, for an annual fee of £2 10s. Ladies could also join, for the lower rate of a pound, but there was a stipulation that they had to dress in full-length skirts, wear hats and leave the courts by 5p.m.

In 1923 the Marquess of Bute – the owner of the land – contacted the club to say that he wanted to develop it for other purposes, and the result was that the club – renamed as Cardiff Lawn Tennis Club – moved to its present location in the Castle Grounds at the rear of the castle, and near the entrance into Coopers Field at the southern end of North Road.

Various members of the Castle household were enthusiastic tennis players, including the Marchioness herself, who, attended by up to half a dozen servants, would grace the courts for several hours whenever the weather was fine on her visits to stay at the Castle. The link between the Butes and the tennis club was further strengthened in 1947 when the Marquess handed over his property to the City, but stipulated that the tennis club should remain where it was.

Over the years, the Cardiff club has also attracted several celebrity players, including artists from the New Theatre, who were keen to pop over from Park Place for a spot of exercise in between shows. On one occasion, Sir Ralph Richardson was amongst the thespians who booked time on court, with a challenge set up between Sir Ralph and women's champion Glenys Bates. Sadly, the Cardiff weather intervened and the special contest was postponed.

With eleven floodlit courts, the Cardiff Lawn Tennis Club is the largest and most successful in Wales and both men's and ladies' teams currently compete against the leading clubs in Britain in the national league.

WILF WOOLLER

'A colossus of Welsh sport'
by Peter Walker

If an opportunity existed to vote on the greatest all-round sportsman ever produced by Wales, it would take a mighty strong candidate to match the case argued on behalf of Wilfred Wooller. Match maybe, surpass, never.

There was nothing of the trim, highly-trained modern athlete about Wilf, neither in his rugby-playing heyday nor as a first-class cricketer and administrator. He cast a huge shadow, particularly during his time as player and captain of Glamorgan County Cricket Club, then its secretary and also as an England selector and respected commentator on the game. All this on top of becoming a rugby legend before his twenty-first birthday!

A huge, powerful man who led from the front – and occasionally with his chin too - in Wilf's language, spades were most definitely shovels and his opinions on all matters, sporting and otherwise, carried no whiff of self-doubt.

Thanks to an extra year in the sixth form and so technically still a Rydal School schoolboy in North Wales, Wilf was picked in the centre for the senior Welsh rugby XV, in the process becoming the first North Walian for forty years to do so. Around 13st 7lbs and 6ft 2ins in height, Wooller was deceptively quick over the ground, his high knee action making him a nightmare to tackle and bring down. His debut, against England in 1933, was doubly important for it was the first time Wales had won at Twickenham. Out of this, the Wilfred Wooller legend was born!

Nor was it just at rugby that the Rydal schoolboy excelled. Virtually every sport he tried, including swimming, tennis, association football and of course cricket, came easily to him. Going up to Cambridge University, where in those days sporting prowess as well as academic excellence still counted for something, Wilf read geography and anthropology – but only in between his growing obligations to the University's rugby and cricket teams. They always took precedence!

The years 1935 and 1936 were memorable ones for Wilf. He was selected in the Welsh side that made history at Cardiff Arms Park by beating the All Blacks 13-12, while the following

Wilf Wooller at a gathering of former Glamorgan players in 1993.

summer he gained a cricketing Blue against Oxford in the university match at Lord's. Nor did his interest in other sports go untested. In later years he was fond of reminding anyone who would listen that he could have won a soccer Blue too if rugby hadn't interfered, and that he was virtually unbeatable at darts!

With limited sporting and business opportunities in north Wales, it was inevitable that the young sporting Colossus, proud of his Welsh roots even though both his parents were English born, should move south. He joined Cardiff RFC in 1936, his presence on the field with Cliff Jones instantly inspiring the rest of the team and massively boosting crowd attendances. He played 71 times for the club and was captain for two seasons. He was also a regular member of the Welsh team in these years, winning 18 caps, and was captain on four occasions. During the summer, he played as an amateur for Glamorgan in the county cricket championship. In between, as war clouds darkened over Europe, he fitted in appearances as centre forward in a number of charity matches for Cardiff City AFC.

What heights might Wilf Wooller have achieved had the Second World War not interrupted this upward spiral? Those six years robbed him not only of his athletic prime, but also his health. Indeed, after four years in a Japanese prisoner of war camp, three in Singapore's notorious Changhi jail, a lesser mortal would have returned broken in mind and spirit. When he was repatriated to Wales, Wilf weighed just over 8st and his sporting career, if not at an end, then certainly seemed at an end at the highest level.

But that was not the Wooller way. His international rugby days may have passed him by, but there was still cricket where an unexpected post-war opportunity presented itself. Tragically, as the war in Europe was about to end, Maurice Turnbull, the pre-war lynchpin of Glamorgan CCC, both as captain and secretary, had been killed in Normandy. During his 14 matches for the county in 1938 and 1939, Wilf had learnt much from the autocratic Turnbull and, providing his own health would stand up to it, Wilf was his natural replacement in both departments.

Together with two other wartime survivors, Johnnie Clay and Cardiff RFC stalwart and life-long friend Les Spence, Wilf, initially as assistant secretary, began the slow process of rebuilding the Glamorgan club and himself. There were many county players from pre-war days who had either fallen in battle or had become too long in the tooth. But around the men

Wilf kicks the ball ahead during Wales' historic victory over England at Twickenham in January 1933.
(Tim Auty)

who had survived, including Emrys and Haydn Davies, Phil Clift, Arnold Dyson, Willie Jones
and Allan Watkins, Wooller and his mentors rebuilt the side. The acquisition of all-rounder
Len Muncer and swing bowler Norman Hever from Middlesex, plus the ageless but now
occasional off-spin of Johnnie Clay and Wilf himself – reduced in pace from his pre-war days
but with increased guile – gave Glamorgan a powerful strike force on the bowling front. So
much so that in 1948 they won the County Championship for the first time since the club
had gained first-class status in 1921,

The team may have been short of big-name players, but under Wilf's inspirational leadership
they were indisputably the finest close-catching unit in the Championship. Typically, Wilf led
from the front. Fearless at forward short leg, he, Clift and Watkins were avaricious predators in
the leg trap, feeding from the bowling of Muncer, Hever and the fifty-year-old Clay, while at
slip, the youthful Gilbert Parkhouse missed precious few chances that came his way.

If this proved to be Wilf's finest hour on the field, it should not be forgotten that through
fundraising campaigns throughout Wales during post-war Britain's impoverished days he, Clay
and Spence succeeded in their financial battle to keep the county afloat. Soon there came
offers for Wilf to captain MCC on tour to South Africa in 1948/49 where, by association,
they became England when Test matches were played. But because of his winter business
commitments he had to decline.

In those days, amateur players in the professional game of county cricket were not
financially compensated for time spent away on tour. But for this, Wilf might well have also
led MCC parties to Australia and India in 1950 and 1951 too, but for the same financial reasons
withdrew his name for consideration.

What made Wilf Wooller an inspirational captain? Principally he was one of the first men to
go 'over the top' when a sporting battle demanded; a risk-taker in pursuit of victory and the
most tenacious of scrappers when defeat looked inevitable. At forward short leg, his favoured

Above, left and right: Wilf Wooller, the cricketing all-rounder.

fielding position, he was physically brave too. On the retirement of Emrys Davies, and now aged fifty, he promoted himself up the batting order from his normal number seven position to open the innings on uncovered, often unpredictable bounce pitches against the likes of tearaway fast bowlers Frank 'Typhoon' Tyson, 'Fiery' Freddie Trueman, Brian Statham and Peter Loader – this in the helmet-free days and with very little body armour!

As a captain he gave – and demanded – the same level of commitment he brought to any game he was involved in. He had a personality that often led to a fierce war of words on the field, particularly with opposition captains. Players in such games often felt the match was between Wilf and his opposite number with the other twenty merely in bystander roles. However, once stumps had been drawn, rivalries ended there and the language became more gentile. As dusk fell, recent foes became close colleagues in heated, albeit friendly verbal exchanges which then took place in pavilions or hotel bars. No sportsman ever carried fewer personal grudges once day was done than Wilfred Wooller.

Nor was he idle in the winter months. For many years he was an often acerbic *Sunday Telegraph* columnist on his schoolboy passion, rugby football. Wilf played his last game for Glamorgan in 1962, but continued his association with the club as secretary until his eventual retirement in 1977. Taking out the war years, this amounted to thirty-nine years of service. He helped to shape and nurture the Glamorgan side which won the club's second Championship title in 1969 and he continued to offer advice, sometimes unsolicited, but nevertheless valuable, to countless young players who followed thereafter.

Wilf ended his days as the president of Glamorgan CCC. It was an honour the young man from Rhos-on-Sea, but Cardiff loyal through and through, never dreamed would come his way. He is remembered for his glittering all-round sporting careers as a player, administrator, critic, commentator, confidant and counsellor. No Cardiffian has left a bigger legacy of sporting achievement and memories than Wilfred Wooller.

ROB HOWLEY

'Another great scrum-half for Cardiff and Wales'
by Gwyn Prescott

Since the Second World War, Cardiff Rugby Club have been particularly fortunate in possessing a succession of scrum-halves who can be counted amongst the greatest exponents of half-back play. Unquestionably included amongst these is Robert Howley. According to Graham Henry, he had it all: he could run, pass, and kick with vision and he was hugely competitive. He was an exceptional player whose game was based on strength and pace from the base of the scrum and he possessed superb distribution skills. It is a measure of his great ability and consistency that he spent much of his career playing behind less-than-exceptional packs.

Rob's first experience of rugby was at Oldcastle Primary School, which Jack Matthews, another Bridgend-born Cardiff great, also attended. After representing Wales at several junior levels, he began his first-class career with Bridgend in 1990/91 and spent the next six seasons with the club. In 1993/94, however, he had a brief spell with Cardiff but Andy Moore was playing well and Rob could not settle so he returned to his home-town club after only five games.

After some sparkling performances for Bridgend, he was eventually rewarded with his first Welsh cap in the 1996 international against England. It was in this match at Twickenham that the twenty-five-year-old's career took off and although Wales lost 21-15, Rob scored a fine try from close range. It would be at the same ground some eight years later that his career would come to a dramatic climax. The highlight of his first year of international rugby, however, was his crucial try as Wales defeated France at the Arms Park by a nail-biting 16 points to 15. He was then named Welsh Player of the Year and he was similarly honoured again the following season.

After winning six caps with Bridgend, in the summer of 1996 Rob decided to rejoin Cardiff, where Terry Holmes was now coach. This, however, was not a popular move with some of the Brewery Field faithful. As a Cardiff player, he went on to win another 53 caps and to captain Wales on 22 occasions. At the end of his first full season with the Blue and Blacks, he played in the Welsh Cup final which was also the last ever match on the National Stadium pitch which had seen over 120 years of rugby football. Since it had been their home for most of those years, it was appropriate that Cardiff recorded a win over Swansea in this historic match. Rob also enjoyed later success with Cardiff when they took the Welsh-Scottish League title in 2000.

Rob Howley, however, had already created his own piece of history a few weeks before the 1997 cup final. When Wales played their last match at the old Arms Park, he recorded the last international try at the ground with one of his characteristic solo efforts. This produced a neat historical symmetry, for the first man to score in an international there, way back in 1884, was another brilliant Cardiff half-back, William 'Buller' Stadden, though he only managed to drop a goal.

That try merely confirmed what everyone believed: Rob Howley was a certainty for the Lions' summer tour to South Africa. And so it proved. However, after only a handful of matches when his stunning displays immediately established his supremacy over Dawson and Healey, disaster struck in the form of a dislocated shoulder suffered in a tackle in the Natal match just before the first Test. His Lions tour was over. Though this was a devastating blow, in 2001 he was again an automatic choice for the next Lions tour to Australia. Here he was in devastating form and again he outplayed his competitors for the Test berth, with his tactical awareness and coolness under pressure and the speed and accuracy of his passing. In the first two Test matches he clearly established himself as a world-class half-back of the highest order but again injury forced him to miss the crucial final Test.

Rob Howley makes a decisive burst for Wales against Scotland. (*Western Mail and Echo*)

Rob Howley scores a vital try for Cardiff. (*Western Mail and Echo*)

Rob first led Wales in 1998 and Graham Henry retained him as captain when he was appointed the Welsh coach later that year. Under this successful partnership, Wales enjoyed a marvellous run of ten victories on the trot in 1999, with Rob creating a new record for successive wins as a captain. This period included the first win in Paris for twenty-four years, the never-to-be-forgotten last-minute defeat of England at Wembley and the first ever Welsh victory over world champions South Africa in the first match at the Millennium Stadium. The historic 2-0 Test series win over Argentina was an achievement of which Rob was especially proud, as it was the first time he had ever won a series or championship in a Welsh jersey.

After Henry resigned in 2002, Rob retired from international rugby to concentrate on his club game. Leaving Cardiff, he then spent two enormously successful years playing for London Wasps, helping them to two Zurich Premiership titles and the 2003 Parker Pen European Challenge Cup and the 2004 Heineken European Cup. It was in the European Cup final against Toulouse at Twickenham that he scored one of the most remarkable tries. With extra time only seconds away, he chased a kick as it bounced towards the in-goal area. Instead of kicking the ball out of play, the French full-back fatally waited for it to run dead, seemingly unaware of Rob racing down the touch-line. The Wasps' scrum-half pounced on the ball and scored the winning try. A more dramatic conclusion to a major cup final could not have been imagined.

It was also a fitting climax to Rob Howley's career since, because of a wrist injury, it proved to be his last game. But in 2005 he was back at the Arms Park again, now using his vast experience as a valued member of the Cardiff Blues coaching team.

AUDREY BATES

Cardiff's finest all-round sportswoman
by Andrew Hignell

During the 1970s and 1980s *Superstars* was one of BBC Sport's most popular mainstream television programmes, as it showed, during a primetime slot, many of the country's famous sportsmen and women taking part in a variety of athletic pursuits. Had the programme been in the corporation's schedules during the 1950s and 1960s, Audrey Bates would surely have been one of its stars, as she was the finest all-round sportswoman to represent both Cardiff and Wales, winning international honours in no less than four different sports in the post-war era.

A regular competitor at Wimbledon in both singles and doubles events, Audrey won several county titles, in addition to being a leading member of the Welsh ladies lawn tennis side between 1947 and 1960. Audrey also won the Carmarthenshire title at Llanelli, and when she retired she was the Welsh ladies number one.

She was also a leading exponent at table tennis, and during the 1950s, she formed an outstanding and highly successful partnership with Nancy Evans, with the pair participating in the Corbillion Cup in 1953 – the official world table tennis championships for women. At the time, the Welsh ladies were ranked sixth in the world – behind Chinese and Japanese opponents – after excellent performances in the World Championships at Bombay in 1952 and Bucharest in 1953.

Audrey also won honours in the world of lacrosse as well as squash, where she represented Wales and also Britain, for whom she appeared against the United States. Audrey was also a highly talented hockey player, and was invited to play for Wales, but had to decline through lack of time.

In later years, Audrey continued her career as an administrator, serving as president of both the Welsh Squash and Welsh Lacrosse associations. After such a glittering career as both a player and an official, it was fitting that Audrey was inducted into the Welsh Sports Hall of Fame.

Audrey Bates.

MARTYN WOODRUFFE

'The schoolboy swimmer who won silver at the Mexico Olympics in 1968'
by Andrew Hignell

When the police knock on your door in the middle of the night, their arrival is often accompanied by bad news. So when Mr and Mrs Woodruffe were woken at 5a.m. at their home in Pentrebane Road in Fairwater in October 1968, they must have feared the worst. But John and Audrey need not have worried as the officer was instead bringing the glad tidings that their eighteen-year-old son Martyn had just won a silver medal at the Mexico Olympics.

In fact, the sixth-former at Cantonian High School had just been pipped to the gold medal in the men's 200 metres butterfly, with Carl Robie of the United States of America winning the race by just a third of a second. Trailing in last in the contest was another American, Mark Spitz – then the world record-holder and someone who four years later would enter Olympic history by winning a record seven swimming golds at the Munich Games.

The Cardiff teenager had showed his good form leading up to the Olympic finals by winning the 100 metres butterfly and 200 metres individual medley in a pre-Games contest against Australia in the Olympic Pool at Mexico. But when, a few days later, the Games began, Woodruffe was narrowly beaten in the heats for a place in the final of the men's 400 metres individual medley.

He made amends soon afterwards by winning his heat – the first of five – in the qualifiers for the 200 metres butterfly, and then took his place along with the other seven qualifiers for the final of the contest. From the outset, Mark Spitz set a fast pace, but the contest soon developed into a duel between Robie and Woodruffe. By halfway Robie had secured a narrow lead, but in the closing length, Woodruffe bravely came back and missed out on the gold by 0.3 of a second. It was a performance which was to lead later to his being voted the BBC Wales Sports Personality for 1968.

Martyn, on the medal rostrum at Mexico, congratulates the bronze-medal winner. (*Western Mail and Echo*)

'I'm thrilled to bits,' he told the watching journalists after the medal ceremony. 'I gave everything I had and it worked better than I had expected. I can't wait to get back to Cardiff to show off my medal to my folks and friends!'

News of Martyn's tremendous achievements in the first Olympics to be held at altitude was received with glee back home in Cardiff. These were the days before the rolling twenty-four-hour news channels and dedicated sports channels on satellite TV, so some were lucky enough to catch news of Martyn's success on the short breakfast-time highlights on BBC One. Others may have heard brief news on the radio reports but, for many of Martyn's schoolfriends, the first they knew that he had won a silver medal was when the headmaster, Mr Harold Davies, announced the news at the morning assembly. Loud cheers and spontaneous applause rang out for several minutes, before the head could tell the school further details about Martyn's wonderful swim.

Woodruffe – who in recent years has been Scotland's National Director of Swimming – began swimming at the age of eight in the Empire Pool. Six years later, he was chosen to swim for Wales for the first time – against Norway – before he won the British Junior 110 yards butterfly title as well as the Welsh 220 yards butterfly crown, before coming within a hair's breadth of an Olympic gold medal.

THE EMPIRE POOL
by Andrew Hignell

Built for the 1958 Games, the Empire Pool stood in Wood Street, just to the south of the Arms Park. It was the city's first championship-sized pool – the building of which had long been a cherished ambition – following the popularity of Cardiff's first baths in Guildford Crescent, opened in 1899.

Right: Martyn receives a wonderful reception on returning to Cardiff after the 1968 Olympics. (*Western Mail and Echo*)

Below: A postcard image of the Empire Pool.

The Pool, built at a cost of around £700,000, was surrounded by seating for 2,400 spectators and there was a full house to watch the swimming and diving events in the 1958 Games, and to cheer on Australia's Dawn Fraser, Scotland's Ian Black and England's Judy Grinham and Anita Lonsbrough as they won their gold medals.

For the next forty years, the Empire Pool was popular with Cardiff's swimmers, and it continued to host major events for many years. The redevelopment of the National Stadium and the creation of the Millennium Stadium resulted in the demolition of the Empire Pool during the winter of 1998/99.

The Empire Pool.

CHRISTIAN MALCOLM

'Cardiff's champion sprinter'
by Clive Williams

On a brilliantly sunny 1998 afternoon in the picturesque south-east French border town of Annecy, the then nineteen-year-old Christian Malcolm – the British team captain – announced his presence on the world athletics stage. He scored an unprecedented sprint double in the World Junior Athletics Championships, taking both events in championship record times. Furthermore, he beat his own Welsh 100-metre record in the semi-final with 10.18 before lowering it again to 10.12 in the final. Following these performances, he was named World Junior Athlete of the Year for 1998.

The previous year the Cardiff AAC athlete had shown a glimpse of his potential by winning the European junior 200-metre title in Yugoslavia. He also took the silver in the 100 metres behind England's subsequently disgraced Dwayne Chambers, who won in a world junior record of 10.06. With his second place, Christian became the youngest ever Welsh 100-metre record-holder with 10.24 seconds – five hundredths of a second ahead of Colin Jackson's record set seven years earlier. For good measure he brought home relay gold as part of Britain's winning sprint relay team.

But since those heady days, he will be the first to admit that he has yet to fulfil his potential, although he was still good enough to be Britain's fastest over 200 metres in 2006 when winning the European Cup 200 metres for Britain in Malaga. He was also Britain's number one in 2005, emulating his position in 2001 and 2003.

Christian's only individual medal at senior level so far has come in the 1998 Commonwealth Games in Kuala Lumpur, where he took the 200-metre silver in 20.29, to lower Cardiff clubmate Doug Turner's Welsh record and set a new European junior record. In the 2002 Commonwealth Games in Manchester he was very disappointed with his eighth place, and had the misfortune to suffer a hamstring injury in his 100-metre heat at the Melbourne Games early in 2006 which prevented him from taking any further part in the competition.

He has yet to make his individual mark in the two premier world events – the Olympics and the World Championships. Although one could argue that a 200-metre fifth place in the Sydney Olympics in 2000 and final spots in both the 100 (fifth) and 200 (seventh) in Welsh record times of 10.11 and 20.08 in the Edmonton World Championships in 2001 would please him. But no, the unassuming Malcolm quickly dismisses these performances and is positive that individual Olympic and World medals are long overdue. At the time of writing, his 20.08 clocking is the second fastest time recorded by a British athlete behind John Regis (19.87), and one hundredth of a second ahead of Linford Christie.

On the domestic scene, he was a good, but not brilliant, athlete as a junior, as he excelled in most sports, particularly football in which he had trials for Nottingham Forest and Queen's

Christian Malcolm winning a race at the Welsh Games. (Clive Williams)

Park Rangers. The only Welsh junior titles he won were the youths sprint double in 1994. But at senior level he has been the star performer at Welsh Championships in recent times, taking a total of seven titles since his first win in 1997, but in 1998 he had to be satisfied with second in the 100 metres behind Colin Jackson. However, he still has some way to go to match the record number of Welsh sprint titles, held by Britain's 1968 Olympic captain, Ron Jones who captured twelve between 1956 and 1970.

The Cardiff-born athlete, who showed his early promise as a member of Newport Harriers, ran a great race to take fourth in the 2002 European Championships 200 metres, won by the Greek Konstadinos Kenteris, who has since been banned for drug offences. But he became one of a select band of Welsh athletes to win a European gold medal when he was part of the UK team that took the sprint relay, joining legends Lynn Davies, Colin Jackson and Iwan Thomas.

His only other gold medal in major international events came in 2000 when he won in Ghent to be crowned European Indoor 200-metre Champion. He became only the third Briton, after Linford Christie in 1986 and Ade Mafe in 1989, to win the title.

BILLY HARDY

'The Cardiff footballer who was the greatest half-back of his era'
by Richard Shepherd

North-easterner Billy Hardy was one of Cardiff City's greatest ever players. His connection with the club lasted for twenty-one years, including that period of the twenties when City were amongst the Football League's leading lights, as they challenged for the League Championship and appeared in two FA Cup finals, beating Arsenal in 1927 to take the famous trophy out of England for the only time to date.

During that golden era for the Bluebirds, Hardy's bald head made him instantly recognisable on top grounds throughout the country in those days well before mass-media coverage of the game on radio and television. He was born on 18 April 1891 in Bedlington, a small mining town near Newcastle and, as a teenager, played for his local club Bedlington United. Scottish club Hearts took note of his abilities and offered him full-time terms. He joined them in the summer of 1910 as a nineteen year old.

In that same year, Cardiff City had just turned professional following their amateur days, first as 'Riverside' before they adopted their current name in 1908, three years after the town of Cardiff attained city status. At the end of Cardiff City's first professional season, they appointed a secretary/manager in May 1911. This was Oldham-born Fred Stewart, who had been connected in a similar role with Stockport County for the previous ten years. Stewart had

Billy Hardy displaying his magical touch
on the training pitch. (Richard Shepherd)

signed Billy Hardy on loan for Stockport from Hearts in January 1911, on the understanding
that if Stockport wanted to sign him permanently, they would have to pay a fee of £200, a
substantial sum for such a young player in those days. But Stockport did not have the money
to spare, so Hardy returned to Hearts in April 1911, just after his twentieth birthday.

The following month saw Fred Stewart joining Cardiff City. He was keen to sign the young
Hardy and somehow persuaded Hearts to accept a fee of just £25! But City did not have
the money for the transfer – finances were very tight at the new professional club in those
days. But Stewart paid the fee out of his own pocket, and the club later reimbursed him. Fred
Stewart was to say years later that Billy Hardy was his best-ever signing.

At that time, Hardy had thick black curly hair, but when he returned from war service
in 1919, he was prematurely bald at the age of twenty-eight. Primarily a left half (midfield
player in today's terminology), Hardy was to play in several defensive positions for the
Bluebirds during the twenties, having gone with the club from the Second Division of the
Southern League to the top of the Football League. He had, in fact, been with City for ten
years (including his wartime service) before he made his Football League debut at the age of
twenty-nine in 1920, when the club was elected to the old Second Division while the rest of
their Southern League colleagues formed the new Third Division.

Extremely fast, and capable of out-jumping most opponents, despite being only 5ft 8ins
tall, he was widely regarded as the finest left half of the twenties throughout League football.
But he was never capped for England because the Football Association were reluctant to
select players with clubs who were outside their jurisdiction. The most famous football
journalist of the period was Jimmy Catton – 'Tityrus' of the *Athletics News* – who wrote an
article describing the treatment of Hardy as a 'scandal'. All that Billy had to show by way of
representative honours was a solitary appearance for the Football League against the Irish
League at Newcastle in September 1927. In later years he was to say that if the price of playing
for such a good Cardiff City side in the twenties was the lack of representative honours, then
it was a price worth paying.

Billy Hardy's greatest moment was undoubtedly the 1927 FA Cup final when he outplayed
the legendary England international and Gunners' captain, Charlie Buchan. The two had been

regular opponents throughout the 1920s, with Buchan being at Sunderland before joining Arsenal in 1925, and the tall forward never got the better of Hardy in all their contests.

Hardy, who lived in the Cathays and Whitchurch areas of Cardiff throughout his time with the club, experienced the highs of football with Cardiff City: promotion and FA Cup semi-finalists in 1920/21, League Championship runners-up in 1923/24, FA Cup finalists in 1924/25 and winners in 1926/27. But then came the lows as the club slid from the First Division to the Third Division (South) between 1929 and 1931. Billy was appointed City's player-coach in September 1930 but, with his advancing years, his appearances became less frequent and his final League game for City was in late March 1932, one month short of his forty-first birthday.

In the summer of 1932, he joined Bradford Park Avenue as coach, and was their manager from March 1934 until April 1936, when he left football to become landlord of the Dolphin public house in Wincanton, Somerset. In 1949 he and his wife, whose brother Charlie Pinch had been one of City's first professionals and a colleague of Billy's when he had first joined the Club, emigrated to Hobart in Tasmania, where they ran a delicatessen store for a number of years.

They returned to Cardiff and the Flaxland Avenue home that they had occupied for much of Billy's time as a Cardiff City player, in February 1963. The *South Wales Echo*, always on the lookout for a good story, brought him to Ninian Park the next day for a reunion with his old City skipper, Fred Keenor.

Billy Hardy's final appearance on the Ninian Park pitch that he had graced for so many years as a player was on 4 January 1969 at the age of seventy-six when he made a special journey from his daughter's home in Iver, Buckinghamshire, as a guest of Cardiff City for their FA Cup third-round tie against Arsenal, a reminder of that great occasion when he was part of the legendary Bluebirds side that captured the FA Cup in 1927.

He maintained an interest in the club's fortunes until the day he died in March 1981 at the age of eighty-nine. There will be hardly any Cardiff City fans today who can recall the bald head, the shirt outside the shorts, the loyal service of more than twenty years as a player – but the name of Billy Hardy will always be a permanent reminder of Ninian Park's 'Roaring Twenties' when the Bluebirds flew high.

DENNIS REARDON

'Commonwealth Games boxer *par excellence*'
by Clive Williams

Dennis Reardon is the last surviving member of arguably Wales' most successful Commonwealth Games team. The Cardiff-born boxer, still going strong at ninety, took the middleweight gold medal as a twenty-year-old, beating England's Welsh born Maurice Dennis in the final in the Sydney Games in 1938.

At the time, the Games were called the Empire Games, and Wales' other medallists were Jim Alford of Roath Harriers who took the mile title, and Jeanne Greenland who struck silver in the women's backstroke. So out of a team of six, they returned with three medals, with Alford just missing out on a second medal in the 880 yards, finishing fourth.

Reardon returned to his North Luton Place home in Adamsdown as a hero and his thoughts immediately turned to becoming a professional. At the time he said:

> We went to the Games without two halfpennies to rub together. They had a whip round at Curran's, where I worked as an apprentice, and they raised £20 which is all that I had. OK, they paid for our fare and meals, gave us a red blazer and Panama hat and that was that – I didn't even get paid leave.

But the Second World War intervened, and Dennis (or Dinny as he has been affectionately known throughout his life) remained in the amateur ranks. He only lost two out of the 200 bouts he had in his career, and finally retired after representing Britain against France at Wembley in 1940, winning his contest. He started boxing at the age of twelve, and amongst his other achievements in a glittering career were British schoolboy titles, in 1930, 1931 and 1932, Welsh ABA middleweight champion 1937-1939 and the ABA middleweight title.

Dinny came from a great Cardiff sporting family. His father Tom played in the centre for Cardiff before the First World War and his brother Billy played 62 games and scored 35 tries for Cardiff. Dennis himself also played rugby for Cardiff and District side St Peter's. As he remarked when returning from Sydney: 'We had no training gear, all I trained in on the deck of the ship on the 12,000 mile trip to Sydney was a pair of daps and my St Peter's rugby jersey!'

In later life he became a publican in Cardiff, firstly at the Criterion in Church Street, then the Royal Oak in St Mary Street, before moving to Rhoose as the first manager of the new Whitbread Wales flagship, the Mayflower.

The following true story is oft told, but is worthwhile repeating as it clearly sums up one of Cardiff's greatest sporting characters. Colonel Harry Llewellyn, who won a showjumping gold medal in the 1952 Helsinki Olympics on Foxhunter, and then became chairman of Whitbread Wales, was making visits to some of his firm's establishments and on seeing Dennis's gold medal in a display case behind the bar asked of Dennis, 'what's that for?' 'I won a gold medal in the 1938 Empire Games for boxing,' says Dennis. 'Ah,' said Sir Harry, 'I won a gold medal in the Olympics,' implying that his medal was of more importance. 'Yes,' said Dennis in a flash, 'but you had a bloody horse to help you!'

THE SOPHIA GARDENS PAVILION
by Andrew Hignell

It was one of Cardiff's more unusual sporting venues – a converted RAF hangar situated at the southern end of the Sophia Gardens pleasure grounds. But, despite its unorthodox origins, the pavilion played host to the boxing and wrestling events in the 1958 Empire Games, as well as many of the country's biggest names in the entertainment world.

The aircraft hanger had originally been erected at Stormy Down near Bridgend during the Second World War and, after the handing over by the Fifth Marquess of Bute of the Sophia Gardens and his other property in the Cardiff area to the City Corporation in September 1947, the hanger was moved to Cardiff and the building was converted into a pavilion for music, drama, exhibitions and conferences.

Formally opened on 27 April 1951, sporting contests were subsequently added to the list of events staged at the Sophia Gardens Pavilion. Its proximity to the city centre and decent size made it an ideal venue for the boxing events at the 1958 Empire Games, and it was at the Pavilion that Howard Winstone became the darling of Welsh sport, as he took the gold medal in the bantamweight division.

Many well-known celebrities from the world of entertainment appeared at the Pavilion including Sir Cliff Richard, Danny Kaye and Gracie Fields, as well as many famous pop groups, but in the winter of 1982, part of the roof collapsed following a heavy snowfall, and the Pavilion was demolished.

The site is now used primarily as a municipal car park, popular with shoppers and other visitors to sporting events at the Millennium Stadium and the Sophia Gardens Cricket Ground.

The Sophia Gardens
pavilion, as seen on a
1960s postcard.

CLIFF MORGAN

'A rugby legend, with either ball or microphone in hand'
by Huw Richards

While the city's wealth is founded upon the hinterland, none of the benefits it has derived from the valleys has been more warmly appreciated than Cliff Morgan. Born in Trebanog in 1930, his darting, scurrying style made flesh of his forerunner Cliff Jones' contention that Rhondda players were forced to acquire the arts of sidestep and evasion in order to escape buses and other potential predators in the narrow confines of valley streets.

A dark, diminutive deceptionist, he was the most archetypal Welsh practitioner of the position outside half that Wales regards as its own. Dai Smith and Gareth Williams called him, 'An amalgam of the social and cultural forces that had shaped modern Wales... his was the Welshness of the nonconformist home where mam ruled and Sunday was for chapel.'

That chapel upbringing made him the choirmaster of the 1955 British Lions touring team in South Africa, while he remained at home in Trebanog well into his senior rugby career, catching the bus – which would make a special stop to pick him up outside his home once he had been picked for Wales in 1951 – down the valley to Cardiff.

Educated at Tonyrefail Grammar School, he benefited from yet another Welsh archetype, the nurturing schoolmaster. Ned Gribble's perception of potential greatness in his star pupil was echoed by veteran journalist Townsend Collins after a schoolboy international, hailing him as a born footballer 'without conscious thought, without instruction, they dodge, swerve, sidestep and are dazzlingly effective in individual attack.'

He joined Cardiff as a schoolboy – still wearing his school cap, he was refused admission to an Arms Park training session by a suspicious gateman – but in 1949 began studies at the city's university. He was neither the first nor the last student to be diverted fatally by sport – a vital examination coincided with an important match and, after making the only choice that seemed possible to him, he was asked to leave the university.

But if studies failed, his rugby blossomed. His arrival was perfectly timed to take up the succession to Billy Cleaver at outside half, forming a partnership with the powerful, protective Rex Willis, scion of a family of cinema magnates and 'my better half' in Morgan's gratefully gracious tributes. He joined a gifted, mature, charismatic team still attracting huge crowds to the Arms Park to watch the midfield elder-statesmanship of superbly complementary centre pairing Bleddyn Williams and Jack Matthews, the rumbustious vigour of Sid Judd and picaresque prop Stan Bowes. Morgan fitted naturally into this environment as, in the words of Bleddyn Williams, 'a darting tackle-defying symbol of all that is great in traditional Welsh

Cliff Morgan.

back-play.' By 1951 he had graduated to the Wales team, where he would remain an all-but-automatic selection until 1958, his 29 caps at outside half a national record until overtaken by Neil Jenkins.

This was a tough era for midfield backs, when, as his national teammate and Swansea persecutor Clem Thomas would recall, back-row forwards 'had a licence to kill outside halves'. Morgan was often pursued, but rarely collared, even as he courted danger with his audacious running, vividly recalled by Smith and Williams, 'with the ball held at arm's length in front of him, his tongue out almost as far, his bow legs pumping like pistons, eyes rolling, nostrils flaring and a range of facial expressions seldom seen north of Milan.'

While he was famed as an attacker, his defensive and tactical kicking skills were equally apparent in the Arms Park epics that saw first Cardiff, in the most memorable of his 202 appearances for the club, then Wales beat the touring All Blacks late in 1953.

He probably peaked in 1955 as the fulcrum of a Lions team who, in an era when touring defeats were routine, went to South Africa and drew a four-match series with a devastating running game perfectly suited to both his talents and local conditions. Off the field he was, in J.B.G. Thomas's words, 'the radioactive particle around which the whole social side of the tour revolved.'

Any great player limits the prospects of deserving contemporaries, denying them international opportunities they might have had at another time. Among the best, and undoubtedly the most perceptive, of Cliff Morgan's contemporaries was Llanelli's Carwyn James, who won only two caps but recognised his rival's superiority: 'I had to think carefully about what I did on the field. Cliff was different. He did everything naturally and quickly, instinctively and expertly. He was a much better player than I was.'

He proved to have similar natural gifts for the broadcasting career that followed his retirement from rugby at the age of twenty-eight after receiving a job offer he simply could not refuse from the BBC, who had recognised the possibilities inherent in a mellifluous voice and a tone-perfect sense for the right word. He became a substantial BBC figure. Rugby fame and the god-given attributes of voice and vocabulary can take you only so far. You do not spend eleven years as head of outside broadcasts, handling fraught negotiations for rights, or three years as editor of current affairs programme like *This Week* if you do not also have considerable qualities of judgment, intellect and gravitas. His indelible moment at the BBC, though, remains perhaps the most memorable piece of sporting commentary ever broadcast from Cardiff, describing Gareth Edwards' immortal try for the Barbarians against the All Blacks at the National Stadium in 1973.

Roy Evans.

ROY EVANS

'The Cardiff-based table tennis supremo'
by Gareth Jones

Table tennis is a sport that rarely makes the headlines. But it played a significant role in changing the face of the modern world, and a Cardiffian was at the centre of it all.

Contact between China and the West had been virtually non-existent as the planet's most populous nation turned in on itself following Chairman Mao Zedong's Cultural Revolution. But by 1971 Mao was a sick man and, as his iron grip on power relaxed, those about him sought a way to reintegrate the country into international affairs.

H. Roy Evans, the president of the International Table Tennis Federation (ITTF), met privately in Beijing with the Prime Minister, Zhou Enlai, and suggested reviving the invitational tournament formerly staged in the Chinese capital – with the US among the guests. No group of Americans had been allowed in since the Communists took over in 1949, but the idea was agreed. The renewal of contact between the two opposing ideologies became known as 'ping-pong diplomacy' – a phrase Evans hated – and paved the way for President Nixon to visit China the following year.

If that was the moment in the Welshman's career which most impacted on the wider world, his chief achievement in a sporting sense was to have table tennis accepted as an Olympic sport in 1988, following a campaign which lasted a decade.

A Roath boy, Harold Roy Evans was born into the sport in 1909. His father, Morgan, was the first treasurer of the Table Tennis Association of Wales and it was he who organised practice sessions between the top male players, which included Roy, and the first women's international side, which included a young lady called Nancy Jackson. The pair clicked, married and went on to, in effect, run world table tennis from a house in Cyncoed.

Roy served as secretary of the Welsh association, later succeeded by his wife, and filled the same position with the ITTF from 1951 to 1967, graduating to the presidency, which he held for twenty years. Nancy, who served as secretary to the European Table Tennis Union for twenty-four years, soon joined him on the ITTF Council, the first woman to become a member. Both also held down day jobs at Guest Keen Nettlefolds. The couple's popularity and influence was reflected in the way the annual Welsh Open Championships became a magnet for the world's top players in the 1970s.

It was also recognised beyond their own sport. They were jointly elected to the Welsh Sports Hall of Fame and each received the Welsh Sports Council Medal of Honour. Roy, awarded an OBE in 1972, was honorary life president of the ITTF until his death in 1998.

Roy's dedication is demonstrated by the tale of his return to Cardiff at the end of the war, after six years in the RAF. He was greeted at the station by Nancy, her foot in plaster after breaking an ankle playing table tennis, and instead of heading for home the pair went to watch a game in the local league. It was straight back to business!

CLIVE SULLIVAN

'A rugby league great'
by Huw Richards

Clive Sullivan may not quite have matched the prodigious statistical feats of his greatest Cardiff predecessors in rugby league but, by any other standards, he had a highly distinguished career. And his achievement in becoming the first black man to captain a Great Britain team in a major sport – in 1972, eleven years before the Welsh Rugby Union included a black player – has a significance extending far beyond the confines of his own game.

Born in Splott in 1943, he was yet another youthful recruit to league, but in rather different circumstances to those attending Jim Sullivan, Gus Risman and Billy Boston. Nobody was pursuing him with league contracts when he turned eighteen, for the simple reason that he had not played rugby for four years.

He had at an early age shown a family talent for athletics – his elder brother Brian would run for Great Britain – as a five-and-a-half-year-old beating seven-year-olds in a race in spite of being left at the start. That pace inevitably translated into great promise as a schoolboy rugby player – as a pupil at Herbert Thompson Secondary Modern, Ely, he was chosen once for Cardiff Schools. His hopes seemed, though, to have been destroyed by a series of injuries. At fourteen he was warned that he might never walk normally again and gave up the game.

At the age of eighteen he joined the Army. Before long, stationed at Catterick Camp in Yorkshire, he was chosen for a game of rugby. To have admitted the extent of his youthful injuries would have led to his being invalided out, so he decided to play. He not only avoided any ill effects, but scored a spectacular long-range try which excited the attention of a watching rugby league scout.

The ensuing trial with Bradford Northern was unsuccessful, but a touch judge in the match recommended him to his home-town club, Hull. Sullivan scored a hat-trick on his debut against Bramley in December 1961 and, still only eighteen, signed professional forms the following day. His early years with Hull were restricted by army duties and a series of injuries, the most serious in a near-fatal car crash in Cyprus.

The 1960s and 1970s, according to one league history, 'virtually passed Hull by', but Sullivan was the saving grace of a dull era, a winger once described as 'running like a deer, daintily and precisely and with an effortless grace'. He was not only a prolific try-scorer – his career tally of 406 tries was seventh on the all-time list at the time of his retirement – but also a formidable defender. Hull teammate Arthur Keegan recalled: 'He was the best defensive winger I have played with or against, not only for his one-on-one tackling, but for his cross-field covering. He made my life easy playing almost as an extra full-back.'

Those all-round talents won him international recognition against France in 1967, when he scored two tries on his debut. In 1972 he was chosen as Great Britain's captain for the World Cup in France and played a vital role in the 10-10 draw against Australia that secured the trophy – the last time Britain won it – with a length-of-the-field run for his team's first try and the break that set up the second.

Clive Sullivan celebrates with his teammates from Hull Kingston Rovers at Wembley in 1980. (*Hull Daily Mail*)

As is sometimes the case with successful black players, he succeeded even in winning over racists among his own club's following. A black player from another club, who pointed to the illogic of Hull fans subjecting him to racist abuse while they cheered Sullivan, was naturally bemused to be told 'he's not black – he's black and white', referring to Hull's colours.

He became red and white in 1974, leaving Hull to join mortal rivals Hull Kingston Rovers. Supporters of the two clubs, who divide Hull on geographic lines, agree on very little but a mutual affection for and pride in Sullivan, the only player to have scored more than 100 tries for both clubs. His last game for Rovers was on the greatest day in the city's league history, the Hull – Hull KR Challenge Cup final of 1980 that prompted one local wag to leave a 'last one out, turn off the lights' notice alongside the road out of the city, veteran at thirty-seven of the team whose 10 5 win secured Rovers' only Challenge Cup.

Five years later that city-wide affection was expressed in shock at his death from liver cancer at forty-two and the naming of the approach road of the newly-opened Humber Bridge as Clive Sullivan Way. His son Anthony followed him as an international winger and one of the most prolific try-scorers of the 1990s before turning to union and winning honours never available to his father when as a Cardiff player, he made two appearances for Wales in 2001.

Ernie Curtis. (Richard Shepherd)

ERNIE CURTIS

'The teenager who won a cup final medal with Cardiff City in 1927'
by Andrew Hignell

Ernie Curtis was a Cardiff man through and through. So imagine his delight in 1927, as the teenage footballer, who had been working as an electrician just a couple of years before, helped his home-town club to create sporting history by winning the FA Cup. Just for good measure, Ernie also created a little bit of history himself by becoming, at nineteen, the youngest player ever to appear in a cup final.

After winning a Welsh Schoolboy cap and showing promise as a Welsh amateur, Ernie was taken onto Cardiff City's books. In September 1926 the midfielder made his League debut in Cardiff's 2-0 home defeat to Manchester United but, despite the reverse, Ernie had done enough to convince the Bluebirds' management of his abilities, and he retained his place in the squad for the remainder of a season that culminated in Cardiff's glorious victory over Arsenal in the cup final at Wembley.

Ten days or so before the final, Ernie was not in the starting line-up, but an injury to right-wing Harry Wake, in the match against Sheffield Wednesday a week before the final, gave the nineteen-year-old the chance he could only have dreamt about during his days as an apprentice electrician. As he later recalled, 'I had no pre-match nerves at all. We had no fear of Arsenal, as our records that season were very similar.'

However, the victory over Arsenal – on St George's Day, 23 April 1927 – was Ernie's final appearance for Cardiff as he was later sold by the Cardiff manager to Birmingham for the princely sum of £3,000. In all he scored 44 goals in six years with Birmingham, but perhaps the most important in Ernie's career came in October 1927 as he won his first full Welsh cap against Scotland at Wrexham, and celebrated his international debut by scoring in the 2-2 draw.

During his time with the West Midlands club, Ernie was lucky enough to make a second appearance in a Wembley final, as Birmingham City met West Bromwich Albion in 1931 in a game that saw Albion defeat City 2-1. In November 1933 Ernie briefly returned to Ninian

Kay Morley. (*Western Mail and Echo*)

Park, but his short-lived stay was marked by contractual disputes which were eventually ended as Ernie joined Coventry City.

The outbreak of the Second World War saw Ernie join the Royal Artillery for whom he served in the Far East, but in 1941 he was taken prisoner by the Japanese and spent the rest of the war in captivity. At the end of hostilities, Ernie rejoined the Ninian Park club where he held the post of reserve trainer until the early 1960s.

KAY MORLEY

'One of Wales' greatest female hurdlers'
by Clive Williams

Although born in Yorkshire, Kay Morley achieved all of her best performances whilst a schoolteacher in Cardiff. In Auckland in 1990, she became only the second Welsh woman – Kirsty Wade is the other – to win an athletics gold medal at the Commonwealth Games. She won the 100-metre hurdles in 12.91, a time which still stands to this day as the Welsh record.

She came to study at Cardiff University in 1983, later taking up a teaching post at Whitchurch High School. Soon after her arrival in the Welsh capital, Kay became part of the Welsh athletics set-up, teaming up with Malcolm Arnold – the then Welsh National Coach, and mentor to Colin Jackson and Nigel Walker.

Her winning streak of seven consecutive Welsh 100-metre hurdles titles is unparalleled at the Welsh Championships. Not even Colin Jackson, Nigel Walker or Berwyn Price, who dominated Welsh and British sprint hurdling over a period of twenty years, can match Kay's feat.

She retired after the 1992 Barcelona Olympics, having married Gareth Brown, the first Welsh athlete to run a sub-four-minute mile on Welsh soil the previous year.

HUGH MORRIS

'A star batsman with Glamorgan who is now a top cricket administrator'
by Steve James

I always knew Hugh Morris was brave. Opening the batting with him for many seasons told me that: never once did he shirk from any challenge. But the biggest challenge of all was yet to come. In early 2003 he was diagnosed with throat cancer. It tells you everything about his remarkable courage and resilience that by September 2004 the man who had become technical director at the England and Wales Cricket Board in 1997 was now stepping in as acting chief executive of that organisation. He is now the ECB's deputy chief executive.

Morris took us all by surprise when he retired in 1997. But as his final match – against Somerset at Taunton – yielded 165 (and 1 not out) to take him level with Alan Jones' Glamorgan record of 52 centuries (subsequently bettered by Matthew Maynard), as his beloved county clinched the County Championship for the first time since 1969, it was a rather fitting manner in which to bow out. In truth, it had looked as if his career might have ended before then because his knees had become increasingly unreliable. But with the greater emphasis on fitness in the county game he had taken the message on board and paid especial attention to the leg muscles that protected his knees. It meant 1997 was one of his most productive seasons, including a career-best 233 not out against Warwickshire at Sophia Gardens. Even then his time at the crease was only ended by a wicked Allan Donald bouncer, forcing Morris to be stretchered off. Meantime, his only words to physiotherapist Dean Conway were, 'What about 300? I fancied that!'

It has almost become a cliché that Morris' appetite for runs matched his desire for food, but there was never any doubt who was going to be first in the lunch queue at Sophia Gardens. Morris always delighted in this reputation. Still now he talks about the wonderful toffee banana desserts served up then. More's the surprise then that his nickname had no gastronomic connotations, instead it was 'Banners', referring to the TV detective Banacek.

Most annoying for me about Morris' departure from the game was that I was just starting to contribute something meaningful to our partnership. Before that I had always been very much the weak link and had watched in something approaching reverential admiration as Morris calmly collected his runs (he ended up with 19,785 of them in first-class cricket), mostly through flowing cover drives with the odd waspish hook supplementing meaty clips off his toes. The

Hugh Morris, after he had led Glamorgan to the Sunday League title in 1993.

Another boundary for Hugh Morris.

biggest compliment I can pay to his batting is to say that I was always surprised when he was out. Always. My insecurity – both mental and physical – was never replicated at the other end.

Of course there had been harder times for the left-hander before I became his opening partner – 'morning partner,' he would say with a smile every morning – proffering untold confidence to this young tyro. Not in his early days, though. Born in Cardiff in 1963, brought up in Cowbridge, schooled at Blundell's and then an education completed firstly at South Glamorgan Institute (now UWIC) and latterly in the Glamorgan dressing room, Morris also captained Young England after breaking all manner of junior records. But county cricket was not initially so simple. Finding the most suited position in the batting order – he initially preferred number three – proved difficult, not aided by the premature elevation to the captaincy in 1986, making him Glamorgan's youngest ever leader at twenty-three. It ended in a mid-match resignation at Bristol in 1989; never the most happy of episodes.

But Hugh was determined to return the stronger for his travails. In terms of his own form, 1990 saw the left-hander amass 2,276 first-class runs and a club-record ten centuries, and then in 1993, another stab at the captaincy resulted in Glamorgan lifting the AXA Equity and Law league title, with their success owing as much to Hugh's careful planning and clear leadership as it did the inspirational presence of the great Viv Richards. Third place in the County Championship and a losing NatWest Trophy semi-final also indicated a more-than-useful season.

Hugh instilled a professionalism, begun by his predecessor and then opening partner Alan Butcher, which lasted for over a decade. His captaincy credentials soared so high that Hugh was asked on no less than three occasions to skipper the England 'A' team on tours abroad.

It was a shame that Hugh only won three Test caps for England. Less capable players have won many more, but Hugh was handicapped by not being especially rated by Graham Gooch who was England captain at the time. Playing against a rampant West Indian attack in 1991 was not particularly timely either, but Hugh's 44 in his second Test appearance at The Oval was an innings of immense value and no little bravery, as England won that Test to level the series.

Many people's memory of Hugh Morris at Test level might consist of little more than the ubiquitous photograph of him leaping high in the air whilst attempting to fend off one of Curtly Ambrose's throat-tickling bouncers. But he was not alone in suffering discomfort at the hands of such a fearsome attack containing Ambrose, Malcolm Marshall, Courtney Walsh and Patrick Patterson. And at least his experiences spawned an entertaining after-dinner tale, ending with Ambrose's mock greeting of 'Have a nice day, man!' after his first bouncer, which from any audience always guarantees a warmth of feeling in keeping with Hugh's engaging affability.

SOPHIA GARDENS
by Andrew Hignell

In the early twentieth century, the Sophia Gardens Field was the recreational heart of
Cardiff, and every Saturday hundreds of sportsmen and women would throng to the field
– to the north of the pleasure gardens – to take part in various sports including cricket,
rugby, soccer, tennis, athletics and hockey. By the early twenty-first century, the field
had become transformed into the headquarters of Glamorgan Cricket. In the course of
the past year, a lavish ground redevelopment scheme has started which will see the next
chapter in the city's sporting history being written as Sophia Gardens hosts the third Test
in the 2009 Ashes series between England and Australia.

Like so many parts of Cardiff, the history of Sophia Gardens is inexorably linked with
the Bute Estate, with the pleasure gardens on the west bank of the Taff, and adjacent to
Canton Bridge, being laid out in the 1850s after concerns over the limited amount of
open space in the bustling industrial centre. Sophia, the wife of the Second Marquess,
oversaw their creation – at a cost of around £2,000 – with the planting of trees and
shrubs, the design of broad avenues and the installation of a bandstand and fountain.
After her efforts, it was fitting that the Gardens were duly named after Sophia, but sadly
she died in 1859, just a year after their formal opening and she never lived to see how
popular they became.

Within a decade, the twelve-acre Recreation Field had been added at the northern
end of the Gardens, with the Bute Estate specifically stating that the area should be set
apart for athletic exercise. In 1878 the Bowling Green was opened, whilst an athletics
and cycling track was also laid out around the perimeter of the Recreation Field. To the
west of the field, Cathedral Road was also created – prompted by the proximity to the
delightful gardens – with many opulent villas being built on the new avenue leading to
Llandaff, some of these properties having their own private entrances into the Gardens.
By the turn of the century, fetes, civic galas, horse shows, circuses and other grand
events were staged at the Recreation Field, including the 1909 National Pageant of
Wales, attended by upwards of 30,000 people each day.

After the First World War, the number of events at Sophia Gardens started to fall, with
fewer people frequenting the Gardens, as the affluent residents moved to a new and
spacious home in the more distant suburbs. The Recreation Field, however, retained its

Sophia Gardens in
the early 1900s.

popularity as a sporting venue, despite the fact that facilities were still quite spartan and the nearest thing to a post-match shower was a dip in the nearby river!

In September 1947, the Fifth Marquess of Bute handed over his entire property, including Sophia Gardens, to the City Corporation. Under the terms of the acquisition, it has remained as a centre for entertainment and recreation and, in the 1950s, the city fathers thought about developing the field and the adjoining Pontcanna Fields – on which the Bute Estate had considered building houses in the nineteenth century. Various plans were submitted for a racecourse, as well as for a multi-purpose recreation complex, including a skating rink, bowling alley and a ballroom. Nothing came of these, but in the 1960s, the creation of the National Stadium saw Cardiff Athletic Club transfer several of its activities from the Arms Park and, in August 1966, Cardiff CC played their first match on the new cricket ground at Sophia Gardens. The following May, Glamorgan played their inaugural Championship match at the ground, and two years later, they clinched the county title as they defeated Worcestershire at their new Cardiff home.

Work also began adjacent to the cricket ground, creating a large indoor sports centre – now known as the Welsh Institute of Sport – which was opened in 1971/72. This was followed a few years later by the installation of various all-weather sports pitches on the strip of land to the west of the cricket ground. In November 1995 Glamorgan Cricket acquired a new 125-year lease of the ground – previously belonging to Cardiff Athletic Club – and work began to develop the ground as a centre of excellence for Welsh Cricket, including an indoor school, nursery and practice facilities, together with new grandstands and enclosures. The National Cricket Centre was opened in 1999, and, in April 2006, following the elevation of Sophia Gardens by the England and Wales Cricket Board to Test match status, work began on the second phase of the development which, by the spring of 2008, will see a 15,000-seater stadium being created.

Tony Cordle and the rest of the Glamorgan team celebrate winning the 1969 County Cricket Championship on the balcony of the pavilion at the Sophia Gardens cricket ground.

Members of Cardiff Cricket Club practice on the newly created wicket at Sophia Gardens in 1966 ahead of their move from the Arms Park. The batsman is Gordon Eccles – a stalwart figure in the club – who for many years was the scoreboard operator at the Sophia Gardens ground during county matches.

The modern face of Sophia Gardens as the crowd enjoys a floodlit Twenty20 match between the Glamorgan Dragons and the Gloucestershire Gladiators in 2006.

DEREK TAPSCOTT

'Record-breaking centre forward with Cardiff City'
by Andrew Hignell

It was a game that saw Cardiff City achieve their highest ever score, and a match in which Derek Tapscott entered the city's sporting folklore by becoming the first – and in all probability the only – man to score six times in a first-team match. The fixture in question, the Welsh Cup fifth-round tie against Knighton Town in January 1961, saw the Bluebirds crush their mid-Wales opponents 16-0, with Tapscott joining the very exclusive club of professional footballers to score six times in a match.

The one-sided contest stemmed from various incidents the previous season when Cardiff, who were going for promotion to the First Division, opted to rest many of their regulars and send instead a reserve team to Swansea for the Welsh Cup tie. Cardiff triumphed 2-1 in an ill-tempered affair and they were subsequently fined for sending this under-strength side to the Vetch Field, and told that in future Welsh Cup ties, no matter what their League position may be, they should field their strongest XI.

So the following year, poor old Knighton were on the receiving end, as Tapscott – the Barry-born striker, created City history by scoring a double hat-trick. He was a lethal finisher

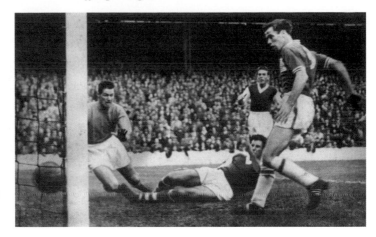

Derek Tapscott scores for Cardiff City in October 1959 in their game against Ipswich Town. (Richard Shepherd)

given any room close to goal, especially to any balls chipped into the box, which he would deftly slot into the back of the net with his trademark header.

As a youngster, he slipped through Cardiff's scouting network, despite a prolific goal-scoring record as a schoolboy for Barry West End, and then Barry Town, who participated in the Southern League. His goal-scoring prowess, however, did not go unnoticed and, in the autumn of 1953, 'Tappy' and Bill Jones – the Barry Town manager – headed up to London to talk to a big club who wanted to sign the teenager, who was working as a bricklayer and odd-job boy. But the youngster Tapscott didn't know that he was on the point of signing for Arsenal until he spotted two underground tickets for Highbury station in Jones' hand. The centre forward subsequently recalled:

> I wasn't really sure what was going on, or where we were going. Bill didn't say much to me on the journey, but when we reached Paddington, he took out two underground tickets to Highbury. That's when I guessed what he was up to. I couldn't believe it. At the time, Arsenal were the biggest club in the country, and the Football League champions.

A fee of £2,000 was agreed upon and, in October 1953, the twenty-one-year-old Tapscott joined Arsenal, for whom he scored 13 times in 15 reserve games, before making his League debut against Liverpool in April 1954 and scoring twice. In the course of the next few years, he continued in his rich vein of goal-scoring form, becoming Arsenal's leading scorer in the 1955/56 season and also winning the first of 14 Welsh caps whilst at Highbury.

His bubble burst when he sustained the first in a series of knee and ankle injuries, and by 1958 Derek was languishing in the Arsenal reserves. With Bill Jones – his former manager at Barry – now in charge at Ninian Park, Derek returned to South Wales when the London club accepted an offer of £10,000 for his services. It soon proved to be value for money, as he renewed his productive partnership with Brian Walsh, who had also moved from Highbury to Ninian Park.

Despite having spent much of the previous season in the reserve team, 'Tappy' was still enthusiastic and he soon showed that he had lost none of his sharpness, as Cardiff enjoyed a successful run in League matches. In the course of the next few years, both Walsh and Tapscott frequently found the net, including the famous match in March 1961 when double-chasing Tottenham Hotspur visited Cardiff, and were defeated 3-2 in an enthralling encounter under the floodlights at Ninian Park.

The match was an evening kick-off because of the Wales–Ireland rugby international earlier in the afternoon at the Arms Park. It became an evening to remember for the City fans, many of whom had travelled up to White Hart Lane earlier in the season, only to see the Bluebirds lose a fiercely contested encounter and then only after a hotly disputed penalty in favour of

Spurs. The City team, and their fans, were eager for revenge on home soil but, after just three minutes, the visitors opened the scoring as Terry Dyson put Spurs ahead. Derek Hogg soon equalised but, shortly before half-time, the visitors scored again and during the interval there were even a few dark mutterings on the Bob Bank about what the second might bring.

But the doom-mongers were silenced as, shortly after the interval, Walsh and Tapscott put City into the lead with a couple of sweetly-struck goals. Whilst Walsh found the net from close range, Tapscott's goal was drilled through a packed goalmouth and, with two titles at stake, Spurs threw everything at City in the final quarter, but their defence held firm, and 'Tappy' was the toast of the town when the referee blew the final whistle.

Despite scoring several hat-tricks for Cardiff, this goal against Spurs was the most important of the 99 Derek Tapscott scored in 233 first-team appearances for Cardiff until 1965. In July that year, he joined Newport County, before subsequently moving into non-League football and, after retiring in 1970, working for a boot manufacturer in the sporting goods trade.

DAVID BROOME

'Showjumping supremo'
by Brian Lee

Born on St David's Day, in the Fairwater district of Cardiff in 1940, David Broome, who was awarded the OBE in 1970 and the CBE in 1995, is without any doubt at all one of the greatest showjumping competitors there has ever been. He competed at the highest level for thirty-five years and had a record 106 Nations Cup events to his credit. He started taking part in senior classes back in 1957 and made his debut on a horse, appropriately called Wildfire, who was considered virtually unrideable by its previous owners, the King's Troop!

However, after a spell with one of the greatest horsemen of the twentieth century, Wildfire became the leading showjumper in the land. Broome, who has a record six wins in the King George V Gold Cup between 1960 and 1991 and on six different horses, was World Champion in 1970 on Beethoven and three times European Champion on Sunsalve (1961), Mister Softee (1966) and Sportsman (1972).

He turned professional in 1973 and the following year won the 1974 Professionals Championship, appropriately held at Cardiff Castle. There were times, in the late 1950s and early 1960s, when he didn't have the really top-class horses to match his ability. Even so, he still headed the list of prize-money winners for Great Britain. Broome won two individual showjumping bronze medals at the Olympics, in 1960 partnering Sunsalve and in 1968 aboard Mister Softee. He was also selected for the 1964 Tokyo Olympics when he borrowed his brother-in-law Ted Edgar's horse, Jacapo. His sister, Liz Edgar, was also a national champion.

Once he had turned professional, he was not allowed to compete at the Olympics until the rules were changed, but he again made the British team in 1988 and 1992. Colonel Sir Harry Llewellyn, of Foxhunter fame, said of him:

> No one could be fonder of his horses – or more solicitous for their care – than David Broome… When it comes to winning the big competition against the clock I would say that David is marginally better than Harvey Smith. He always clocks up very quick times over courses because he jumps off a longer stride than Harvey.

Praise indeed from the Welshman who put British showjumping on the map with his Olympic gold medal. Voted the BBC Television Sports Personality of the Year in 1960, Broome – who now farms at Chepstow – is truly one of the all-time greats of British sport and a legend in showjumping circles.

A caricature sketch of David Broome.

GWYN NICHOLLS

'Prince Gwyn of Cardiff and Wales'
by David Parry-Jones

An unsuspected obstacle lay in store when I was researching my biography of Gwyn Nicholls in 1998. There appeared to be little or no original writing by him concerning the events and issues that accompanied his outstanding career. The sad explanation for this was given in *Cardiff Rugby Club: History and Statistics*, written by the club historian Danny Davies. He wrote that Nicholls left a large volume of personal papers to the club that were stored in the little old cricket office at the Arms Park. They were totally destroyed by the floodwater of 4 December 1960 when the Taff burst its banks.

Hence much of the detail, infuriatingly, has to be best-guessed. We do not know which school Nicholls attended in Cardiff, though it may have been the Wesleyan School in Working Street, where his brother Sid went, or the old Howard Gardens. As adults, little is known about where he and his friends liked to go for their evening entertainment – where they ate out and what plays and films they enjoyed. And how was marriage with Emmeline – 'Nell'?

What do we know about essentials? Erith Gwyn Nicholls was born in 1874, the fifth of seven children, to Gloucestershire parents at Westbury-on-Severn. In 1876 the family came to Cardiff to settle in Constellation Street in Roath. The father, Hartley, was described by the town council as a 'cattle inspector'.

As he grew up, Gwyn saw himself as 'a true Son of Wales in all things except birth.' But there is no doubt that he enjoyed living in Cardiff, too, soon to achieve City status and drooling with prosperity. His elder brother Sid, already an international player with four caps, introduced him to Cardiff RFC, for whom his first game took place on 1 January 1894, and his 242nd and last in 1909. He loved the club, which he captained for four seasons, and the fans loved their tall, rangy, classical centre.

Two years into his senior career, in January 1896, Nicholls junior was named in the Welsh teams to meet Scotland, who were defeated, and Ireland, who were not. But the young hopeful had made his mark upon the Welsh selectors and, by the time he chose to retire, he had a won a healthy 24 caps.

His reputation was growing in the British Isles and in 1899 he was Down Under, enchanting hard-nosed Aussie crowds with the immense skill levels that he was parading. The sole Welshman in a 'British' touring party which won its series 3-1, he was also its most charismatic and effective player.

AUSTRALIA		CARDIFF	
Full Back	... C. J. WINDSOR (2)	(1) FRANK TROTT	Full Back
Left Wing	... C. C. EASTES (3)	(2) LES WILLIAMS	Left Wing
Outside Centre ...	T. ALLAN (6)	(3) BLEDDYN WILLIAMS	Left Centre
Inside Centre ...	M. L. HOWELL (7)	(4) JACK MATTHEWS	Right Centre
Right Wing	J. W. T. MacBRIDE (8)	(5) D. H. JONES	Right Wing
Five-eighth	... N. A. EMERY (11)	(6) W. B. CLEAVER	Outside Half
Scrum Half	... R. M. CAWSEY (14)	(7) HAYDN TANNER (Capt.)	Scrum Half

Kick Off 3.15

Referee:
Mr. GEO. GOLDSWORTHY
(Penarth)

THE ROATH FURNISHING CO BRANCHES EVERYWHERE

Next Saturday at Home
October 4th
NEWPORT
Kick Off 3.15

Forwards—		Forwards—	
E. TWEEDALE (27)		(8) CLIFF DAVIES	
W. L. DAWSON (26)		(9) MALDWYN JAMES	
R. E. MacMASTER (28)		(10) W. G. JONES	
G. M. COOKE (18)		(11) ROY ROBERTS	
N. SHEHADIE (24)		(12) W. E. TAMPLIN	
G. J. WINDON (20)		(13) ELVET JONES	
A. J. BUCHAN (16)		(14) LES MANFIELD	
W. M. McLEAN (Capt.) (15)		(15) GWYN EVANS	

Linesmen: D. F. KRAEFT (Australia)   Mr. R. A. CORNISH (Cardiff);

There was also a dark side to Nicholls' character. Personnel on this short tour made their own way safely home – the exception being their Welsh teammate, who was rumoured to have disembarked at Cape Town to take a look at South Africa. With a signal disregard for courtesy, he failed to return in the late autumn as promised, missed Wales' match with England, and reached Cardiff in January. He immediately offered his services to the WRU for the game against Scotland on 27 January – they were accepted, he was forgiven and Wales won.

It is true that selectors were becoming irritated by Nicholls' unpredictable behaviour. More than once he told friends that he was retiring, before changing his mind. Sometimes he also declined a cap because his presence was needed at the laundry business he had started in Llandaff North with his Cardiff and Wales teammate Bert Winfield. The great man's attitude was becoming hard to take: 'I'll turn out – if you insist.'

But the whole of Wales – selectors, press and public – deemed it imperative that he should front the Welsh cause against the all-conquering New Zealanders of 1905. The Nicholls preparation, his strategy, his generalship, his inspiration, and his dashing play on the day were hugely positive. The 3-0 victory he delivered – the First All Blacks' only defeat – will never be forgotten by Welsh rugby.

His last international year had something of an anti-climax about it – victories over England and Scotland being followed by defeats at the hands of Ireland and, in December 1906, by the first Springboks, whom Cardiff defeated on 1 January by a stunning 17 points to nil. Thereafter, his first-class games were intermittent, and tongues wagged when in 1909 he refereed the Calcutta Cup game between England and Scotland – an experience which he chose never to repeat.

In 1919 he lost his business partner Winfield in a motorcycle accident, but stayed with the Victoria Laundry until his death – a peaceful one – in 1939. Cardiff RFC commemorated him by siting the Gwyn Nicholls Memorial Gates, first opposite Quay Street and latterly at

Right: The front of the unofficial match programme for the historic match between Wales and the All Blacks in 1905 – a match which saw Wales beat New Zealand for the first time.

Opposite: An advert for Nicholls and Winfield adorns the centre pages of the match programme for the encounter between Cardiff RFC and Australia in 1947 at the Arms Park.

The Angel entrance to Cardiff Arms Park. They are a worthy tribute to one of the first greats of Welsh rugby, alongside Frank Hancock, the pioneer of the four three-quarter system at Cardiff, James Bevan, the first man to captain a Welsh team, and 'Monkey' Gould of Newport, arguably Wales' first rugby superstar.

Why does Gwyn Nicholls belong in this august company, and that of the other greats who have come after his time? Space dictates that I should choose no more than two from a manifold number of reasons. One is that Nicholls should be remembered as the first Welsh captain to write or talk about 'The Spirit of the Team'.

This is the phenomenon that has since come to be known as 'team spirit', and about which he wrote after his retirement:

> It is telepathic communication if you like… in an ideal Welsh game you really see fifteen great chess masters working in a partnership and without consultation. How is it done? Well, there you have me: I know that it is done, and we all of us [his players] know it is done, although 'how' we could never explain.

The team talk, you will agree, is alive and kicking in every changing room in 2007.

The second, tactical, advance made by Welsh rugby and prompted by Gwyn Nicholls, I would argue, appears to have been support play, in which forwards and backs alike were urged by him to get involved. The four three-quarter system was generally used by clubs and national teams all over the rugby-playing world by the turn of the century. Nicholls perceived that, for it to work to maximum effect, men should not stop running after delivering a pass, but should strive to stay with the new ball carrier.

He is complimentary about the great skill of Gould, but implies that the objective of the Newport centre was to run as far as he could before dying with the ball:

The whole essence of a successful attack lies in its uncertainty. You must get the other fellows' minds more or less in a whirl. They should be expecting all sorts of terrible things, and horribly uncertain as to which trick is going to be played on them next.

All in all, I suggest, it is no way surprising that teammates at Cardiff RFC, and in the Wales teams which he led ten times, had a special name for their captain. They always referred to him as 'Prince Gwyn'.

MATT ELIAS

'Cardiff's star athlete in relay events'
by Clive Williams

Matt Elias is one of the most ebullient and flamboyant of Wales' star athletes. He has suffered many highs and lows during his brief but illustrious career, but he has always remained determined to recapture the brilliant form which saw him almost snatch the 4 x 400-metre relay gold for Wales in the 2002 Manchester Commonwealth Games. In a pulsating and inspired last leg on the final day of the Games, he lost out to Chris Rawlinson of England by just one hundredth of a second.

Earlier in the Games, he ran an outstanding individual race to take the 400-metre hurdles silver medal behind Rawlinson in 49.28 seconds, after setting a new Welsh record in the semi-final of 49.11 – a time that would last as the Welsh best until beaten by Cardiff AAC teammate Rhys Williams in the Melbourne Games four years later.

However, in those Melbourne Games – his third Commonwealths – he was ill and failed to reach the final. But just before, he had showed that he was in fine shape running 49.50 in an open meeting in Australia, a time that was still good enough to rank him third fastest in Britain in 2006.

It is unique that the fathers of two of Britain's leading 400-metre hurdlers should come from the same mid-Glamorgan village of Nantyffyllon. Both dads were outstanding athletes – Matt's father John was one of Britain's leading long jumpers with a best of 7.47 metres, whilst the rugby and athletics exploits of Rhys Williams' father 'JJ' are well recorded. And the family link doesn't end there, as Matt's mother, Kath, a former Welsh Schools Hurdles Champion, is the current secretary of Cardiff AAC.

In an injury- and illness-filled career, his only major individual championships win so far has been when he was crowned European Under-23 Champion in 2001 in Amsterdam. In winning, he dipped under the magical 50 seconds for the first time in his heat before winning the final in 49.57, adding a second gold later when he anchored the British 4 x 400-metre team.

He has been one of the mainstays of the British 4 x 400-metre team in recent years. He was part of the team that took fifth in the Athens Olympics, although his finest run for the squad came in 2002 when the team, including Cardiff colleague Jamie Baulch, took the European gold.

Another relay triumph came in the European Cup Super League in Florence in 2003, where the British team was seventy-five per cent Cardiffian. Chris Rawlinson was the only non-Cardiff runner in the squad, the others being Tim Benjamin and Jamie Baulch.

After a couple of years concentrating on the 400 flat, he returned to his first love of 400-metre hurdles at the 2005 AAA Championships to take his first national senior title, after winning several in the younger age groups. Happily, Matt is over the illness that blighted his 2006 season, returning for a fine second place in the 2007 Welsh Indoor 400 metres and he now looks forward with relish to the challenges ahead.

Matt Elias winning a title in an indoor event.
(Clive Williams)

MAINDY STADIUM
by Brian Lee and Clive Williams

Maindy Stadium was built on the site of an old clay pit, known as Maindy Pool, which was said to have been eighty-five feet deep in parts. Several adults and at least nine children were drowned in its murky waters and some bodies were never recovered.

Over the years, the stadium has hosted a variety of sports including professional boxing, baseball, football, rugby union and rugby league. But it is best known as a venue for cycling and athletics.

With its 600-metre cycle velodrome, the stadium was the home of Cardiff Ajax, the largest cycling club in Wales. Maindy hosted the cycling events in the 1958 Empire Games, and it was here that Cardiff's own Don Skene won the second of his bronze medals. In fact, former world champion Reg Harris expressed the opinion that the track was one of the best he had ever ridden on and he set a flying lap record there of 27.8 seconds.

Although the running track was not the best in the world, Welsh rugby international Ken Jones clocked even time there for 100 yards against a strong wind. Dubbed 'The Welsh White City', the Welsh AAA used to hold their annual championships at Maindy and the Welsh Games were also staged there. Hundreds of world-class athletes competed at Maindy, which was also the headquarters of Roath Harriers and Birchgrove Harriers before they amalgamated in November 1968.

The creation of the new Cardiff AAC was followed by a period of huge success with Cardiff dominating not just Welsh but British club athletics. The British Athletics League was formed in 1969 and after being a close runner-up in that first year, the Maindy-based club went on to win three consecutive British League titles from 1972. In 1974, Cardiff also won the British League Cup, becoming the first club to win the league and cup double.

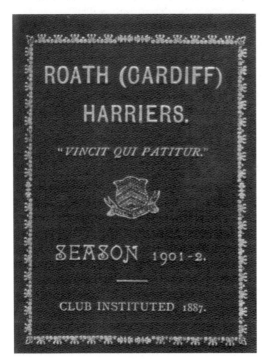

Above: Maindy Stadium.

Left: A membership card for the Roath Harriers for the 1901/02 season.

Although it has not won the league title again, Cardiff is one of the few British League clubs to have retained its place in the league without a break, and remains to this day one of the leading clubs in Britain. Additionally, Cardiff's women's team entered the top flight of women's club athletics in 2006, with promotion to division one of the UK league. One of the club's finest achievements came in 1974 when they won the AAA marathon team title, beating the Japanese national team.

After many years at Maindy Stadium, Cardiff AAC moved to the Leckwith Stadium in 1989. A new chapter now begins with the creation of a new athletics stadium on the opposite side of the road, with the old Leckwith facility being redeveloped as Cardiff City's new stadium.

JACK PETERSEN

'Cardiff's prized fighter'
by Gareth Jones

Even in these days of multiple titles, few boxers can have signed up simultaneously for two championship bouts. Jack Petersen did. And he won both, becoming Britain's heavyweight king just fifty days after winning the light-heavy crown. But the unexpected was almost to be expected from the handsome Cardiffian.

His Welsh blood spiced with Irish and Norwegian, Jack was born in 1911 into a fighting tribe – father John first put on gloves at ten – yet turned to the ring against paternal wishes. 'Pa' Petersen would have preferred his son to study medicine and join the health club he ran in St John Street. But once it was clear the youngster wanted to box, Pa determined that he would be the best, and he was well equipped to transform the dream into reality.

Although the concept was alien to the age, Petersen was one of the first athletes to be commercially marketed. The basic material was ideal. Charming, intelligent and articulate, Jack could play his part outside the ring, appealing to the followers of fashion; within the ropes he became the tiger whose bravery and untamed aggression made him the day's top attraction for the grass roots fight fan.

Jack had a mere twenty amateur bouts over three years, becoming ABA champion at light-heavyweight, before the Petersens turned to the money side. Again ahead of his time, Pa secured sponsors to guarantee his son's immediate future. A chance remark during a round of golf at Porthcawl led London Scotsman William Blackwood and Cardiff businessman Harry Jones into partnership as Jack's backers; they forged an alliance with Fred Howard, of the Stadium Club at Holborn, and it was there the prodigy was unveiled in September 1931. Even in his debut he topped the bill – as he did in every fight of his career. By the end of the year, the tyro had accumulated eleven straight wins and Pa was already issuing open challenges to any British opponent.

Cardiff's Greyfriars Hall was overflowing as Jack lifted the Welsh heavyweight crown from the giant Dick Power in just twenty-one seconds. Victory over tough Charlie Smith put Petersen in line for a shot at British champion Reggie Meen, but the Welshman was still a natural 12st 7lbs man, and Pa decided on an unprecedented double assault: Jack would meet Yorkshireman Harry Crossley for the light-heavy crown, then step up to tackle Meen.

Petersen faced Mexborough miner Crossley at his familiar Holborn Stadium, flooring the older man twice on the way to a points decision. Strike one! Strike two came at Wimbledon Stadium. Petersen decked Meen in the opener, finishing him off with a bludgeoning right uppercut in the second. The twenty-year-old was a double champion, less than ten months after making his professional debut.

Staying at heavyweight, he saw off challenges from big Jack Pettifer and charismatic Irish teenager Jack Doyle, who disgraced himself with a series of low blows and was disqualified in front of 70,000 fans at London's White City.

Next up was Len Harvey, a pro since the age of twelve, who had already held titles at middle and light-heavy. With Pa insisting that his boy was well paid, promoters were loath to cough up much for his opponents, and Len was only given his chance at the heavyweight honour after his wife, Florence, agreed that her husband would box for no more than his training expenses. After that, he simply had to win! Before a record Albert Hall crowd of 10,000, the Cornishman duly upset the Welshman's applecart – despite being on the deck in the first – taking a controversial points verdict.

Jack did his penance with stoppage wins over three former victims – Smith, Meen and Crossley – followed by another against the tough South African Ben Foord to earn a return shot at Harvey, by now the Empire champion as well. The future King George VI was among

45,000 at the White City who saw a titanic struggle eventually decided when a loose lace on Petersen's glove is said to have grazed Len's right eyeball. His vision now clouded, the holder fought on for two rounds, but retired at the end of the twelfth.

The Welshman now had two titles to defend. He forced Canadian Larry Gains to yield after thirteen rounds and another veteran, Australian George Cook, was clearly outpointed. So much for the Empire; Europe was to prove more difficult.

Germany's Walter Neusel stunned the Wembley crowd by battering the bloodied Petersen around the ring and prompting a concerned Pa to toss in the towel in the eleventh round. A rematch four months later proved another thriller, in which only the desperate pleas of manager Paul Damski persuaded Neusel off his stool for the tenth: he shipped more punishment, but managed to find two wild swings near the bell which had Petersen out on his feet. Pa, unlike Damski, had seen his charge suffer enough and signalled the end.

Six months later Jack faced another challenge from Harvey. The clash lacked the excitement of their previous meetings, the champion boxing within himself to claim a surprisingly easy victory. He repelled the middleweight champion, Jock McAvoy, before facing former victim Foord, now eligible for the British as well as the Empire title. The one-time lifeguard from Durban cut Petersen in the second and charged out for the third to force the referee to step in.

Petersen demanded an immediate return, but it was called off when Ben went down with flu. The show went on, however, with another familiar face in the opposite corner: that of Walter Neusel. The outcome, too, was familiar. By the ninth round only courage kept Jack on his feet, and he was bleeding badly from nose and mouth when the towel fluttered in during the tenth.

It proved the last hurrah for Petersen. He had damaged the retina of his left eye, and after an eye specialist warned that to continue boxing could run the risk of permanently impairing his sight, the Cardiff man, still only twenty-five, announced his retirement.

Yet more than half a century on, Jack Petersen, awarded the OBE in 1978, was still playing a leading role in the sport he loved. Years of service to the Board of Control were rewarded in 1986 by his election as its president – the first former professional to fill the post – and he was still in office at his death in 1990. Boxing could have had no finer representative.

JACK LUKE

'Cardiff's speedway ace'
by Andrew Weltch

Cardiff hosted a minor league speedway team in the 1950s and the Millennium Stadium has staged the British Grand Prix since 2001, but we have to go to back to the pioneering days of the 1920s and 1930s to find a real Cardiff speedway great.

Jack Luke was among the best in Wales. Such was his celebrity status that his wedding to Josephine Hampson – sister of a fellow racer – took place in Llandaff Cathedral, with riders in leathers and helmets, holding race flags as a guard of honour.

The son of a family of Canton bakers, he was among sixty local riders who joined established stars for the first dirt-track meeting in Wales on Boxing Day 1928. Some 25,000 reportedly deserted their firesides for this new sporting curiosity at the Welsh White City Stadium in Sloper Road, and they saw Luke finish second in the Cardiff City Trophy.

Race wins in subsequent meetings led to Luke's selection for a Cardiff team which beat Bristol in April 1929 and he scored an easy win in the Golden Gauntlet competition that night. Press reports described his 'splendid riding' as 'delightful to watch'. He retained the title later that month, and achieved further success in winning the *Western Mail* trophy and Golden Sash.

Jack Luke prepares to challenge Fay Taylour in a special challenge race. (Andrew Weltch)

Jack Luke has a special guard of honour on his wedding day. (Andrew Weltch)

Although listed as 'J.H. Luke' in early reports, by the end of April 1929, he had reluctantly accepted the nickname 'Lightning' in preference to the alternatives of 'Lively' and 'Lurid'. Such was the price of fame for South Wales' competitors in those publicity-fuelled days. Others had already acquired such epithets as 'Whirlwind' Baker, 'Hurricane' Hampson and fellow Cardiffian 'Champ' Upham.

Now Lightning Luke was being billed as 'Cardiff's champion' and was pitched against visiting stars in high-profile match races – most notably Fay Taylour (dubbed 'the world's lady champion'), who had broken the lap record at Wembley in front of 40,000 fans the previous week, and whom Luke beat convincingly.

Although not part of the burgeoning league competition, Cardiff took part in team challenges against other track sides. Luke helped them to a draw at home to mighty Wembley on 8 June 1929 and to a famous victory in the return match in London four days later. In further Wales–England clashes, he was involved in wins over West Ham, the Midlands and Salford.

In 1930 he regained the *Western Mail* trophy, won the 'All-Star' match race championship and helped Wales to victories over Coventry, Crystal Palace, Preston and Portsmouth. A return visit by Preston saw a rare defeat for the Welsh, with Luke the only Welshman to win his race, and going on that night to win a thrilling Golden Sash final ahead of Preston captain Joe Abbott.

His success was not confined to his home city – he was a regular winner at Wales' other short-lived dirt tracks, Pontypridd (where he won the 1929 Cambrian Dash), Tredegar (where he led Cardiff in a four-team championship against Bristol, Salford and the Valleys), and Caerphilly (where he set the track record).

Luke rode further afield too – he was one of a handful of Cardiff-based riders invited to appear regularly at Portsmouth Speedway and he was picked for an unofficial 'England' team that beat the touring Australians at Exeter in October 1930.

SPEEDWAY IN CARDIFF
by Andrew Weltch

Motorcycle speedway – or dirt-track racing as it was then known – arrived in Britain from Australia in 1928 and it reached Cardiff just before the end of that pioneer year.

White City Stadium, Sloper Road, hosted the city's first speedway races on Boxing Day in front of some 25,000 spectators, and the venue went on to hold regular meetings – twice a week at their peak – until 1930.

Racing was revived at the track with a single charity meeting in 1934, watched by 3,000 spectators and, after further events in 1935, the owners extended the track for Cardiff's first entry into league competition in 1936. However, the team withdrew from the Provincial League before the season was over and, although a lone event was held in 1937, speedway was lost to the city until the 1950s.

A new purpose-built stadium, alongside the railway line in Penarth Road, was opened for the 1951 season, but Cardiff was rejoining a sport in decline. Speedway's post-war boom – peaking in 1949 with 12.5 million spectators attending Britain's thirty-four tracks – was over, and the Cardiff Dragons would have only a short life.

Five-figure crowds were not uncommon for the first two seasons, but Cardiff never got beyond the sport's lower levels. Falling attendances – hitting a low of 1,800 – and entertainment tax took their toll, and the Dragons failed to complete the 1953 Southern League campaign. The stadium was also the home at the time of the similarly short-lived Cardiff Rugby League Club. It remained derelict for many years before being developed in 1969, and it is commemorated today in the name Stadium Close.

Speedway returned on a grander scale in 2000, when the Millennium Stadium hosted the British Grand Prix – the UK's round of the world championship. It was reckoned to cost £500,000 to install the temporary track and safety fence. Some 31,000 attended the event, and support has continued at a level sufficient to bring the meeting back to Cardiff each year since.

BRADLEY DREDGE AND STEPHEN DODD

'Wales' World Cup-winning golfers'
by Andrew Hignell

Golf's World Cup – the premier men's event contested by teams of two representing their country   in November 2005 was the occasion for one of the greatest moments in the history of the game in Wales, as Bradley Dredge, a resident of Cardiff, and Stephen Dodd, the finest golfer produced by Barry, won the world title in Portugal.

Heavy rain may have fallen over the course in the Algarve, with the added risk of lightning, giving tournament officials no other option than to abandon the fourth and final round. But the rain could not dampen Welsh spirits as Dredge and Dodd emulated the feats of Ian Woosnam and David Llewellyn in Hawaii in 1987, by winning the world title for Wales.

Dredge – on his fourth appearance in the World Cup event – and Dodd – in his first in the competition – were two shots ahead of England's Luke Donald and David Howell and Sweden's Niclas Fasth and Henrik Stenson when the rain washed out the final round. 'It was the best rain I've ever watched,' commented Dodd to journalists shortly after the Welsh pair had been presented with the winners' cheque amounting to a whopping £800,000. 'It would have been nice to have won over four days, but we'll take winning over three days.'

A delighted Dredge added:

It is obviously huge for us and for golf in Wales. Anytime you pull the Welsh jersey on it gives you an extra incentive, so it was great for Steve and I to win a title like that for our country. Hopefully we'll see a knock-on effect, and get some more Welsh winners in the future.

Dredge – who was born in Tredegar in July 1973 – had turned professional in 1996 after a highly successful amateur career which saw him win the Jacques Leglise Trophy in 1991, followed by the Welsh Amateur Championship in 1993, the St Andrews Trophy in 1994, and an appearance in the 1993 Walker Cup, representing Great Britain and Ireland. In 1998 Dredge became a member of the European Tour, and has since won the 2003 Madeira Open and, in 2006, the European Masters. His end-of-year position saw Dredge finish in fiftieth place in the world rankings, clinching a start in April 2007 in the US Masters in Augusta.

Dodd learnt his golf with the Brynhill club in his native Barry, and, in 1989 at the age of twenty-three, he won the Amateur Championship at Royal Birkdale. That same year he was also the Welsh Amateur Champion. He turned professional soon afterwards, but it was not until late 2004 that the Barry man won his first event, as he took the Volvo China Open title in Shanghai after ending at 12 under, just ahead of Denmark's Thomas Bjorn, whose late surge petered out on the final hole as he made a mess of the eighteenth. The victory was Dodd's first tournament win in 166 starts, but throughout his barren spell, Dodd kept believing in himself: 'I thought I would win given time,' he later told journalists, 'but it's obviously taken longer than I thought. I never believed I wasn't good enough. If I didn't think that, I would have stopped a long time ago.'

His optimism was further rewarded a few months later as he tied in second place in the Dubai Desert Classic, before adding the Nissan Irish Open to his title tally in May 2005. At the

Carton House Golf Club in Maynooth, County Kildare, he beat Englishman David Howell in a play-off by birdieing the first extra hole – the par-five eighteenth – after reaching the green in two with a drive and three iron, before calmly putting for a birdie from five feet. The Emerald Isle has proved to be a happy hunting ground for the golfer, described as the 'quiet man of the European tour', as this victory was followed by the Smurfit Kappa European Open at the K Club in 2006, where he shot a final-round 70 to lift the title at the course near Dublin.

Bradley Dredge. (*Western Mail and Echo*)

Stephen Dodd. (*Western Mail and Echo*)

THE GOLF CLUBS IN CARDIFF
by Andrew Hignell and Gwyn Prescott

The first steps towards the formation of Cardiff Golf Club were taken on 24 May 1921, at a meeting held in St Margaret's Church Hall in Waterloo Road. Around 500 people attended and expressed a strong interest to join, should a club be formed and an eighteen-hole course be created.

Consequently, a committee was formed and three sites were considered. Two were quickly discarded – a rather small area near the 'Three Arches' railway bridge, and a second plot on the Marquess of Bute's Estate to the east of Roath Park. The latter would have been very expensive to acquire, but not the third alternative – the land of Ty-to-Maen farm, adjacent to Cyncoed Road, owned by Ewan Davies, and adjoining land owned by Wyndham Clarke.

Both landowners were amenable to its sale, and on 23 November 1921 Cardiff Golf Club came into being with the inaugural captain being R.J. Pugsley, who, along with Trevor Williams, had first mooted the formation of the club. This overcame the problem of the long journey the pair previously undertook, at first by train from Cardiff and then by pony and trap for a couple of miles, to The Leys course at Gileston in the Vale of Glamorgan. Robert Walker, the former Southerndown professional, also helped lay out the course and, in 1923, the clubhouse was opened.

In 1936, R.M. de Lloyd won the Welsh Amateur Championship and a year later two Cardiff members – David H. Lewis and Roy Glossop – contested the final, which Lewis won. All three were Welsh internationals, as was Hew Squirrell, who remarkably played for Wales from 1955 until 1970 and who also won the Welsh Amateur Championships on five occasions during the 1950s and 1960s. Two other club internationals later won the Welsh title, T.J. Melia in 1979, followed by S.P. Jones in 1981. Cardiff has been the Welsh champion club on two occasions, in 1963 and 1989.

Amongst the long-serving professionals at the course have been Peter Johnson, Bill Smalldon and his son Denis, who acted as assistant professional and represented Wales in the Canada Cup, besides winning the Welsh professional title in 1953, 1956 and 1959. But in the latter year, Denis was tragically killed in an accident en route to a tournament.

One of the most curious events at the Cardiff course – regarded as one of the finest inland courses in Wales – took place on 9 August 1964, when brothers John and Roger Sanders each had a hole-in-one in the space of five minutes, with John's feat coming on the 135-yard eighteenth, whilst Roger followed suit shortly afterwards on the 171-yard twelfth!

Cardiff's oldest golf club, Radyr, celebrated its centenary in 2002. The course has one of the most impressive settings in South Wales with magnificent views over the Bristol Channel. Four-times Welsh champion club – most recently in 1981 – Radyr Golf Club also produced the 1969 and 1975 Welsh Amateur Champion, J.L. Toye. Founded only three years after Radyr, Llanishen Golf Club possesses a wooded mountain course near Parc Cefn Onn, and also enjoys spectacular views over the Channel.

On the eastern edge of the city is the St Mellons Golf Club – the course is located partly inside the city boundaries, but the clubhouse is situated just outside, hence the club's affiliation to the Gwent Golf Union, rather than to that of Glamorgan. St Mellons is the youngest of the clubs in the Cardiff area, having been formed in 1936.

The Whitchurch Golf Club was founded in 1915. Since 1966, it has won the Welsh club championship on no less than ten occasions, the most recent success being in 2005. That year, Carl Wakely won the Welsh Amateur Championship, which had previously been held by John Povall in 1962 and 1967. Povall also reached the final of the British Amateur Open in 1962.

Cardiff Golf Club. (David Edwards)

Whitchurch currently possesses one of Wales' leading amateurs in Nigel Edwards, a Walker Cup player and the 2006 South African Amateur Champion. With panoramic views over the city, the Whitchurch course is greatly admired amongst golfers and it has hosted many top tournaments, including the Welsh Professional Championship and the Welsh Ladies Open.

RON JONES

'World-record athlete and managing director of Cardiff City'
by Clive Williams

In the eyes of athletics fans, Ron's claim to fame is undoubtedly being part of the British team that set a new world 4 x 110 yards record in 1963, being Britain's athletics captain at the 1968 Mexico Olympics, and winning more Welsh sprint titles than anyone else, including Ken Jones, Christian Malcolm and Colin Jackson.

But to the wider world, he is probably best known for achieving distinction in football. He was appointed chief executive of Queens Park Rangers in 1976, having spent the previous nine years on the QPR staff as a part-time coaching adviser, before moving to Ninian Park in 1980. He then became the first paid managing director of a Football League club in 1982, having first joined the Bluebirds in 1980 at the invitation of chairman Bob Grogan. He left Cardiff City in June 1988 to rejoin John Gregory, his former boss at QPR and now owner of Portsmouth FC, to become managing director at Fratton Park.

However, there is no doubt where his sporting loyalties lie – with athletics. Cwmaman born, but a member of Cardiff's Birchgrove Harriers, he took his first sprint Welsh title at Cardiff's Maindy Stadium in 1956, beating the eventual 1960 Olympic sprint relay bronze medallist, Nick Whitehead. In total Ron won twelve Welsh sprint titles between 1956 and 1970, which is still a record. However, his first win in 1956 was remarkable in the circumstances:

I was a late starter in the sport and, after knocking on the front door of Bernard Baldwin, the former Welsh AAA secretary, at his Mountain Ash house for advice, he suggested that I ran the Glamorgan championships of that year. With very little training or preparation I won the 440 yards but came nowhere in the 100. At that time I had already entered for the Welsh championships in both the 100 and 440 yards and as the 100 event came before the 440 I ran that and, to my great surprise, won. It was only the second or third 100 I had ever run! Perhaps if the 440 had come first I would have just run in that, and not bothered with the 100 again!

Ron's most pleasing moment in a glittering athletics career spanning fifteen years was when he bettered 1948 Olympic sprint relay silver medallist Ken Jones' total of seven Welsh 100 yards titles in 1970. Ron rates this performance even above the occasion in 1963 when, as a member of one of the most famous British sprint relay quartets of all time, he equalled the world 4 x 110 yards record at the White City beating the mighty USA. Their quartet, which included Bob Hayes, the man destined to win the 1964 Tokyo Olympic 100 metres, hadn't been beaten for many a year.

Another satisfying moment came in 1969 at the ripe old age of thirty-four when he took the AAA (British) 100 metres title to follow in the footsteps of fellow Welshmen Fred Cooper (1898) and Berwyn Jones (1963).

He set his first Welsh 100 metres record with a hand-timed 10.5 seconds in 1959, beating the 10.6 set at the 1948 Olympics by Ken Jones. He held the Welsh automatically timed 100 metres record for a phenomenal twenty-seven years, until Colin Jackson beat it with 10.29 seconds in 1990.

Altogether Ron won 31 British international vests. In many of those international matches, he was handing the baton over in the sprint relay to the current leader of the Liberal Democrats, Ming Campbell. 'I had to be careful in placing the baton firmly in his hand, because even in those days he was liable to change direction,' quips Ron. Staying in political mode, Ron adds that if he had to hand over to another famous (or infamous!) political athlete, Jeffrey Archer, he would have asked for a receipt!

Ron took part in nine major championships – four Commonwealth, three European and two Olympics. Retirement came at the end of the 1970 Commonwealth Games in Edinburgh just a month ahead of his thirty-sixth birthday. Recalling those 1970 Games, Ron says that he was foolish to run, as he was suffering from an injury which subsequently brought about his retirement. Says Ron: 'We had a chance of a sprint relay medal, but I felt that if I ran, I could break down and let the team down, so I reluctantly withdrew from the team.' Wales finished fifth, just 18 hundredths behind bronze medallists England.

Now in his seventy-third year, he is still very active as director of the sports charity SportsAid Cymru Wales, which he joined in 1990, and was appointed governor in 1997 on the retirement of Cadfan Davies. He was awarded the MBE in the 2001 New Year's Honours List for his services to sport and charity.

Ron Jones wins the Welsh 100 yards sprint at Maindy Stadium in 1968, beating J.J. Williams who later found fame as a Welsh rugby international and British Lion. (Clive Williams)

JACK MATTHEWS

'The Welshman who fought Marciano'
by Gwyn Prescott

With Bleddyn Williams, 'Dr Jack' Matthews formed a centre partnership which many regard as one of the finest ever seen in the game, though owing to injury and the perversity of the selectors, they only appeared five times together at centre for Wales. But although he is always associated with his lifelong and inseparable friend, the Cardiff GP was an outstanding player in his own right.

Dr Jack is one of those many gifted sportsmen whose career was drastically curtailed by the Second World War. As a result, he was approaching twenty-seven before he was awarded his first official Welsh cap. Nevertheless, the following six years would see him established as one of Wales' great post-war players.

Born in 1920, he first showed his potential whilst still at Bridgend County School. Following three seasons in the Welsh Secondary Schools team, he played in a senior Welsh trial when only eighteen. Extremely fast – particularly for his build – Jack was already gaining a reputation as a promising sprinter. In 1937, he won the Welsh AAA Junior Men's 220 yards title and two years later he came second in the Senior Men's 100 yards and third in the 220 yards.

Representative honours would have soon followed had the war not intervened. He planned to serve in the RAF but was required to train as a doctor at the Welsh School of Medicine and so he played most of his wartime rugby in south Wales. Eventually, Jack was commissioned in the RAMC.

Dr Jack Matthews.

Representing Wales against England in 1940, he took part in several subsequent wartime internationals and also in the unofficial Victory international series, including the win over France when he was captain. He won his first official Welsh cap in the first post-war international and went on to win 17 in all between 1947 and 1951. In 1948, playing on the wing, he was one of ten Cardiff men in the Welsh team against England and later that year he participated in the victory over Australia. Jack was also a crucial member of the 1950 Welsh team which won the Triple Crown for the first time in thirty-nine years.

Extremely fast off the mark and well built for a centre, Jack was difficult to stop. Taking the ball on the burst, he could crash through defences. It was one such contribution which led to the first try against Scotland in the Triple Crown year. He was, however, also particularly renowned – and feared – for his totally committed and ferocious tackling. Not for nothing did he have the reputation of being virtually indestructible on the field. This was the Welshman after all who, during the war, had boxed a draw in an amateur bout with the future world champion, Rocky Marciano.

His hardness and physical presence on the field was particularly valued during the 1950 Lions tour to Australasia. In the third Test, for example, the All Blacks' skipper was forced to leave the field following one of Jack's tackles. Not surprisingly, as a hard player who never spared himself, he was greatly admired in New Zealand where he was acclaimed as the 'Iron Man', a distinction not lightly conferred on visitors to that country. One of the outstanding successes of the tour, he played in all six Tests and captained the Lions on three occasions.

Jack Matthews is a member of that small and distinguished band of players who have captained Cardiff for three seasons. Much of the club's great success over the first post-war decade stemmed from his period of captaincy between 1945 and 1947, when he imbued his players with an attacking spirit. During his third season as captain in 1951/52, Cardiff were narrowly defeated 9-11 by the Springboks when Jack had a fair try cruelly disallowed by a bad refereeing error. That South Africa were later awarded a try in identical circumstances only increased Jack's indignation and disappointment. He retired at the end of that season but maintained his active involvement with the club and still regularly attends matches at the Arms Park.

He was medical officer to the Welsh Boxing Association for many years and in 1980 he again participated in a Lions tour, this time to South Africa, where he was the official team doctor. A year later, he was awarded the OBE. In an appropriate historical link with an earlier distinguished club centre and captain, Dr Jack officiated at the re-dedication of the Gwyn Nicholls gates when they were moved to their new location at the Arms Park following the building of the Millennium Stadium. One of the great characters of Welsh rugby, Dr Jack remains highly respected throughout the game, not least for his forthright and strongly expressed views.

NORMAN RICHES

'The Cardiff dentist who was Glamorgan's first Championship captain'
by Andrew Hignell

Having been Glamorgan's finest batsman in their Minor County days, it was fitting that, in May 1921, Norman Riches should lead out the Welsh county at the Arms Park – the scene of so many of his graceful innings for both the county and the town club – as they played Sussex in their inaugural fixture as a first-class county.

It was, in fact, a fairytale start for Riches and his Glamorgan colleagues as they defeated Sussex. After the final wicket fell, he and his team were mobbed by their delighted supporters before Riches led a series of impromptu speeches on the pavilion balcony, in which he paid fulsome

Left: N.V.H. Riches.

Opposite: Norman Riches walks out to bat with Tom Whittington to open the batting for Glamorgan in their inaugural County Championship match against Sussex at Cardiff in 1921.

tribute to all those people who had supported Glamorgan in their days as a Minor County between 1897 and 1920, and had engineered their elevation into the County Championship.

At the time, Riches was thirty-seven years old, and working as a dentist in Cardiff. But he was by no means past his best as a batsman – as he proved in 1928 when making a superb century against Lancashire who at the time possessed one of the most potent bowling attacks in the country. They held no terrors though for Norman Vaughan Hurry Riches, as he crisply struck a series of boundaries in a magnificent innings, before returning a few days later to the family's dental practice at 24 Dumfries Place where he worked until the mid-1950s, and successfully mixed his duties with playing cricket for Cardiff and Glamorgan.

Born in Cardiff in 1883, Riches was one of seven children, with his sister Beryl later becoming a famous actress and ironically living close to Lord's cricket ground in St John's Wood. From a young age, he showed great prowess as a right-handed batsman, having been coached by his uncles, who themselves had played with distinction for both the town and county clubs.

Like so many other well-to-do young Cardiffians, Norman's sporting ambitions were first nurtured at Monkton House School, whose headmaster – Mr Henry Shewbrook – had been an instrumental figure in the formation of Cardiff RFC in the mid-1870s. Norman subsequently completed his education at Abingdon School and then Guy's Hospital, where he gained the necessary qualifications that allowed him to embark on his dental career. His father, though, was always generous enough to give him sufficient time off so that he could play plenty of county and representative cricket.

Norman made his county debut, aged seventeen, in 1900 and, within a couple of years, he had secured a regular place in the county's line-up. He subsequently enjoyed many productive seasons both for Cardiff CC and Glamorgan.

His most successful summer at county level came in 1911, when he struck three centuries and became the first man to amass over a thousand runs in a season for any Minor County side. Not surprisingly, Riches was highly regarded at Lord's and viewed as one of the finest amateur batsmen in the country.

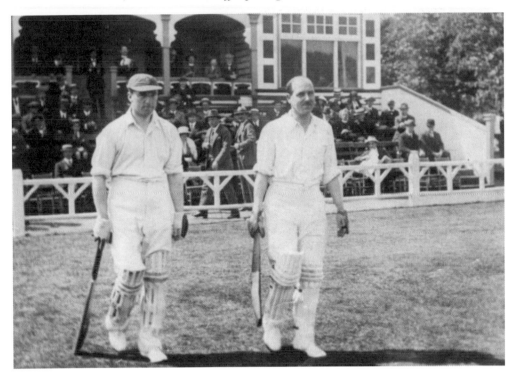

When available, he turned out for the MCC against touring teams and other first-class sides, and in 1912 a few discreet enquiries were made about his availability for the winter tour to the West Indies. Rather than speaking directly to the Cardiff dentist, the MCC officials spoke to another leading figure with Glamorgan who, in an off-the-cuff remark, suggested that he doubted Riches would get time off to tour abroad in the winter. In truth, his father would have been only too pleased to grant his son leave of absence, but sadly no invitation ever came his way from Lord's.

After retiring from county cricket in 1935, Riches became a stalwart figure in Cardiff Athletic Club and he was Cardiff CC's venerable president in their centenary year in 1967, as together with the county club, the Cardiff cricketers moved from the Arms Park to their new home at Sophia Gardens. His son John also played for Glamorgan in 1947 and, like his father, was a mainstay of the Cardiff side for many years.

CARDIFF ATHLETIC CLUB
by Andrew Hignell

For several generations, Cardiff Athletic Club has been the powerhouse of amateur sporting activity within the city, the organisation which helped to preserve the use of the Arms Park for the benefit of so many Cardiffians and the body which oversaw the operation of the city's premier cricket, rugby, hockey, lawn tennis and bowls club.

The club was formed in 1922 through the amalgamation of the city's rugby and cricket clubs who, for the previous half century, had been granted the use of the Arms Park at a peppercorn rate by its owner, the Marquess of Bute. There had been previous attempts to merge the clubs, starting in November 1892, whilst between 1902 and 1904 the two clubs worked closely to finance the erection of a spacious pavilion to serve the needs of both the burly rugby players and the gentlemen cricketers.

However, the merger did not take place until 1922 – a time when the Marquis was starting to dispose of his property in South Wales. Eager to preserve their hallowed turf, the cricket and rugby clubs joined forces, and through the help of leading solicitor and sportsman Hugh Ingledew, the newly-created athletic club purchased the Arms Park – except for a strip of land adjoining Westgate Street – for the sum of £30,000 on the understanding that it should be preserved for recreational purposes.

Shortly afterwards, a limited company was formed after discussions by the athletic club with the Arms Park (Cardiff) Greyhound Racing Company and the Welsh Rugby Union. Until the early 1930s the athletic club was operated under licence, revocable at short notice, from the limited company, but the situation changed in 1933 as they secured a ninety-nine-year lease from the limited company at a rental of £200 per annum.

This arrangement gave the athletic club greater security but, even so, several changes took place, starting in 1935 when the Marquis of Bute decided to build a large block of flats on his land adjoining Westgate Street. The three grass tennis courts were lost, and the cricket ground was slightly reduced in size. However, greater changes took place in the 1960s with the creation of the National Stadium. As a result, the cricket and hockey sections of the athletic club moved, initially to Sophia Gardens in 1967, and then in 1995 the Diamond Ground in Whitchurch became the home of Cardiff Cricket Club. The club may have become fragmented in terms of location, but its influence amongst the corridors of civic power has remained undiminished.

The Arms Park in 1930 showing the tennis, rugby and cricket grounds before the flats in Westgate Street were erected. (Local Studies Department, Cardiff Central Library)

PADDY HENNESSEY

'Cardiff's baseball legend'
by Andrew Weltch

One of the most impressive aspects of Welsh baseball is the speed obtained by the bowlers with their distinctive underarm technique, and the man who impressed more than any was Paddy Hennessey. The Irishman's ferocious right arm put fear into batsmen in the Welsh League and on the international scene, and even came close to earning him a call-up into first class cricket.

Born in County Cork on 6 October 1929, Richard Christopher Hennessey's early sports were hurling and Gaelic football but, having migrated to Wales, he came across baseball while working in the Connies and Meadon factory in Cardiff and watching the game played by his colleagues in their breaks. The twenty-one-year-old decided to try it himself and in his first competitive game for the works team, he removed St Mary's of Canton for no runs and 13 extras. After a couple of seasons in the lower levels of the league, he was signed by Splott US (University Settlement), and he was an instant success at the top level.

In 1957, he made his debut for Wales in the annual international against England in Liverpool. He opened the bowling and had the English at 33 for 7, but was removed after a protest was made over his bowling style and a series of no-balls was called. John Clements replaced him in the bowler's box and finished the English off for 43, but their efforts counted for nothing, as the match was abandoned because of heavy rain.

The following year saw the big game on home soil at Maindy Stadium. Hennessey was again selected and bowled England out for just 17 in their second innings, taking Wales to a comfortable win. The match marked the golden jubilee of the first international in 1908 and Hennessey had an extra reason to celebrate that season, as he was named Welsh Baseball Union player of the year.

By 1962, he had joined Grange Albion, and in that year's international he dismissed England for just 11 in their first innings and 14 in the second, with only four batsmen hitting the ball. Two years later, his performance in the international was even more impressive, removing England for just six runs in their first innings, a feat which again helped him to the WBU player of the year award, becoming the first man to achieve the honour twice.

His devastating form also came to the attention of Glamorgan CCC who considered that a super-fast underarm bowler could give them an advantage in the new limited-overs version of their game. As the first round of the new Gillette Cup loomed, Ossie Wheatley, the Glamorgan captain, invited Hennessy for a trial in the nets at Cardiff Arms Park, with the thought of recruiting him as a secret weapon.

As Peter Walker recalled:

We watched in amazement as he ran up and with a whirl of his bowling arm delivered a 75mph (estimated by me) underarm delivery which was still rising to near head height as it reached the batsman's end! I put the pads on and went into the net to face him. It was unusual and, indeed, unnerving to find a bowler running up and letting it go at me underarm as they used to in the eighteenth century! I spent the first half a dozen or so balls ducking and weaving out of the way – this, remember, was in the pre-helmet days – and so didn't lay a bat on the ball except once when I glanced it over what would have been the men fielding in the slips in a cricket match.

However, the laws of cricket required the ball to bounce before it reached the batsman, and the trajectory of the baseball delivery made that almost impossible to achieve. 'If he'd bowled as he usually did in his game, in a cricket match he would almost certainly have been no-balled by the umpire,' said Walker.

Paddy Hennessy. (*Western Mail and Echo*)

So Hennessey was not considered for selection. If he had been, he would have become the first man in over 100 years to have been selected as an underarm specialist bowler in a county cricket match – a development which could have changed the face of the modern game, and brought the formidable talents of Paddy Hennessey to a whole new sporting public.

RHYS WILLIAMS

'Wales' promising sprinter'
by Clive Williams

On a damp afternoon in Gothenburg in August 2006, Cardiff AAC youngster Rhys gave an insight into his potential with an outstanding performance in the European Championships, becoming one of only two members of the British team to win two medals. There is little doubt that he is one of the brightest prospects on the British athletics scene. This is underlined by him being voted third most popular athlete in Britain in 2006 in two polls conducted by *Athletics Weekly*, the bible of the sport in Britain.

In Gothenburg, with a typically late burst, he took the bronze medal in the 400-metre hurdles, before returning on the final day to be part of the British 4 x 400-metre relay team, along with his Cardiff teammate, Tim Benjamin, which took the silver medals.

The two Gothenburg medals were his first as a senior, although winning medals at European Championships has become a bit of a habit. He first announced his presence on the international stage with a gold medal in the European Youth Championships in 2001. He then followed this with wins in the 2003 European Junior Championships in Tampere, Finland and then took the European Under-23 title in 2005 in Erfurt, Germany to emulate his Cardiff clubmate, Matt Elias, who won in 2001.

There is no doubt that in 2006 he came of age. He was unlucky to miss a medal in the Melbourne Commonwealth Games, finishing fourth, but had the great satisfaction of lowering Matt Elias' Welsh record by two hundredths of a second to 49.09, the fastest time by a British athlete in 2006. He also took his first AAA (British) title, and is clearly established as the British number one for his event.

Sport runs in the family. Father 'JJ' is, of course, best known for his exploits as part of the great Welsh rugby team of the 1970s. But many people forget that he won four Welsh sprint titles, and ran in the 1970 Commonwealth Games. But more to the point, elder brother James and sister Kathryn are great stalwarts of Cardiff AAC. James, the 2006 Welsh indoor 1,500-metre champion, has been men's captain since 2002 whilst Kathryn, a former British junior 400-metre hurdles international, was the club's female athlete of the year in 2004. So the blue vest of Cardiff AAC is not exactly unfamiliar to Rhys.

The former Loughborough student, who has restarted his studies at the University of Glamorgan now that he is being coached in Leckwith by Colin Jackson, the double world champion and still holder of the 60-metre indoor and joint holder of the 110-metre outdoor hurdles world record. But Rhys is the first to admit the invaluable coaching help he received in his early days from Rob Green, and former Welsh 400 metre hurdles champion Wyn Leyshon. And he recognises the part that former Welsh 110-metre hurdles champion Nick Dakin gave him whilst he was studying in Loughborough.

Rhys' first sporting love was swimming, winning the Welsh Schools 200-metre backstroke and racing against Olympic bronze medallist David Davies. But he quit the pool at sixteen, and hasn't looked back since. He was also a member of the Welsh Schools rugby squad. But there is no question of him changing sports again. He is undoubtedly the finest athletics prospect Wales has seen for many a year.

HARRY BOWCOTT

'Classical rugby player for Cardiff, Wales and the British Lions'
by David Parry-Jones

I came to know Harry in his retirement days after he had been a London-based civil servant – he loved to hold court in Cardiff RFC's clubhouse bar. Anyone could buy Harry a gin and tonic to lubricate the flow of reminiscences that was guaranteed, but I possessed a special entrée to his company – membership of Cardiff High School, which I attended from 1945 to 1952, and in whose New Hall the honours boards featured H.M. Bowcott (1921-27) and his onward move to St Catharine's College, Cambridge. He always wanted to hear titbits of news about the high school that I could bring in.

In fact, it was a remarkable and very important change in the school's sporting curriculum that, arguably, underwrote Harry's progress on the rugby field. In 1921 eleven Welsh grammar schools, led by Cardiff High School, switched from soccer as a keynote winter sport to rugby, and so impressively did Harry take to the handling code that by 1927 he could force his way into the Cambridge teams that beat Oxford that year and the next.

The Bowcott family, which included rugby-playing brothers Jackie and Bill, ran a butchery business in Cardiff, which meant that Harry could stay in Wales initially, riding the economic depressions of the day, playing for Cardiff over eight seasons during the twenties and thirties. His total dependability on a rugby pitch was appreciated by clubmates and praised by the press. 'Classy' and 'cultured' were amongst the words used by the hacks to describe his performances.

Although his place in the Welsh team was never guaranteed, the 1929 season saw him winning three caps against Scotland, Ireland and France. In January 1930 he captained Wales in Cardiff but, following an 11-3 defeat, there was to be no continuation of his leadership. Out of favour he went, and his final four caps in the Five Nations tournament were sporadic.

It was possibly because of the good profits made by the butcher's shop that Harry could accept a most agreeable invitation to tour with the 1930 British side in New Zealand and Australia. Captained by F.D. Prentice, the side won the first New Zealand Test 6-3, but lost the next three – and the series – by narrow margins. Although quiet in his youthful days, he

A cigarette card depicting Harry Bowcott.

fitted in well. 'We had no coach, no doctor, no physiotherapist, and – thank goodness – no pressmen, so we could do as we liked with nobody looking over our shoulders,' he smiled when questioned about the tour by journalists.

The Kiwis liked his game. In his book of the tour, the former All Black Geoffrey Alley wrote, 'He was a most extraordinarily consistent player. Bowcott appeared in sixteen matches, including the four Tests, and scored eighteen points.' He also played in the single Test against Australia.

But back home, Harry would have been the first to concede that between the wars, Welsh rugby was not enjoying a grand period in its history. Sustained by clever backs like Rowe Harding, Windsor Lewis, Guy Morgan and Jack Bassett, total disgrace was avoided. On the other hand, Welsh forward play was untutored and rough and ready, especially when compared with the well-presented English packs under inspirational Wavell Wakefield's leadership.

A sensational compensation in the midst of mediocrity was Wales' first victory at Twickenham in ten visits since 1910. Winger Ronnie Boon got the try and dropped goal that won the January 1933 game, but Bowcott too was at his supreme best, beating back from stand-off frenzied efforts by the English to save the game.

Harry had one final match to play for Wales, against Ireland at Ravenhill, which contained a first, and last, score for his country – and one that Cardiff RFC historian Danny Davies described as 'one of the best tries seen in international rugby for years.' The match programme also noted by now that Bowcott had joined London Welsh, where he was to see out his rugby days. Having played 113 matches for the Blue and Blacks, he had left Cardiff to pursue careers as a civil servant in Whitehall and a rugby player at Herne Hill, where he was captain in 1934/35.

After the Second World War, Bowcott also found time to involve himself in the higher echelons of Welsh rugby. President of the Welsh Rugby Union in 1974/75, between 1963 and 1974, he was a member of the 'Big Five' selection committee – a time when a large number of the 'Exiles' began to win caps, and seven of the London Welsh players were picked to tour with the 1971 British Lions, who remain the sole British tourists to win a Test series in New Zealand.

Harry talked endlessly and fruitfully to the London Welsh coach, John Dawes, later the captain of those same Lions, as the two men travelled to and from Cardiff to committee meetings at the Arms Park. Memorably, he answered a question about selection by explaining, 'when the claims of London Welshmen are under scrutiny by the Big Five, I simply keep my mouth shut, confident that my four co-selectors will pick them for me.'

In 1968, and at the age of sixty, he was a surprise choice as 'coach' to the Wales side bound for Argentina where, in the absence of the eleven top Welsh players on tour with the Lions, the two unofficial Tests against the Pumas ended in one defeat and one draw. His appointment was highly controversial, for the WRU had just appointed a professional coaching organiser in Ray Williams, and were now perceived to have ignored recommendations for the tour management made by him. In the end, genial Harry got his tour, in the role of assistant manager, while Clive Rowlands was chosen to wear the track suit at training.

No love at all is lost when Cardiff RFC play Newport RFC (or as it now is, under regional rugby, the Blues playing the Dragons). This 130-year-old, ever-smouldering feud survives into our time, and the relationship continues to be prickly. Therefore, I judge it a felicitous idea to conclude this profile of a Cardiff great with a Newport judgement. In *Rugby Recollections*, written in 1948, W.J. Towsend Collins ('Dromio' of the *South Wales Argus*) lavished almost lyrical praise upon Harry Bowcott:

> As a schoolboy star, H.M. Bowcott was a youthful prodigy, whose play had classic perfection of technique. The correctness was something to wonder at. It seemed unnatural in a boy. In 1929 he was selected against Scotland and in a very hard game which Wales won by a goal and three tries to a dropped goal and a penalty, he displayed coolness and judgement, revealed a sense of position, and kept the opposition on tenterhooks by well-judged individual efforts, while the length and judgement of his kicking were especially admirable. H.M. Bowcott may have over-done the kick ahead, but overall was certainly among the cleverest of players.

I am sure that, if Harry read that, his response would have been a satisfied smile – coupled with a generous reloading of his pipe.

SONIA LAWRENCE

'International gymnast and pole-vaulter'
by Andrew Hignell

Sonia Lawrence is one of a rare breed of athletes to have represented Wales in the Commonwealth Games in two different sports. She initially competed as a schoolgirl in the gymnastic events at the 1994 Commonwealth Games, where the Cardiff AAC youngster from Bedwas won a silver medal in the vault.

This was a deserved reward for the youngster who, after fire had destroyed her initial training facility in Cardiff, had to travel regularly to south-east England to train at the gym owned by the Welsh National Coach. Her long hours of travel were rewarded by selection for the World and European Championships in the mid-1990s, as well as the Atlanta Olympics in 1996, before another appearance in the 1998 Commonwealth Games in Kuala Lumpur.

A modest performance in the latter Games was a watershed in her career, and as she later explained in an interview, she started to contemplate a change of direction:

> After getting the medal in Canada, I was disappointed with my display in Kuala Lumpur in 1998. It got so bad that I started thinking about giving it up. I was talking to Jamie Baulch and he suggested that I should try pole-vaulting, which was a new sport for women at the time. That stuck in my head, really. I took a year out and then decided to go to UWIC in Cardiff where I began pole-vaulting for the first time.

After three years study at UWIC and intensive training at their facilities, as well as with the Cardiff club, and winning the senior womens indoor pole-vault championships in 2002, Sonia won a place in the Welsh pole-vault team at the Commonwealth Games in Manchester. However, she failed to reach the finals, being eliminated in the qualifying rounds after a best vault of 3.90 metres.

Nevertheless, the following year she won the Welsh Championships with a vault of 4.02 metres, and she later improved on this in 2003 to record a new personal best of 4.05 metres – the second highest ever recorded by a Welsh athlete. In 2006 she won the Welsh Championships for the second time.

GEORGE LATHAM

'A Ninian Park legend'
by Richard Shepherd

One of the legendary names of Cardiff City and Welsh international football in the 1920s and 1930s was First World War hero George Latham – a man who was connected with the Bluebirds from 1911 until 1932, and then from 1934 to 1936. George had been a well-known player at club and international level in the period leading up to the First World War, but it was as an outstanding trainer and personality that he left his mark on the game, becoming one of the most respected and best-loved men behind the scenes.

In fact, such was his reputation that, in the summer of 1924, he was invited to travel to Paris with the British Olympic squad as their masseur for the 'Chariots of Fire' Games and, as a token of the athletes' appreciation of his services, he was awarded a special medal by them.

Born in Newtown, mid-Wales on 1 January 1881, George first played for the Newtown Night School team, becoming a noted local player who could appear in most positions. He worked as a tailor in a local shop and went on to play for Newtown FC, before volunteering his services in the South African War, which broke out in 1899, by joining the South Wales Borderers and rising to the rank of non-commissioned officer.

On his return from war service, he continued his football activities and, after a spell as an amateur with Liverpool, was a professional with them for six years before joining Southport Central. He played nine times for Wales between 1905 and 1910 before going to Stoke as player-trainer in 1910/11. At that time, Cardiff City were in their first season as a professional club, playing in the Second Division of the Southern League. In February 1911 George joined the Bluebirds as player-trainer, and he helped the club win the Welsh Senior Cup in April 1912 – the first time that the competition had been won by a club from South Wales. George played at right-back in the replay of the final when City beat Pontypridd 3-0; it was in fact his first appearance in the competition that season, and after the game he gave his medal to injured defender Bob Lawrie, who had missed the replay having appeared in every round.

By that time, George was concentrating mainly on his trainer's role that included not only getting the players fit, but also treating them for various injuries. Although he was not formally qualified in physiotherapy (hardly any trainers were back in those days), he had a remarkable knowledge of the human body, much of it derived from his mother who had been matron of the Montgomery County Infirmary. George became an expert masseur and was skilful in the treatment of injuries – so much so that many sufferers of rheumatism and people recovering from broken limbs would seek his aid. Local footballers, rugby players, and cricketers would all come to him at Ninian Park, and he would give them his time and services for nothing.

A physical fitness expert, George would often send his City players on demanding cross-country runs. A typical route would be along Leckwith Road, up the hill to Dinas Powys and back again, finishing off with an intensive session involving heavy medicine balls. It is not surprising, therefore, that City easily won the Second Division of the Southern League in 1912/13.

George Latham.

It was in that season that George also made his final Welsh international appearance, albeit in somewhat unusual circumstances. He had travelled with the Wales team to Ireland as their trainer, and, on the sea crossing from Fleetwood to Belfast the day before the game, the sea was so rough that two of the players were extremely ill. One of them recovered by the next day, but Manchester City left half Teddy Hughes showed no sign of improvement. Wales had travelled with just eleven players and it was too late to send for a replacement. George was sent for by Ted Robbins, secretary of the FA of Wales (no self-styled fancy title of secretary-general or whatever back then). 'George, you will have to play,' said genial Ted to his trainer, and play he did, helping Wales beat Ireland 1-0 in what was his first international appearance for three years.

Just over a year after that win over Ireland, with Cardiff City by then having won promotion to the First Division of the Southern League, the First World War broke out in August 1914. George enlisted in the Army and, at first, acted as an instructor in the 7th Battalion Royal Welsh Fusiliers. He received a commission as a second lieutenant in August 1915, and was promoted to lieutenant in May 1916. He fought with the Seventh Army in Palestine and Egypt, eventually reaching the rank of captain, and it was whilst involved in action against the Turks in Gaza that he won the Military Cross after capturing an enemy position and a number of highly-ranked prisoners. In a later action at Beersheba, he was also awarded a Bar to his Military Cross.

During his time in the Army, George also became 'acquainted' with rugby union, and he took part in a recreational game behind the lines. But when he headed the ball over the opposition crossbar, his teammates soon decided that rugby was not for Captain George Latham MC and Bar!

On his return to civilian life and Ninian Park in 1919, there were exciting times ahead. Cardiff City had been elected to the Football League in 1920 and they were soon to become a successful League club with numerous international players. George, in fact, became City's oldest League debutant when, on 2 January 1922, at the age of forty-two, he had to appear for the Bluebirds at Blackburn Rovers. Once again he answered an SOS call after two players – Jack Evans and Jimmy Gill – had been taken ill on the way to the game, leaving City with just ten fit men. George was hastily registered with the Football League by telegram and played at inside right, helping his side to a 3-1 win.

In the latter stages of the game, he moved to a right-wing position in order to take a breather, but his teammates made him chase long passes at every opportunity and, at the end, he was somewhat struggling! In fact, George nearly scored in the game, hitting the post with one effort and going close with another. Whenever he was with the team at Blackburn in succeeding years, home officials would enquire if he was playing. When told that those days were behind him, they would smilingly reply, 'Well – we might have a chance of winning then!'

'Gentleman George', as he was popularly known, never married – Cardiff City, Wales and his home town of Newtown were his life. He would often be at Ninian Park from early morning to late evening, attending to training, kit, injuries and various other matters. Throughout his time with the Bluebirds he did not live too far from the ground, lodging with a family in Clive Street.

George was also instrumental in Cardiff City playing a regular end-of-season match against Montgomeryshire at Newtown in aid of the County Infirmary, and in 1926 he was awarded an inscribed gold watch and chain by his friends in the town as a token of his efforts on behalf of the hospital. Another measure of his popularity came when Wales toured Canada at the end of the 1928/29 season. George travelled with the team as trainer, and in the words of FAW secretary Ted Robbins, 'he was as big an attraction to Welsh exiles out there as the team itself. Everybody who came to see us asked for George, saying that their parents or grandparents had originally come from Newtown.'

But with Cardiff City's slide in the late 1920s and early 1930s, times were tough at Ninian Park and George was made redundant at the end of the 1931/32 season. The club's directors said that they very much regretted having to take such a step, but they faced severe financial difficulties, and had to offload several of their long-serving backroom staff.

George joined Chester as trainer, and spent two years with them before returning to Ninian Park at the club's request in May 1934. Two years later, though, he met with a serious accident whilst cycling to work from his Clive Street digs. He was forced to brake violently in Sloper Road to avoid a vehicle, and fell off his bike. He was quite badly hurt and had to retire from his work as a trainer. He also returned to Newtown but never really recovered from the accident, and died aged fifty-eight on 10 July 1939.

He was very much missed by everyone with whom he had come into contact, having made such a massive contribution to Welsh football and especially Cardiff City. He was buried in Llanllwchaern Churchyard, just outside Newtown, and when the latter's football club opened their new ground in the early 1950s, they had no hesitation in naming it 'Latham Park' in memory of the man who made his mark in everything that he did.

THE GRANGETOWN STADIUM
by Andrew Hignell

The Grangetown Stadium, which flourished either side of the First World War, was one of Cardiff's unique sporting centres. Situated at the lower end of Clive Street, it played host to rugby, football, professional running and whippet races.

Some of the best sprinters in the world at that time appeared in the races at the Grangetown Stadium, including Jack Donaldson, a world champion from Australia, and Bombardier Billy Wells, the ex-heavyweight boxing champion, who won a £200 handicap – at the time, one of the largest prizes ever offered in Great Britain for a sprint handicap.

The Stadium was quite spartan by modern standards, but it was a popular meeting place with a colourful and animated atmosphere all of its own. The regular band of spectators were mightily disappointed when its promoters, two Cardiff bookmakers, Duggan and Dye, closed down operations so that the land could be developed for housing.

A caricature of Nicky Piper drawn by Dorrien of the *Western Mail*.

NICKY PIPER

'The Mensa member who became a king of the ring'
by Gareth Jones

At first it seemed as though his membership of Mensa was more important than his boxing, as Nicky Piper became the poster boy for a sustained campaign to prove that fighters did not necessarily lack intelligence. But his ring achievements on their own proved him worthy of respect and admiration.

Born in 1966, the lanky lad from Culverhouse Cross was just nine when he followed big brother Cliff to the Victoria Park gym. While Cliff won a Welsh amateur title, Nicky captured four, going on to win the British ABA final on his twenty-third birthday before opting to turn pro. Guided by the wise old head of trainer Charlie Pearson, Piper linked up with Frank Warren, a decision which was to bring him three world title opportunities in an eight-year paid career.

His punching power soon grabbed the headlines: a nineteen-second demolition job on Dave Owens was surpassed when he knocked out American serviceman John Ellis in twelve seconds, including the count. Only future British champion Maurice Core, given a controversial draw despite hitting the deck twice, lasted the distance in the Welshman's first ten contests.

Perhaps it had been too easy. Piper rashly agreed to face the much heavier Carl Thompson as a short-notice replacement and was himself halted inside three rounds. Thompson went on to become WBO cruiserweight king, while Nicky learned a painful lesson.

But, after six more wins, he was offered a surprise shot at WBC super-middleweight ruler Nigel Benn. Many thought it was another step too far, but Piper boxed superbly before the 'Dark Destroyer' eventually forced a stoppage in the eleventh round, with Nicky actually ahead on one judge's card.

After dabbling with the minor Penta-Continental belt, Piper stepped up to light heavyweight and was soon given a crack at WBO champion Leeonzer Barber at the National Ice Rink. The American, his right eye swollen shut, was told by his corner that he had one more round before they pulled him out; he responded with a stunning left hook and Nicky was the man needing rescue. The same venue saw a thriller for the British title, but veteran Crawford Ashley emerged with the decision. Within a year, however, Piper acquired the Commonwealth belt, halting Ulsterman Noel Magee on the Naseem Hamed–Steve Robinson bill at the Cardiff RFC ground.

Two years later the Cardiffian was granted a third chance to collect the ultimate prize. But taking on unbeaten Dariusz Michalczewski before his German fans in Hanover was always a big ask. Nicky was floored inside the first ten seconds and only immense courage took him as far as the seventh round, after which his corner ended the torture.

If that was his last appearance inside the ropes, it did not mean a farewell to boxing. As well as his role as a respected analyst on television, he became an administrative steward on the Board of Control, for whom he now acts as marketing consultant. He also served on the Sports Council for Wales and was given an MBE in the 2006 New Year's Honours List.

JIM SULLIVAN

'Cardiff's rugby league legend'
by Huw Richards

When the Rugby League Hall of Fame, celebrating the greatest contributors to the code in Britain, was inaugurated in 1988, a panel of experts chose nine charter members. Two were Australians. There were three Yorkshiremen, a Lancastrian and three men from Cardiff. Nothing in the city's sporting history is more remarkable than this contribution to a game that was played only rarely and intermittently there until the student-led growth of the late twentieth century.

They formed part of what Phil Melling has called one of the greatest migrations of sporting talent in history. The traffic between Wales and the North of England reached its peak between the two world wars when nearly 400 players, including seventy internationals, 'went north'. Among the earliest and perhaps the most remarkable of this group was Jim Sullivan, who signed for Wigan in 1921.

Like his successors, he mirrored Cardiff's ethnic diversity, as one of many sportsmen of Irish descent from the city. None of the hall of famers had played international union – none could afford to wait for the honour when an opportunity to turn their greatest talent into cash was pressing, and all went north in their teens.

Sullivan, who was born at 35 Elaine Street, Splott in December 1903, went earlier than any of them, aged seventeen. Yet even at that age he had come close to a Welsh cap, placed on standby as a reserve before an injured player recovered in time for the match. A product of St Alban's School, he made his debut for Cardiff aged sixteen and immediately became a regular, playing 35 matches in his single season. He became the youngest ever Barbarian, playing against Newport less than a month after his seventeenth birthday and was also the only player ever to knock out the man who, in his absence, would become the greatest Welsh player of the 1920s, Llanelli legend Albert Jenkins. Cardiff club historian Danny Davies recorded that 'had he remained an amateur he would most probably have become Cardiff's greatest of all full-backs'. He also played baseball for Wales and was a good enough golfer to consider turning professional.

Wigan were convinced enough of his talents to pay £750. At the time the record transfer for an established league player was only £600, although the first four-figure fee was paid a little later in 1921. It might, Geoffrey Moorhouse has pointed out, be regarded as the greatest bargain in league history. He joined a club that had won a single Championship and no Challenge Cups. A second title was won in his first season, and the first Challenge Cup followed two years later. Wigan have rarely stopped winning trophies since.

Sullivan became interwar league's defining figure – like Yorkshire and England cricketer Herbert Sutcliffe, his career coincided almost exactly with the era. The danger in considering his league life is of bemusement by an avalanche of statistics – his 922 matches and 2,858 goals remain all-time records, while his 6,001 points have been eclipsed only by Neil Fox. His

Right: Jim Sullivan, cheerfully and proudly holding some valuable silverware.

Far right: A cigarette card of Jim Sullivan.

kicking statistics had a Bradman-like quality, as he led league's goal scorers – often by massive margins – in every season but two between 1921/22 and 1938/39, on those two occasions headed only very marginally by Joe Thompson, formerly of Cross Keys.

He would, though, have been remembered as a great player if he had never kicked a goal. One of those best qualified to judge, his fellow Cardiffian and hall of famer Gus Risman wrote of him that, 'so many full-backs are either good in defence or good in attack. Hardly any are good in both departments. Yet Jim Sullivan… was simply brilliant in both'. He was a 14st 7lbs man quick enough to join three-quarter movements with an impeccable sense of timing and angles, an impregnable tackler and, in an age when kicking duels between full-backs were an integral part of the game, unmatched for the length and direction of his clearances. To Risman he was also, 'a master tactician, a great student of the game and perhaps the most brilliant captain the game has known. With Sullivan in command you were playing under a general who was quite willing to do as much work as the private'.

He played in an unmatched total of 60 international matches, 26 of them for Wales and 25 for Great Britain. He took part in five consecutive winning Test series against Australia, was captain on the 1932 tour and would have led again in 1936 had his wife not been expecting a child.

His tactical and leadership skills were apparent when he took over as Wigan's coach after the war and built a team reckoned to be among the three or four greatest in league history, winning three Championships and two Challenge Cups while monopolising the Lancashire county trophies in the first seven post-war seasons. His signings for the club included Billy Boston.

After a falling out with the Wigan board, he moved to St Helens and lifted a club previously counted among the game's also-rans to the status among its giants that it has enjoyed consistently ever since, winning its first Challenge Cup in 1956. He died in Wigan in 1977, aged seventy-three.

REG BRADDICK

'Cardiff's Mr Cycling'
by Andrew Hignell

Reg Braddick, the Welsh Sprint and British Road Race champion, just loved riding bikes. Even after retiring from running his cycle business in Cardiff, Reg continued to ride and

Reg Braddick, pictured on one of his beloved cycles in 1981. (Suzy Braddick)

raise money for charity, with his journey, at the age of seventy-five, from Land's End to John O'Groats, raising £25,000 for various causes.

Born in Cardiff in 1913, his love affair with cycling began when he was a young boy, working in a butcher's shop in Whitchurch Road and making deliveries by bike. It continued several years later as he joined the Raleigh Bicycle Company and worked as a toolmaker in their cycle factory in Nottingham, although he returned each weekend to Cardiff, cycling back and forth in order to woo his girlfriend Betty, whom he later married in April 1941.

By this time, he was a regular in both sprint and road race competitions, and Reg's outstanding performances led to an Olympic trial in 1936 at Crystal Palace, but he broke his collar bone in a crash and did not make the final team. However, two years later he was one of six athletes chosen by Wales – and the only cyclist – for the 1938 Empire Games in Sydney, and he travelled by boat to Australia with his five colleagues.

Although it was a decent liner, there were few facilities on board where the Welsh team could train, never mind anywhere that Reg could adequately practice with his racing bike. Salvation came when the vessel had to pass through the Suez Canal, and Reg was able to ride his bike along the road from Cairo to Port Said at the southern end of the canal. In fact, it proved to be a much quicker route and Reg sped to the end of the canal, arriving in Port Said well before the boat and the rest of the Welsh party. But bad luck struck again, this time in the 100km Road Race in Sydney, as Reg sustained a puncture and finished in sixth place. Forced to give up his job to attend the Games, it was then he went to work for Raleigh in Nottingham, spending the war as a munitions worker. During his time there he won the 1944 British Amateur Road Race Championship, taking the title in the final sprint.

In 1945 Reg returned to Cardiff and set up his cycle shop business on Broadway, which has subsequently become one of the city's longest-running and successful sporting businesses. In the flat above the shop Reg also helped to found the Cardiff Ajax Cycling Club and, despite the heavy demands of running the business, he always found time to support the club at grass, track, massed start and time-trial events.

In recent times Reg also helped to inaugurate the *South Wales Echo*'s 'On Your Bike' charity cycle race, which, amongst others, has raised vast sums for Barnardo's Cymru. His lifetime of enthusiastic support and encouragement to cyclists of all ages, as well as to charitable causes, was deservedly recognised in July 1989 with the award of the British Empire Medal. He died in 1999.

BILL PHILLIPS

'The father of Cardiff Rugby Football Club'
by Gwyn Prescott

When Cardiff RFC instituted a hall of fame some years ago, they did not elect the man who, arguably more than any other, helped to establish the club and whose range and depth of contribution to rugby in Cardiff and Wales is unlikely ever to be matched.

William David Phillips, more usually known as Bill, was born in the heart of Cardiff in 1855 at the Greyhound in Bridge Street. His father was presumably successful as the licensee of this well-known pub, as he was able to afford to educate Bill privately at Bridgend School. This was one of Wales' earliest rugby-playing academies, and so when Bill left at seventeen, he immediately set about founding Cardiff Wanderers in 1873.

The club played at the Arms Park and Bill was its captain throughout its short life. In September 1876, the Wanderers merged with Glamorgan to form the Cardiff club and Bill was elected its first vice-captain. Remarkably in Cardiff RFC's first nine seasons, Bill Phillips was either its captain or vice-captain. He captained the club for three seasons, including 1880/81 when Cardiff won the South Wales Challenge Cup for the first and only time by defeating Llanelli in the final. This record alone should have earned him instant hall-of-fame status. But there was more: much more.

Bill Phillips was a versatile player. Though generally known as a forward who was difficult to stop, he also played in the backs. He had played in both positions several times for South Wales, the predecessor to the Welsh team, and it was no surprise when he was selected for the first ever Welsh international match against England in 1881. Wales were overwhelmed that day, but Bill was one of the five players whose reputation remained relatively unscathed and who went on to play for Wales again. In all, he played at forward in five of Wales' first seven internationals between 1881 and 1884. He also represented Wales in 1882 in the two non-cap matches against the North and the Midlands, playing as a back in the latter.

During his last two seasons with Cardiff, he was vice-captain to Joe Simpson, and together they began to experiment with the four three-quarter system. Though the name of Frank Hancock is normally associated with this, it was Phillips and Simpson who were responsible for its introduction at the club. Bill retired in 1885, having been captain or vice-captain of his club throughout his entire adult career. He served on Cardiff's committee from the club's inception right up to the First World War, but for some time Bill also retained an active involvement in rugby as a referee and he officiated in two international matches during the later 1880s.

Bill Phillips represented Cardiff at the historic meeting in March 1881 held at the Castle Hotel, Neath when the Welsh Rugby Union was founded. In 1885, he was elected vice-president of the WRU and, from then on, he served on the union until his death in 1918. For twenty years from 1887, he was also Wales' representative on the International Rugby Board.

Despite his loyal and lengthy service to the wider game, Bill Phillips was first and foremost a Cardiff stalwart. A brilliant and witty raconteur, he was always in great demand at social functions, especially at Cardiff RFC, where he was universally acclaimed by his contemporaries as 'the father of the club'.

PETER WALKER

'One of cricket's greatest ever fielders'
by Don Shepherd

Born in Bristol and raised in South Africa, Peter travelled to South Wales – where his family had originated – during the mid-1950s and, in the course of the next twenty years, he became one of county cricket's finest fielders close to the wicket. He also set up home in Cardiff and, ever since, Peter has lived in the Welsh capital, establishing a highly successful video and television company, as well as being an outstanding administrator for the Cricket Board of Wales, and a magnificent ambassador both for Glamorgan cricket and the city of Cardiff.

His father, Oliver, had played club cricket for Cardiff in the 1920s and, as a talented violinist, he went on to become the music and literary editor of *The Star* evening newspaper in Johannesburg. Peter's mother Freda had also played the piano to near concert standard and younger brother Tim became an internationally acclaimed classical guitarist and composer. So it was hardly surprising that Peter inherited both musical and sporting genes.

However, there was also an inbuilt restlessness within him that became so intense that, aged sixteen, he decided to run away to sea! Many adventures and experiences followed during his time in the Merchant Navy, as vividly recounted in his recently published autobiography, *It's Not Just Cricket*. As far as Glamorgan cricket was concerned, the most important leg of Peter's journey came when he was on a Swedish tanker that visited Barry Docks for a refit. It didn't take Peter long to find his way to Cardiff and to the county's offices – then in High Street – seeking to renew acquaintances with Allan Watkins, the England all-rounder who had coached him at school in Johannesburg.

An unexpected invitation from Allan, Wilfred Wooller, Johnnie Clay and coach George Lavis to join in a practice session in the indoor nets, then high up in the now demolished North Stand of Cardiff Arms Park, led to him being offered a summer contract as a junior professional. In 1954 and, with the feeling he was returning to his ancestral home, Cardiff, Peter began an on-the-field association which lasted eighteen years, followed by an open-ended commitment to the well-being of the club which extends to this day.

Early on, playing alongside his schoolboy hero, Allan Watkins, one of cricket's finest short-leg fielders, provided the young Walker with all the inspiration he needed. From his first-class debut in 1957 until his last game in 1972, and bar the odd period or two when his restless temperament got the better of him, Peter remained an outstanding all-rounder throughout a career of 487 first-class games for Glamorgan. In 1960 he played in the first three Tests against South Africa, all won by England, but then was left out, never to be selected again. Many critics of the day thought he should have won many more international caps.

The peak of his career came the following season when he achieved arguably the finest treble in the history of first-class cricket. His record of 1,347 runs, 101 wickets and 73 catches in 1961 remains unrivalled and with the modern game now dominated by one-day, limited-over matches, it is highly unlikely his all-round performance will ever be beaten. For the twenty-five-year-old, that summer was indeed a momentous season.

Peter was a right-handed batsman with attacking instincts, particularly on the front foot, where he made full use of his 6ft 4ins height. He could bowl either left-arm medium pace with swing or seam movement, or orthodox, slow left-arm leg-spin. It was in the latter vein that he won his three England caps.

But, it was his close catching ability that was truly astounding. I should know and appreciate better than most, for the club scorebooks read, 'caught Walker, bowled Shepherd' 178 times! He broke Maurice Turnbull's pre-war Glamorgan record of 49 catches in a season during Glamorgan's 1959 match against the Indian tourists at Swansea. His fiftieth victim was off my

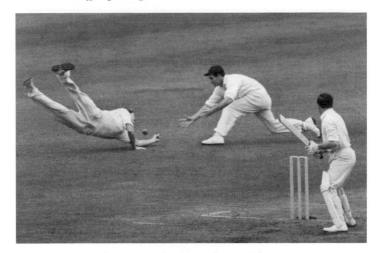

Peter makes a fine diving stop in the slips whilst fielding for England against South Africa in 1960.

Peter Walker (right) practises his catching skills in a training session with other members of the Glamorgan ground staff in the mid-1950s.

bowling as we combined to dismiss opening bat Nari Contractor. It prompted Peter's father in Johannesburg to send the following telegram – 'the Lord is thy Shepherd, thou shall not want!' And, when I took my 2,000th first-class wicket against Worcestershire in the 1969 game at Sophia Gardens which won the championship, inevitably it was the 'old firm', caught Walker bowled Shepherd, who saw Jim Yardley head back to the pavilion.

Many batsmen owed their dismissal more to Peter's phenomenal catching abilities than to my, or any other Glamorgan bowler's, skills! What a comfort it was for us all to know that any edge, or even full-blooded stroke above the grass, which went in Peter's direction a mere few yards from the bat, was likely to be his last! His predatory presence on either side of the pitch made an unnerving impression on batsmen's minds, particularly at the start of their innings.

However, because of how close he dared to field, bowlers too were under pressure to keep a precise line and length, otherwise they would put at stake Peter's life, and the lives of others who crouched in close positions near the bat. In those days, fielders in these 'danger zones' did not wear the protective clothing felt essential by today's cricketers. Sure, like them all, Peter took some unavoidable blows, but so fast were his reactions and hand/eye co-ordination that I don't ever recall him suffering a major injury while fielding at short square leg, otherwise known as 'Death Alley'.

Playing in an age of wonderful specialist close catchers like Tony Lock, Arthur Milton, Mike Smith, Mickey Stewart, Phil Sharpe, Mike Edwards, Peter Sainsbury and Brian Close, Peter was simply outstanding; certainly the best all-round close to the wicket fielder I ever played with or against. As a team, we Glamorgan colleagues always enjoyed sharing in the bottles of champagne awarded each month by Gillette to the fielder with the most catches. Invariably it was they and Peter who enlivened our Saturday night parties – thankfully there were no Sunday League matches to think of in those days!

From a Glamorgan perspective, was he better than his mentor Allan Watkins? For me, on figures alone, (656 versus 390), Peter certainly wins the contest. Unlike Allan, and most of the ones named above, I believe this was because Peter was equally adept fielding either on the off- or on-side. He was able to 'follow the ball' depending on which side of the pitch a bowler took most of his wickets.

Indeed, when the occasion required, he was no slouch in the deep either. I can still picture him under a 'steepler' at Sophia Gardens, Cardiff: a casual wipe of the hands on his invariably dirty flannels – caused by him diving around after every half-chance when fielding close to the bat – before the ball entered them smoothly and cleanly!

He was the most predatory catcher in Glamorgan's history, with unmatched skills. Wherever he was, Peter made catching look the most simple of exercises. Glamorgan's greatest ever leg-trap? How about Watkins, Walker and Wooller – the Welsh version of the famous 'Three Ws': West Indian batsmen, Everton Weeks, Frank Worrell and Clyde Walcott?

Peter Walker was to use his experience and 'know how' to develop the skills of many Glamorgan fieldsmen who played with and followed him, including most notably his successor at short square leg, Roger Davis and, more recently, Mike Powell. He has put much back into the game he lived and loved, including a spell as chairman of the Professional Cricketers' Association and, in 1996, as the first Director of Development for the newly-formed Cricket Board of Wales.

Despite his many other achievements in sports journalism, radio and television, I suspect he always harboured a desire to be a professional golfer. However, Cardiff-domiciled Peter Walker will always be remembered for his phenomenal close catching. Golf's loss was cricket's undoubted gain!

Right: Peter Walker (left) interviews Doug Insole (right), with umpire John Langridge (middle) during a live BBC broadcast of a Sunday League match at Hove in the late 1970s.

Opposite: Peter Walker, the broadcaster, in the studios of BBC Radio Wales in the 1980s.

JAMIE BAULCH

'Cardiff's silver medalist at the 1996 Olympics'
by Clive Williams

Born in Nottingham in 1973, Jamie is one of a select band of only twelve Welsh athletes to have won an Olympic athletics medal, winning silver in the 1996 Atlanta Games. He cut his athletics teeth with Newport Harriers, before moving to Cardiff AAC in 1993.

For such a diminutive athlete – he is 5ft 9½ins tall – he had a brilliant record as a 400-metre runner, an event more suited to athletes in excess of 6ft. His size obviously was more appropriate to the smaller indoor arena where tightly banked 200-metre tracks are kinder to his shorter stride length. So it was as an indoor performer that he made the biggest impact.

His finest achievement came in the World Indoor Championships in Maebashi, Japan in 1999, when he won in 45.73 seconds, beating Milton Campbell of the USA by just over a quarter of a second. An indication of his superb form as an indoor 400-metre runner can be gauged by the fact that the UK record of 45.39, set when he won the UK indoor title in 1997, still stands today.

Whilst the indoor arena was clearly his favourite, he was a key member of the UK 4 x 400-metre relay team that took an Olympic silver medal in Atlanta in 1996 and also European golds in 1998 and 2002. He also won silver as part of Britain's 4 x 400-metre team in the 1997 Athens World Championships. He competed 29 times for Britain in full international matches in a career spanning twelve years.

From a Welsh perspective, he was a member of the brilliant Welsh Commonwealth Games teams that took 4 x 400-metre bronze in Kuala Lumpur in 1998 and silver in Manchester in 2002. In Manchester, the Welsh squad of Iwan Thomas and fellow Cardiffians Tim Benjamin and Matt Elias missed out on the gold to England by just one hundredth of a second, despite Elias's heroic last leg. In Kuala Lumpur the sight of Jamie midway down the home straight sharing a grin with eventual 400-metre winner Iwan Thomas was one of the highlights of those 1998 Games. Jamie finished fourth before going on to the relay bronze with Thomas, and fellow Cardiff teammates Paul Gray and Doug Turner. Turner was destined to win the European 200-metre silver medal some weeks later in Munich.

Jamie Baulch, out in front again. (Clive Williams)

Altogether in his career, Jamie won five senior Welsh Championship titles, including four at 200 metres, and he set nine senior Welsh records at 200 and 400 metres.

His best 400-metre time of 44.57 set in Lausanne in 1996 still ranks him as the seventh fastest by a British athlete and he is the third fastest Welshman of all time behind UK record holder Iwan Thomas (44.36) and Cardiff clubmate Tim Benjamin (44.56).

Jamie retired in 2005 aged thirty-two, and had already started to forge a career in TV whilst still competing. He has hosted his own show and appeared on the television programme *Superstars*. Nowadays he runs his own marketing company.

BARTLEY WILSON

'The father of Cardiff City'
by Dennis Morgan

Bartley Wilson was a lithographic artist from Bristol who was born with a club foot, forcing him to use crutches throughout his life. Bart was unable to play an active role in any sport but, after moving to the Riverside district of Cardiff, he became the secretary of the Riverside Cricket Club.

Looking for an activity to keep the players together during the winter, Wilson called a meeting in the autumn of 1899, at 1 Coldstream Terrace in Riverside, to discuss the formation of a football team. After a second meeting, the decision was taken to form the Riverside Association Football Club. Though rugby was the major winter sport in South Wales, football was gaining in popularity and, despite his handicap, Wilson had a sound knowledge of the game.

Riverside's first match was against Barry West End at Sophia Gardens and it ended in a 9-1 defeat. A year after this unpromising beginning, the team entered the Cardiff and District League. Playing in their chocolate and amber shirts at Sophia Gardens, players were only expected to provide their own boots. To pay for other equipment, collections were taken at matches or members were charged twopence a game to use the billiard table at the club's headquarters in Mark Street.

A man of great determination, already Wilson's ambitions were moving towards a higher level. In 1903 he entered his team in the South Wales Amateur League and, when Cardiff was declared a city two years later, he made an application to the South Wales and Monmouthshire Association, requesting permission to change the club's name to Cardiff City. The request was rejected on the grounds that the team was not playing in high enough standard of football.

So in 1906, driven by Wilson's enthusiasm, the club entered the South Wales League, usually losing more matches than they won. Perhaps worn down by Bart's persistence, an Association meeting on 5 September 1908 agreed that Riverside could change its name to Cardiff City, provided that the name would be relinquished if a professional team was formed in Cardiff at some future date. Wilson had no doubts what that team would be. Friendly matches against Crystal Palace and Bristol City at the Cardiff Arms Park, and against Middlesbrough at the Harlequins ground, indicated public support for entry into the Southern League.

First it was essential to find a ground that could be enclosed. In January 1910, Bartley negotiated with the Cardiff City Council for the use of five acres of land at Sloper Road as a football stadium. The Council agreed on condition the club found guarantors to ensure payment of the £90 ground rent. The most famous of these guarantors was Lord Ninian Stuart, son of the Marquis of Bute. The ground was named in his honour and he kicked off at the opening match – a friendly against Aston Villa, the League Champions. Now fully committed to professional football, Cardiff City became a limited company with Wilson as its secretary. He was given the task of finding suitable players and his first signing was Jack Evans from North Wales, who was paid a signing-on fee of six shillings.

Other people, more wealthy than Bart, were to steer Cardiff City through the years ahead, but he continued to be associated with the club he had done so much to create. For many years he was a director and secretary of the club. Before 1914, Cardiff City won promotion to the First Division of the Southern League. After the First World War, Bart saw a dream fulfilled when he and his fellow directors took Cardiff City into the Football League. One can only imagine his delight on that never to be forgotten day at Wembley when he saw his beloved team lift the FA Cup by defeating Arsenal.

In the dark days of the 1930s, when Cardiff finished bottom of the Third Division and were in dire financial straits, Bart took on the thankless task of combining the posts of manager and secretary. After the Second World War, he continued to serve the club as assistant secretary until May 1954 when, it is pleasing to note, the City were once more in the First Division. Six months later, at the age of eighty-five, he died. The club had come a long way since its humble beginnings in 1899, but there is no doubt that it was the hard work and inspiration of Bartley Wilson that set it on its road to becoming a force in the world of football.

Bartley Wilson. (Richard Shepherd)

Right: Lord Ninian Crichton-Stuart.

Opposite: Ninian Park as seen in an aerial photo in June 1930. (Local Studies Department, Cardiff Central Library)

NINIAN PARK
by Andrew Hignell

The Bute Estate left their mark in so many diverse ways on the city of Cardiff. Although the Marquis handed over his estate to the city fathers shortly after the Second World War, the legacy of the Butes has remained on the city landscape, with a plethora of roads named after family members and estate workers, in addition to Sophia Gardens – named after the wife of the second Marquess – and Ninian Park – named after the son of the third Marquess. Indeed, there was a link between the two Bute grounds as Cardiff City began their life at Sophia Gardens, before moving in 1910 to Ninian Park.

In fact, Cardiff City FC had their origins in Riverside Cricket Club, who like so many other amateur teams during the closing years of the nineteenth century had based their activities in the public recreation ground at Sophia Gardens. In fact, the members of the cricket club so enjoyed themselves that in 1899 they decided to maintain their camaraderie and sporting friendships during the winter months by forming a football club.

Riverside AFC were too late to join the recently-formed Cardiff and District League in 1899/00, which included some of the other football teams that used the Sophia Gardens Field. Nevertheless, they joined the League the following year before amalgamating with another local club – the Riverside Albions – in 1902/03 in order to join the South Wales Amateur League, and participate in the various knock-out competitions sanctioned by the South Wales and Monmouthshire Football Association.

After some success in the League, the club's officials mounted a campaign for their team both to be called Cardiff City and to become a professional club, and on 5 September 1908, they got the backing of the South Wales and Monmouthshire Football Association. This was a massive triumph for Bartley Wilson and the other founders of the Riverside club, which had grown from a local parks side – playing in a rugby stronghold – to an organisation that could lay claim to be the footballing representatives of the 'Coal Metropolis'.

With an upswing in interest in professional football, the time seemed ripe for Riverside AFC in their new guise as Cardiff AFC to join the Southern League. But one of the

requirements was an enclosed ground, and with Sophia Gardens serving the needs of thousands of young sportsmen and women each year as a public recreation area, this was completely out of the question and the Marquess – whose family had created the Recreation Field for the enjoyment of the city's inhabitants – was not ever going to agree to part of the field being converted into the home of a football club, least of all one that harboured ambitions of turning professional.

The attitude of the Bute Estate changed slightly when it came to requests for using the Arms Park for exhibition matches, thereby allowing the Bute officials to charge an entrance fee, and cash in on the growing demand to watch association football, and all without threatening the standing of Sophia Gardens. An agreement over the share of gate receipts was drawn up and on 5 October 1909 Cardiff City FC played out a highly creditable 3-3 draw against Crystal Palace.

Six weeks later, the Cardiff club, augmented by various amateurs from other local clubs, returned to the Arms Park to play Bristol City, and despite a 7-1 drubbing, the game continued to fuel the aspirations of Bart Wilson and his colleagues, who approached the Bute Estate for a plot of land that they could develop into their home ground, and, at long last, turn professional.

Sites at Leckwith Common and in Sloper Road, Grangetown were discussed, and in February 1910 the football club were offered the latter on a seven-year lease by the City Corporation, providing they had guarantors for the annual rent of £90. Shortly afterwards, one of the club's backers withdrew, and for a while it looked as if the scheme would fold. But after protracted discussions, Lord Ninian Crichton-Stuart – the son of the third Marquess – stepped in to secure the land, and in recognition of his efforts, the new ground was named in his honour and the newly incorporated Cardiff City Association Football Club Limited played their inaugural professional match on 1 September 1910 against Aston Villa, the First Division champions, watched by a crowd of 7,000.

The following March, Ninian Park staged its first international match as Wales played Scotland. At the time, the ground boasted only a small grandstand, with a canvas roof on the Sloper Road side of the pitch, and after the First World War, various ground improvements took place, with the erection in 1920 of the Canton Stand, followed in 1928 by a roof over the Grangetown End Terrace, funded by profits from their triumph in the FA Cup.

Ninian Park, the home
of the Bluebirds, as seen
in two photographs
from 1975. (Hills Welsh
Press and Local Studies
Department, Cardiff
Central Library)

   After a fire in January 1937, the Main Stand was replaced by a modern brick and steel
structure, followed in the years after the Second World War by further improvements
and extensions. During the summer of 1960, floodlights were installed and on 14
October 1961 Ninian Park recorded its highest all-time gate as 61,566 attended the
home international between Wales and England.
   Besides playing host to the Bluebirds, Ninian Park was also used in the early 1980s by
the Cardiff City Blue Dragons Rugby League Club. Formed under the managership of David
Watkins – the former Newport and Wales rugby union player – the Blue Dragons played their
home games for three seasons at Ninian Park, in front of quite sparse crowds, before moving
to play at Bridgend. Showjumping and American football, as well as games of floodlit rugby
union in the 1960s, have also been staged at the home of Cardiff City FC.

MALCOLM COLLINS

'The Cardiff boxer with a knockout punch'
by Dennis Morgan

Malcolm Collins was born in Cardiff in May 1935 and, when he left school, he joined the *Western Mail*, first as a journalist and then as a compositor. His interest in boxing was aroused by his father, Hector, whose wisdom and advice guided him throughout his career. When he began boxing, it was soon clear that Malcolm had real ability.

At the Melingriffith Boxing Club, Whitchurch, he was coached by Ernie Hurford and in 1950 won the Welsh Schoolboy Championship. The following year he was the Welsh Youth champion. Collins went on to win three Army Cadet titles in successive years, registering first-round knock-outs in each case. Though he normally fought as a featherweight, Collins had a devastating left hook and most of his victories were won within the distance. Paul Morgan, writing in the *South Wales Echo*, referred to him as 'Knockout Collins' and at one time he registered fifteen consecutive knockouts. Such feats were not obtained without pain, as the power of his punches sometimes resulted in fractures to his hands and wrists.

In 1954 Malcolm was the only boxer to be selected for Wales in the Empire Games at Vancouver. He reached the final but had to be content with the silver medal, as the judges voted 2-1 in favour of his South African opponent, Len Leisching. Malcolm might have achieved even more honours in his chosen sport, but friction with the hierarchy of the WABA sometimes created problems. In 1953 he declined to box for Wales against England because the date clashed with a promise he had already made to fight in the Army Cadet Championships at Cardiff. It seems the authorities never completely forgave him for making this decision. In 1956 the WABA did not support him when the British team was being selected for the Olympic Games in Australia. This was despite the fact that Collins had recently defeated Tommy Nicholls and Freddy Theit, both of whom went on to win silver medals at Melbourne, and Dick McTaggart who won the lightweight gold medal.

There were other times when the WABA did not select Malcolm to fight for his country and, on one occasion, his father bluntly commented, 'Quite honestly, I believe those in authority are sidestepping Malcolm'. Collins retired in 1958 at the tender age of twenty-three. His problems with the WABA may have influenced his decision, as he was not always the automatic choice he should have been for the Welsh team.

However, in 1957 Malcolm won the Welsh and British ABA Featherweight Championships. In the semi-final of the British Championship, Malcolm broke two bones in his right hand against Billy Calvert. In spite of the pain, Malcolm fought the final virtually one-handed to defeat Roy Beaman of England on points. Later that year he was chosen by the Welsh Amateur Boxing Trainers' Association as the Boxer of the Year.

Selected for the Empire Games at Cardiff in 1958, Collins once again reached the final, only to lose on points to the Australian Wally Taylor. Shortly before going into the ring, Malcolm's coach, Ernie Hurford, was taken ill and could not be in his corner. Malcolm relied a great deal on his coach's advice and this may have contributed to his defeat.

The famous boxing promoter, Jack Solomons, tried to persuade Malcolm to become a professional but, after consulting his father, he opted for the security of his job with the *Western Mail* rather than the uncertainty of a professional career. In his retirement, Collins has kept in touch with his sport. He is one of the four Welsh team managers who look after the welfare of Welsh amateur boxers when they are involved in competitions. He also writes for a number of newspapers and magazines. Looking back, Malcolm is grateful for the opportunities amateur boxing gave him. He made many friends, travelled all over the world at a time when this was denied to most people and, perhaps most important of all, won the respect of everyone who followed his sport.

Malcolm Collins.

GERALD DAVIES

'The Artful Dodger of Cardiff rugby'
by John Billot

T.G.R. Davies – a man who could sidestep in a paper bag! This was just one description of Gerald Davies, the Cardiff, London Welsh, Cambridge University and Wales winger who, after retiring, has become one of the shrewdest and most articulate observers of the oval-ball game.

Gerald's classical sidestep was a terrifying trademark – as deadly as a cobra bite – and one that he put to great effect on so many occasions at the Arms Park whilst playing for Cardiff and Wales. He could also swerve, sidle and dodge, as well as sell as sweet a dummy as any as the great Bleddyn Williams distributed, in addition to generally outwitting opponents in a one-to-one situation with majestic ease.

Once he had cut up a tackler, Gerald's renowned sizzling burst of pace frequently brought tries or created them for his support runners. Not until sugarfoot Shane Williams of the Neath-Swansea Ospreys arrived on the international scene twenty-two years later did we witness similar bewitching skills. Both these gifted wingers might have earned a substantial living dancing Swan Lake for the Sadler's Wells Opera Company, but rugby is a more physically challenging way of expressing their talents and the old rough and tumble on the rugby pitch beats a pretty pirouette every time.

Born in Carmarthenshire in 1945, Gerald won 46 caps for Wales and like his Cardiff and Wales colleague, Gareth Edwards, he scored 20 tries for his country, with the first two of his illustrious career coming whilst he was playing in the centre. Indeed, it was here that he began his time in the Welsh jersey, against Australia in 1966, and in all he played 11 times at centre before switching to the wing – a decision made not through choice, but one borne out of injury on Wales' tour Down Under in 1969.

It is indeed a sobering thought that Gerald may never have been discovered as a wing of sensational ability had not the selectors' initial choices been unfit for the second Test against New Zealand. With Stuart Watkins and Alan Skirving out of action, it left Maurice Richards as the only fit winger. Compared with the other centres, John Dawes and Keith Jarrett, Gerald was by far the fastest and the obvious candidate to switch. His country called and the man from

Gerald Davies, seen on the left chatting to another great Welsh rugby international, Cliff Morgan.

Llansaint, near Kidwelly, a schoolboy outside half and then a centre, showed his versatility by playing in unfamiliar territory on the wing.

At first, he was lonely and horribly exposed, but a new era was dawning both for this tricky runner and for Wales. Gerald did not score during his first experience on the wing, but a week later, he sped across Australia's line in Sydney – like a rat racing up a drainpipe – as Wales won a thrilling contest 19-16. And all after a bruising and battering time in New Zealand on a tour with an itinerary which compelled the visitors to appear in three Tests in the space of seven fixtures. The first warm-up match – a drawn game against Taranaki – came just four days after an unbroken flight from the UK. The very next encounter was the first Test against Brian Lochore's man-eating pack, which included Colin Meads, as ferocious an opponent as ever pulled on an All Black jersey, and a man who, if he had trudged out into the Colosseum in Roman times, would have caused the lions to flee at a mere glimpse of his threatening visage.

Gerald admits that he was never comfortable making head-on tackles but, at just over 11st, he developed a successful method of checking bigger and more robust opponents, using their weight to drag them down. It is always as attackers that exciting players are remembered, and Gerald was a truly extraordinary attacker, as he showed on a heavy pitch at Pontypool Park in a third round Schweppes WRU Cup tie in 1978 when he achieved the seemingly impossible whilst leading Cardiff against the revered home team. In front of 15,000 mainly hostile onlookers, Cardiff's forwards endured a terrible roasting, seeing so little possession that their backline could only launch five worthwhile attacks. Yet Gerald was able to scamper over the try line on no less than four occasions as Cardiff won 16-11. After that, he could walk on water!

After his schooldays at Queen Elizabeth Grammar School, Carmarthen, Gerald attended Loughborough College and, after qualifying as a teacher, he joined Cardiff RFC in 1965/66. Soon after, he was awarded his first cap, playing alongside John Dawes against Australia in 1966 – a decision that Gerald heard whilst watching television in a Cardiff pub with his friends, who proceeded to shower him with the pub's best beer!

His debut, though, ended in defeat, as Australia won 14-11 to record their first success over Wales since the two countries initially locked horns back in 1908. In fact, Gerald's first seven games in a Welsh jersey brought just two successes. But the glory days were just around the corner, and when they arrived, Gerald figured in three Grand Slams, five Triple Crowns and a 24-0 victory over Australia. And on top of that was a glittering tour to New Zealand with the British Lions in 1971 when Gerald appeared on the wing in all four of the Tests against the Kiwis.

Gerald had gone to South Africa with the Lions in 1968, but he was subsequently dogged by injuries to his elbow and ankle, and appeared in only a single Test, and then as a centre. Down under in 1971 he made amends for his earlier disappointments, and the Lions' unique series triumph was a richly deserved reward for one of the finest wingers to ever play for Cardiff and Wales.

After the 1968 Lions tour, he went up to Cambridge University, where his dazzling displays and touch of class won him three Blues. In 1970, Gerald joined London Welsh where he was a member of one of the most remarkable club teams of all time, so remarkable, in fact, that no fewer than seven 'Exiles' were included in the 1971 Lions tour party. Returning to Cardiff in 1974, he captained the Blue and Blacks during their Centenary Year in 1976/77 – one of three successive seasons when he was at the helm at the city's famous rugby club. He also led Wales on his final appearance in Welsh ranks, against Australia at the Sydney Cricket Ground in 1978. The Wallabies won 19-17 but suitably Gerald signed off with a try, and we can safely say that in modern times at least there has never been a Welsh wing to match the magic of the Artful Dodger from Llansaint.

STEVE BARRY

'Cardiff's greatest walker'
by Brian Lee

They say that behind every good man is a good woman, and this is certainly true in Steve Barry's case. For if it wasn't for his wife, Sue, Wales wouldn't have had its greatest ever walker. As family man Steve recalled:

> I had fallen by the wayside smoking and drinking and, when I was twenty-four, my wife Sue bought me a tracksuit and told me it was time I got myself in shape. I started jogging, entered and won a walking race, and it all snowballed from there.

Right: Steve Barry.
(*Western Mail and Echo*)

Opposite: Gerald scores a try for Wales against England at the Arms Park in 1967. (*Western Mail and Echo*)

Snowballed is the right word, for Steve went on to win the gold medal in the 30k walk at the 1982 Commonwealth Games in Brisbane, after finishing eleventh in the 20k walk at the European Games in Athens. In a world-class field at Brisbane, he led early in the race to win by more than two minutes and, in so doing, smashed the Commonwealth Games record by nearly twelve minutes. His winning time of 2:10:16 beat his own 30k British record by a substantial margin. He had proved himself to be the best walker in Britain for many years. As well as being voted the BBC Wales Sports Personality of the Year, the Welsh AAA presented him with a Meritorious Plaque for services to Welsh athletics.

Born in Cardiff in 1950, Steve was the son of nine-times Welsh walking champion Dai Barry. Steve went on to hold every British walking record. As a young lad, he was a more than useful cross-country runner competing for his school and county. He then literally began to follow in his father's footsteps when he the won Welsh walking titles as a youth. After returning to athletics in his mid-twenties, Steve claimed his first Welsh senior titles in 1978 at 3k and 10k and went on to complete the double for the next two years.

It was in 1980 that he won his first AAA title at 3k and went on to win the 10k titles at the AAA and UK Championships. The year 1981 saw him being awarded the Road Walking Association Trophy for a brilliant victory in Lugano. In the same year, during an international track race at Brighton, he gave what was described as the greatest display of walking ever seen in Britain. He covered 13,987 metres in an hour beating Phil Embleton's record set back in 1972 and continued walking to clock 1:26:22 seconds for the 20k mark which beat Ken Matthews' record set in 1964. During the race, he broke every record from five miles upwards.

In 1983 in a 20k road walk in Douglas, Steve won in a time of 1:22:51 seconds beating the British record which had been set by the legendary Paul Nihill in 1972. And for the third year on the trot – although trot is not the right word in Steve's case – he won the AAA and UK 10k titles, bringing his British record down to 40:54.7. In winning a 15k event in Paris in 1984, he increased his collection of British records to eight and set new British times for 5k, 10k and 15k in the process. In the 20k race at the 1984 Olympics he finished twenty-fourth. However, operations to his knee and hamstring eventually put paid to his wonderful athletics career. It will be a long time before Wales produces another world-class walker like Steve Barry.

BILLY SPILLER

'Cardiff policeman, Glamorgan cricketer and Welsh rugby international'
by Andrew Hignell

'Excuse me officer — aren't you the man who scored Glamorgan's first Championship hundred?' Anyone arrested by PC Billy Spiller of the Glamorgan Constabulary would have been entitled to say this after the policeman's exploits with the bat in 1921. But being a supporter of Glamorgan was — and still is — no defence in a court of law, and if the county's supporter ended up being fined or doing a stretch inside, it may have been a small crumb of comfort to know that the arresting officer was none other than the man who entered the club's record books as their first batsman to reach three figures in a Championship match.

Spiller's century came in July 1921 against Northamptonshire at the County Ground in Northampton, and it occurred during an extended break that the thirty-five-year-old was having in an attempt to assist the Welsh county during their inaugural season as a first-class club. The prolific batsman at club level had told Norman Riches, his Cardiff colleague and county captain, that he would do his best to get eight weeks leave during July and August, and he did not let his friend down. On 26 July, he duly made his maiden Championship hundred, and the first for the county, with an all-run four on the legside after batting for a shade under three hours.

It had been sixteen long years earlier that the St Fagans-born cricketer had first appeared for the county, in what was then the Minor County Championship. However, his police duties restricted his subsequent appearances and, in the years leading up to the First World War, Spiller mixed regular games of club cricket for Cardiff CC and Barry CC, with occasional matches for Glamorgan.

During the winter months, PC Spiller also found time to play rugby for Cardiff RFC, and his strong running in the centre and deft handling skills won him ten caps for the Welsh side. He made his first appearance for Wales in 1909/10, scoring a fine try against Scotland on his debut. The following season he played in the last Welsh team to lift the Triple Crown and Grand Slam for thirty-nine years. He had a particularly brilliant season in 1911/12, when the press referred to him as the best centre in the country. The next season he was appointed captain of the Cardiff side. He celebrated his elevation by scoring the only try of Cardiff's match against the touring Springboks at the Arms Park, touching the ball down barely a six-hit away from the cricket square where he had shone during the summer months.

PAULO RADMILOVIC

'The great Olympian'
by Andrew Hignell

Like many young Cardiffians growing up in the hurly-burly Dockland community in the early years of the twentieth century, Paulo Radmilovic loved swimming in the Glamorganshire Canal, which ran close to his parent's home in Bute Street. But whereas most of the young men and boys who enjoyed a dip alongside Paulo went on to work in the docks or in other labouring jobs in South Wales, their frolics in the canal were the start of a glittering career that saw 'Raddy' become one of the true Olympic greats, competing in five consecutives Games and winning four gold medals between 1908 and 1924.

The legendary Paulo Radmilovic.

Born in Cardiff in 1886, and educated at Howard Gardens School, Paulo was brought up in the heart of the bustling 'coal metropolis'. Surrounded by the smoke, dirt and noise of the city's industry and docks, how pleasant it must have been, especially in the summer months, to plunge into the cool, and relatively clear, waters of the canal. His parents ran the Glastonbury Arms pub at the northern end of Bute Street, next to the Cape Horn Inn, run by the stepfather of Jim Driscoll, and one can only imagine what the two lads must have talked about when they bumped into each other and talked about their aspirations.

Whilst 'Peerless Jim' worked his way towards boxing glory, young Paulo only thought about fame in the water, and he was even prepared to walk all the way out of town to Blackweir where he could swim against the strong feeder currents and strengthen his shoulder muscles.

Despite this somewhat unorthodox training regime, Paulo took his first steps towards sporting glory as a raw, yet very eager, twenty-year-old at the unofficial 'interim' Olympics held in Athens in 1906, where he competed in the freestyle races over 400 metres and a mile, and finished fourth in the 100-metre sprint. Two years later, at the London Olympics, 'Raddy' won his first gold in the 4 x 200-metre relay, as well as a gold in the water polo event leading the triumphant British team, and a place in the semi-finals of the freestyle swims over 100 metres, 400 metres and 1,500 metres.

Although he took part in the freestyle sprints at the 1912 Games, 'Raddy' focused on water polo in the years leading up to the First World War, and his gold medal as the captain – yet again – of the British team in the Stockholm Games was a worthy reward for the many long hours of training he put in at the baths in Guildford Crescent and with the Barry club. He subsequently made regular appearances in the Taff Swim, where his prowess in the race from Canton Bridge to the Clarence Road Bridge also earned him another nickname – 'Shark of the Taff.'

He continued to lead the British team to a water polo gold at the Antwerp Games in 1920, but only after a most feisty encounter with the home team in the final. In fact, Paulo scored the winning goal, much to the displeasure of the home crowd, who vented their partisan feelings to the extent that Paulo and his colleagues had to be escorted away from the pool by armed guards.

'It was a tough contest,' he later recalled, 'and the entire team was covered in scratches and bruises. The crowd booed and hissed our every move, and nobody hoisted the Union Jack at the end of the final. The Belgian Secretary of State apologised the next day.'

This proved to be his final gold in the Olympics, but the thirty-four-year-old continued to win swimming honours in British Championships. By 1925 he had won every ASA freestyle title from the 100 yards to the five-mile event – apart from the quarter-mile race – and was still good enough to win a place in the British team at the Amsterdam Games in 1928 where they just missed out on a medal as they finished fourth, ahead of the USA, whose team included a strapping young lad called Johnny Weismuller, who later went on to win fame and fortune in Hollywood, starring in, amongst others, the Tarzan films.

In 1930 – at the ripe old age of forty-four – Paulo travelled to Canada with the Welsh party to compete in the first ever Empire Games at Hamilton, Ontario, but he returned empty-handed, and soon afterwards retired from competitive events.

Besides his remarkable prowess in the pool, 'Raddy' was also a prize-winning athlete, a decent golfer and a fearless boxer who, like most of the other young men brought up in Butetown, knew how to look after himself, either in the ring or out on the streets.

After his days of competition were over, Paulo moved the focus of his attention across the Severn Estuary to Weston-super-Mare, where he owned and managed a hotel, yet he still found time to swim, and even aged seventy-eight could still manage a decent time over a quarter of a mile. In 1967, Paulo was inducted into the International Swimming Hall of Fame in Florida, the only previous British swimmer then to have been so honoured being Captain Matthew Webb, the first man to swim the English Channel. To receive this honour, a year before he died, was a most fitting tribute to the Cardiff man who won four Olympic golds.

GRAHAM MOORE

'The schoolboy soccer sensation with Cardiff City'
by Andrew Hignell

In April 1960 Graham Moore, the teenage centre forward for Cardiff City, achieved what every soccer-mad schoolboy has dreamed about – scoring the match-winning goal which clinched for the Bluebirds promotion to the First Division.

His feat in the 1-0 victory over Aston Villa – which also won him the BBC Welsh Sports Personality of the Year Award – was witnessed by a massive crowd of 55,000. For the Ninian Park faithful, the name of the young Welsh international will forever be associated with the rise in the club's fortunes, and their return to soccer's top flight under the guiding hand of manager Bill Jones.

The emphasis at the time was most definitely on attack and, in their promotion-clinching season alone, Cardiff's players scored a total of 89 goals as they finished runners-up to Aston Villa, and a full eight points clear of Rotherham United back in third place. Derek Tapscott – the former Arsenal striker who had moved to Highbury from Barry Town in 1953 – was Cardiff's leading League goalscorer, finding the net on 20 occasions, with the talismanic Moore adding a further 13 himself, including a series of goals in the first three matches of the season. With his team riding high in the League, the eighteen-year-old was undoubtedly the 'Golden Boy' of Welsh football.

Born in Hengoed in March 1941, Moore had first made a name for himself as a prolific goalscorer with Bargoed YMCA in 1956, before agreeing terms with Cardiff City, and adding further to his reputation with the club's reserve side. A series of impressive displays saw the schoolboy international make his first-team debut at Brighton and Hove Albion in September 1958, and the seventeen-year-old had an immediate impact as he scored the last-minute equaliser as the game ended 2-2.

After his *annus mirabilis* in 1959/60, Moore came down to earth with a bump – literally – the following season as he broke a leg and spent many weeks on the sidelines. But he was still very hot property and, after drawing the attention of scouts from leading clubs, Cardiff's management agreed terms with Chelsea in December 1961, which saw Moore move from Ninian Park for Stamford Bridge.

At the time, his transfer fee of £35,000 was a club record, but the twenty-year-old's move was criticised by many fans who felt that the sale of the youngster who had helped carry the

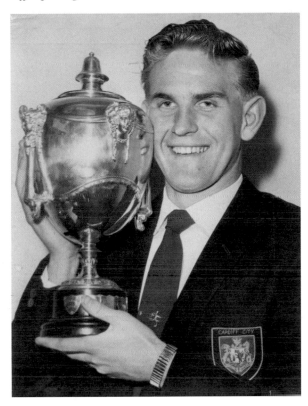

Graham Moore and the BBC Wales
Sports Personality of the Year Award in
1960. (Richard Shepherd)

Bluebirds into the First Division was a sign of the club's lack of ambition – a claim that was
to be repeated in 1970 with the sale to Liverpool of John Toshack, who had been amongst the
adoring crowd of supporters when Moore found the net against Aston Villa.

But whereas Toshack went on to bigger things with the Merseyside club, Moore did
not really find further fame with Chelsea, or indeed the other clubs – Manchester United,
Northampton Town, Charlton Athletic and Doncaster Rovers – for whom he played in the
1960s. In all, Moore won 21 Welsh caps, with the highlight of his international career coming
on his debut in a Wales shirt, as he scored a goal with a header in the final minute of the match
against England at Ninian Park in 1960 to earn a 1-1 draw for his side.

THE MEMORIAL GROUND, ELY
by Gwyn Prescott

Though its importance is frequently overlooked today, there can be no doubt that
Monkton House made a crucial contribution to the introduction and establishment of
rugby in Cardiff from the early 1870s onwards.

The school produced many of the city's first rugby players and, by 1893, there was
a sufficiently large number of them to form the Old Monktonians RFC, who played
at Sophia Gardens and Roath. Twenty years later, reflecting the changing nature of
its membership, the club adopted a new name and so 'Glamorgan Wanderers' first
appeared on the fixture lists of local clubs.

Between the wars, still a somewhat socially exclusive club, the Wanderers moved to
Whitchurch, playing at the Fox and Hounds Field and later at the Polo Grounds, using

the Three Elms pub on the Common as the club's headquarters. After the Second World War, the Polo Grounds were taken for housing development, so the Wanderers decided to create their first permanent home by purchasing and developing land in Ely.

The Memorial Ground was named in memory of all the members of the club who had lost their lives in the two world wars. Amongst these was the 1913/14 captain Edgar Jenkins, who led the club in its first season playing under the Glamorgan Wanderers name.

The Memorial Ground has seen visits by many of the game's leading clubs from Wales and beyond. The Wanderers were strong enough in 1990/01 to be allocated a place in the first ever Premier Division of the WRU's new Welsh League and they currently play in the top level of Welsh club rugby. In the days before organised coaching, the Memorial Ground was used as the training base by the Welsh XV prior to international matches. It has also been the venue of women's international matches. Amongst the more memorable club occasions witnessed there was the Wanderers' splendid 25-6 defeat of the United States touring team in 1987.

For many years, however, the Wanderers maintained their social headquarters in the city centre in premises above some shops in Wyndham Arcade. This may seem rather strange for what was then Wales' largest club, running six senior sides but, as a playing member in the mid-1960s, I can confirm the arrangement worked wonderfully well at the time. Since then, however, the character of the Wanderers has changed, particularly after the arrival of new social facilities at the Memorial Ground, which enabled the club to develop much stronger links with their local area. Glamorgan Wanderers have always been at the heart of rugby, but they can now also justifiably claim to be at the heart of the community.

JOHNNIE CLAY

'The man who helped Glamorgan clinch their first county title'
by Andrew Hignell

In an illustrious career spanning almost three decades, Johnnie Clay took 1,292 wickets for Glamorgan and, with his clever off-spin, he teased and tricked several generations of county and Test batsmen. But, had it not been for his efforts off the field with his great friend Maurice Turnbull, the Welsh county side might have folded because of financial difficulties in the early 1930s – a situation brought upon through poor results and a downturn in the economy.

Indeed, the position was so grim in the winter of 1932/33 that the county's treasurer resigned and, as the club attempted to stay afloat by dispensing with the services of several professionals, a few cynics started to prepare Glamorgan's epitaph. But Clay, whose family had long been linked with sport in south-east Wales, was determined that the club should survive and, unlike the club's previous management, he opted for a proactive, as opposed to the reactive, approach towards fundraising and promoting the good name of Glamorgan Cricket.

For the next couple of years, Clay helped to mastermind the fundraising scheme that eventually helped the club out of this pickle. Like his good friend Turnbull, Clay's family owned a highly successful business in the bustling Docks at Cardiff and, with these dynamic and debonair personalities at the helm, a host of special events were staged across the region, with both men drawing on their vast range of contacts in the commercial and sporting community of Cardiff and further afield.

A measure of their success was that Glamorgan rose up to seventh place in the County Championship in 1937, with Clay enjoying an outstanding season, taking 176 wickets and establishing a club record which still stands to this day, and is unlikely to be beaten. He was widely regarded as amongst the country's leading spin bowlers, although his prowess with the

Johnnie Clay.

ball had to be tempered at times with the financial needs of Glamorgan, especially when it came to a decent gate against the Australians in 1938.

The first two days of the game were badly interrupted by the weather, but the prospect of seeing the great Don Bradman bat at St Helen's had attracted a bumper crowd on the third morning, and during the afternoon, the crowd got their wish as out walked the great man in his baggy green cap. 'Don't get Bradman out too quickly, as there are still a few places in the crowd,' was the instruction from Turnbull to Clay and the rest of the Glamorgan team.

Dutifully, Clay followed these instructions, as word spread like wildfire in Swansea that 'The Don' was finally at the crease. Scores of people headed for St Helen's – some, no doubt, with the flimsiest of excuses for leaving work – and many were rewarded with a glimpse of the great batsman playing himself in as a record crowd now filled the historic ground.

With the crowd now over a dozen deep around the boundary edge, and the enclosures almost bursting, Turnbull had a quick word with Clay and said that he could now try to get Bradman out. It didn't take Clay very long either as Bradman – like so many other batsmen before and after – was lured down the track by Johnnie's subtle bowling and smartly stumped by wicketkeeper Haydn Davies for 17. The Australian maestro departed somewhat crestfallen, but the crowd were happy as they had seen the great man bat, whilst the county's treasurer was equally gleeful, counting the huge pile of coins in the pavilion!

With a thin and wiry frame, Clay remained fit during the winter months by regularly hunting with the Glamorgan Hunt, for whom he also acted as secretary, as well as riding in his youth in point-to-points. His methods worked as season after season he was one of the county game's most successful bowlers and in 1935 his outstanding achievements resulted in his inclusion in the England squad for three of England's Test matches against South Africa. Having been twelfth man for the third and fourth Tests, he made his Test debut in the fifth Test at The Oval and, although remaining wicketless in 32 overs, he bowled with typical guile and accuracy.

Above left: Johnnie Clay demonstrates his action for a photo shoot in 1948.

Above right: Johnnie Clay – batsman – in front of the Arms Park pavilion in 1924.

Over the next few years, the English selectors sounded Clay out about his availability, but each time he politely turned them down, telling the selectors that they should play a younger man instead. It was clear evidence – if ever it was needed – that his heart lay with Glamorgan, but even so, in 1938, after Maurice Turnbull had been appointed as an England selector, Clay was included in England's party for the first Test against Australia at Trent Bridge.

A few days before this announcement, Clay had injured his leg, ironically in the garden of his home on the outskirts of Cardiff, as he attempted to demonstrate to his children how Golden Miller had won the Cheltenham Gold Cup by leaping over a chair. But, unlike the racehorse, Clay came to grief and he duly had to withdraw from the squad as he feared his strained leg would not stand up to the rigours of a five-day Test.

This typified Clay's attitude in not wanting to let anyone down, least of all his great friend, Turnbull. Sadly, the Glamorgan captain was to lose his life serving king and country during the Second World War and, when cricket resumed in 1946, Clay's determination to maintain the highest standards was evident once again, as he readily took over – at the age of forty-eight – the captaincy of Glamorgan, and oversaw the assembly of a new squad of players, thereby ensuring that his friend's efforts before the war would not be in vain.

The next few months saw Clay groom Wilf Wooller as the county's next leader. A measure of Clay's skill and judgement – both on and off the field – was that Glamorgan, under Wooller's command, won the Championship in 1948. At the start of the summer, Clay had slipped into semi-retirement, having been appointed the previous year as a Test selector. But Wooller persuaded the spinner to return to the county side for the decisive match in August against Surrey at the Arms Park, and he responded to his recall in a magnificent way, taking 10/65, as Glamorgan won by an innings and 24 runs.

The fifty-year-old remained in the side that travelled to Hampshire needing one more victory to clinch the title, and took three cheap wickets as Hampshire were forced to follow on. Wickets continued to tumble as the Glamorgan bowlers worked their way through the Hampshire batting and, after all that had happened during his illustrious career, it was most fitting that Clay should take the final wicket as he trapped the last batsman lbw, before

Johnnie Clay and the Glamorgan team are congratulated by their jubilant supporters as they arrive back at Cardiff General after beating Hampshire at Bournemouth to win the 1948 County Championship.

Johnnie Clay walks out from the Arms Park with Wilf Wooller and the rest of the Glamorgan team that won the Championship in 1948.

returning to the pavilion, with tears of sheer joy running down his cheeks, to join in with the celebrations as Glamorgan became county champions for the first time in their history.

This was the crowning achievement in a playing career that had begun in 1921, when the former Winchester schoolboy was a tearaway fast bowler. But, after being plagued by various ailments, Clay wisely experimented with spin during 1924, trying both leg-breaks and off-spin. He subsequently developed into not only one of Glamorgan's greatest bowlers, but also one of the finest exponents of off-breaks in county cricket. His immaculate flight and unerring accuracy lured thousands of batsmen to their downfall. Yet throughout, Clay remained as modest and as happy-go-lucky as when he had first played Minor County cricket shortly after the First World War for Monmouthshire.

He was also a good enough batsman to record a couple of first-class hundreds, including one in swashbuckling style against Worcestershire at Swansea in 1929 which saw Clay race to a hundred in just over an hour and a half as he added 203 for the ninth wicket with Joe Hills – a stand which still remains a club record.

Clay played his final county game in 1949 but, in the following years, he still turned out for the MCC and the South Wales Hunts, as well as serving as a trustee and president of Glamorgan. He also acted as a steward and a director of Chepstow racecourse – which had been laid out close to his family's home during the 1920s – and a long-distance steeplechase was regularly run at Wales' premier National Hunt course in memory of this most outstanding and talented sporting gentleman.

BLEDDYN WILLIAMS

'The prince of centre three-quarters'
by Gareth Williams

Since its foundation in 1876, Cardiff RFC has owed much to the contributions of well-known families. We think of the Bowcott, Turnbull and Roberts brothers in the inter-war period; even earlier of the Hancocks, and the Biggs family who, in the late nineteenth century, were represented in the Cardiff side for twenty-two successive seasons with sometimes three and once four brothers in the same team. The remarkable Williams family of Taffs Well can go even better: they spanned nearly forty years, and there were several occasions in the early 1960s when four of the eight brothers appeared together in the same Cardiff fifteen.

The most famous, however – Bleddyn – was not one of them for he had retired in 1955, after a career which brought him every honour in the game since his first Welsh Schoolboys cap in 1937 at full-back, a position he had never played in before and never would again. Born in 1923, he first attended school in Taffs Well, a village on the banks of the river whose name it took, a few miles north of Cardiff where his father worked as a coal trimmer on the docks. Though hardly well off, the family – through dint of hard effort and parental care – was not poor, and it was as much by virtue of neighbouring Castell Coch, where the coal-owning Marquesses of Bute indulged their fake-medieval fantasies in the woodland overlooking the Taff, as by his father's occupation, that the Williams family was locked into industrial South Wales. Bleddyn's own childhood, however, was more rural than urban. It was spent on the hillsides around Castell Coch and the Black Cock inn, visiting local farms, helping with the hay, churning milk and cheese, taking the horse to the blacksmith and travelling with freight on the Glamorgan canal where in summer he swam.

Just as his rugby always bore the aristocratic features of the Norman nobility whose tenant, supposedly, he was – though Bleddyn is a name potently resonant of medieval Welsh princes and poets – it also reflected something of the serenity of those boyhood days when he had been, like Wales' most famous writer, 'young and easy under the apple boughs and happy as

Bleddyn Williams.

the grass was green.' In his playing career he would always be the tranquil eye at the centre of the storm, apparently imperturbable, an inspiration to his fellow players through the force of his calm, dignified personality, and an iconic figure, as he still is, to the thousands in both hemispheres who swarmed to see 'the prince of centre three-quarters' deploy his sublime skills.

Had it not been for the Second World War, he might have been capped in his late teens, perhaps too early; as it was, his international career spanned the entire post-war decade. He came from durable stock. When his grandfather developed a cancer of the tongue, he walked to the Cardiff Royal Infirmary to have part of it cut out, then went to dusty work the same night loading coal on the docks. While most of the boys passed through the nurturing hands of sports teacher Del Harris, at Taffs Well School, none of them was especially academic, though several (Lloyd, Cenydd, Elwyn and Tony particularly) were, in rugby terms, scholarship boys; Bleddyn, of course, became what was rugby's equivalent of a university vice-chancellor. Elder brother Gwyn was idolised by his younger siblings – there were also four sisters – though the bright future foretold for him after he played for Cardiff as a seventeen-year-old against the 1935 All Blacks, watched by an admiring Bleddyn, was prematurely and permanently dimmed by a near-fatal wartime bullet through his head.

The same war proved to be Bleddyn's making. At fourteen, on the recommendation of former pupil Wilfred Wooller, he attended Rydal School at Rhos-on-Sea on the North Wales coast. Initially disoriented, his rugby ability brought him peer esteem and national attention, while on the outbreak of war his short-lived public-school background helped secure him a commission in the RAF, where he trained in the USA, learned to fly gliders and enjoyed, as he later recalled, 'happy days of rugby under floodlight watched by the expressionless Apaches on their Arizona reservation.' From Arizona he went to Operation Varsity and the Rhine Crossing, where the opposition was stiffer; but only after more rugby.

The lifting of the ruling that forbade amateur and professional rugby players from mixing meant that during the wartime 'international' games, organised for morale-boosting as well as charitable purposes, he was able to hone his skills in the company of some of the Welsh stars of the thirteen man game like W.T.H. Davies, Alan Edwards, Gus Risman and the incomparable Cardiffian, Jim Sullivan. The play was exuberant, the passing fast and accurate, the angles of running mesmerising. These wartime internationals, in front of large and appreciative crowds, enabled Bleddyn to develop a formidable suite of skills. John Gwilliam confessed he 'had never seen anything like Bleddyn at eighteen or nineteen. He'd got it all – speed off the mark, and perfect passing, kicking and sidestepping. He was quite alarming really.' Not to mention a musculature that would have taken a Renaissance chisel to do it justice.

Soon, however, those Michelangelo thighs would prove to be Achilles heels, and the injury alarm bells, which eventually restricted Bleddyn to no more than a modest 22 Welsh caps, began their intermittent tolling as soon as the Five Nations tournament resumed in 1947. Chosen at fly-half in the first post-war international at the Arms Park, he pulled a thigh muscle in the opening minutes and spent a miserable afternoon in a position which the selectors, like their schoolboy counterparts in 1937, were not disposed to try again. Restored to his favourite position of left centre, where he always played for Cardiff, his mere name on the team sheet added thousands to the gate everywhere, even in tribally suspicious West Wales, and especially in England.

The post-1945 period can be romanticised; they were in fact years of austerity, shortages – rationing did not finally end until 1954 – and limited opportunity. Sport did much to illuminate the gloom, especially the feats of Compton, Finney, Matthews, and Bleddyn Williams. His prowess gripped the sports-starved thousands, who now thronged to the rugby grounds of South Wales and beyond to gorge themselves on the performances he was regularly turning in for Cardiff: the display of calm judgment, the tactical awareness, the strong defence, the diverse portfolio of grubber kicks, punts, and touch finders, and above all the attacking weapon which Bleddyn made uniquely and imperishably his own – his rippling, breathtaking jink. He may not have invented it but unquestionably he raised it to an art form: at speed, on the attack, a check, then a devastating transfer of weight – all 13st 7lbs of it – from one foot to the other that left would-be tacklers floundering like firemen at the wrong fire.

It was not just a matter of controlled footwork but of a distinctive twist of the shoulders as Bleddyn would lean in, pulling his wing (Haydn Morris for Cardiff, Ken Jones for Wales and the Lions) that half-yard inwards as he straightened up and delivered a perfectly timed pass to the flyer outside. The *Western Mail*'s J.B.G. Thomas vividly described how Bleddyn 'liked to jink through the gap as if starting to rip a page at the edge, and then tear through it with increasing speed to make a try for his wing or race on to score himself.' Against Scotland in 1948, from loose play Glyn Davies at outside half suddenly changed the direction of the attack and fed Billy Cleaver who then transferred it for Bleddyn to rip through the Scottish defence to score in exactly that way. So was the crystalline try at Ravenhill that year when, from twenty yards out, the ball as always held in two hands, he applied his stiletto sidestep and left the Irish defence in tatters; and in 1949 one of his very best – how do you choose? – when from a scrum on the Scottish '25' (the twenty-metre line today) Glyn Davies went to the narrow side and Haydn Tanner (shades of Dicky Owen in 1905) threw a reverse pass to Bleddyn who jinked through the midfield to score a marvellous try under the posts.

Bleddyn was, of course, fortunate to play in the great Cardiff side of the post-war era. In the late forties he was served from scrum-half by the slowing but ever wily Tanner, while at pivot was Billy Cleaver, who rarely won a game for Wales – Bleddyn could do that – but often saved her from defeat. His co-centre was his still inseparable friend Jack Matthews. Shorter, squatter, even speedier – a Welsh schools sprint champion, Dr Jack was as fast as some of the poisons in his medical cupboard – the crash-tackling 'iron man' was the ideal foil to Bleddyn's rapier. Together they formed a devastating centre pairing for their club and – though curiously less so for Wales – for the 1950 Lions whom Bleddyn captained in three Tests.

The 1951/52 Springboks knew all about Bleddyn too, after he scored beautiful tries against them for both club and country, the latter from a sparkling scissors move engineered with Malcolm Thomas in a late attempt to save a match lost, Bleddyn reckons, through Gwilliam's inflexible instruction to a novice Cliff Morgan to kick throughout the game, which Cliff did, poorly, until at Bleddyn's insistence he let the ball out for the Welsh centres to do the rest; too late.

Bleddyn in action for Cardiff.

Two years later and 1953 is remembered for many things, the Coronation, the conquest of Everest, the Matthews Cup final. But for Bleddyn, for Cardiff and Wales, it was the crowning of a career, the scaling of a personal peak and an overflowing cup as Bleddyn led his club (8-3) and country (13-8) to double victories over Bob Stuart's All Blacks. It was his tactical astuteness and inspiring leadership that won it for Cardiff, and his coolness under intense pressure which held the national side together, though he played the last twenty minutes in considerable pain with torn ligaments at the top of his well-muscled thigh. This meant he had to withdraw in January 1954 for the third successive time at Twickenham, only to return, for the last international to be played at St Helens, to face the Scots against whom he had scored two jinking tries at Murrayfield (his happiest hunting ground) the previous year. This time he put the Stradey greyhound Ray Williams in for a try with two stabbing sidesteps.

Though reluctant to admit it, even to himself – he believed that at thirty-two he could still have cut it on the bone-hard grounds of the high veldt of South Africa with the 1955 Lions – his best days were behind him. Perhaps even 1953 had been an Indian summer. In January that year J.P.W. Mallalieu had gone to the England game at the Arms Park primarily to watch Bleddyn. It was not an inspiring occasion, the magnificent pre-match singing apart, but one other memory of it remained for the visitor:

Of all the golden lads in rugby football the one has who has shone brightest in my eye has been Bleddyn Williams. He could see openings where no opening seemed there. He could sidle, or jink, or glide through a forest of opponents without touching one tree. He could flash to the left, taking all his opponents with him; then flash to the right leaving all his opponents behind. For eighty minutes he was unruffled grace, and all I could wish to see. But on Saturday he was no more. Except just once. With ten minutes to go for time, and England leading by eight points to three, the ball came to Bleddyn on the halfway line and suddenly Bleddyn became what he used to be. A shake of one hip, a twist of one shoulder, and his immediate opponent was grasping the January air while Bleddyn was wisping himself towards the England line...

I'm not sure that Bleddyn, with that powerful physique, 'wisped' himself anywhere. Nor was it his fault that, after feeding Malcolm Thomas, the final pass should have hit Ken Jones on the side of his head and the scoring chance, like the game, was lost.

For Bleddyn won far more often than he lost. In fact he never lost as captain of Wales. Since 1999 the active president of the Cardiff Athletic Club, Bleddyn Williams MBE (an honour belatedly offered, delightedly received, in 2005) remains a living legend, a glorious reminder of another age, an era when we could still beat the All Blacks. 'I am, of course, happy that our achievements [note the 'our'] are remembered,' he wrote on the fiftieth anniversary of his famous double, 'but would have been shocked beyond belief had anyone suggested at the time that we would still be waiting for another Wales victory after more than 50 years.' And with a modesty as characteristic as his immortal jink he added, 'Proud as I am of being Wales' last winning captain against New Zealand, it is a distinction that I would very much like to lose.'

It is the earnest wish of his myriad admirers in Cardiff and around the world that he continues to enjoy the good health to be able to do so.

IRENE STEER

'The first Welshwoman to win Olympic gold'
by Andrew Hignell

For the first ever time in the history of the modern Games, the Olympic administrators added women's events to the swimming schedule held in the pool at the 1912 Stockholm Games. Two freestyle competitions duly took place during mid-July – one was an individual sprint over 100 metres and the other a team event encompassing a 4 x 100 metres relay.

Cardiff's Irene Steer took part in both. Unfortunately a collision in the heats prevented her from contesting the medals in the individual freestyle final. However, on 15 July 1912, the twenty-two-year-old carved herself a name in Olympic history (alongside teammates Isabella Moore, Jennie Fletcher and Annie Spiers) as she swam the fourth and final leg of the Great Britain relay to win the first ever gold medal for the British ladies swimming team. Their time of five minutes 52.8 seconds was no less than 12 seconds ahead of Germany who won the silver medal and 25 seconds ahead of Austria who took the bronze. In 1913, Irene went on to win the ASA 100 yards freestyle title in a time which equalled the then world record.

Born in Cardiff in August 1889, Irene was the second daughter of Cardiff draper George Steer. The family lived in the early 1900s in The Parade in Cardiff – a prosperous inner suburb to the north-east of the city centre – and like other well-to-do Cardiff families, the Steers enjoyed taking time off from the hurly-burly of city life at Roath Park, especially during the summer months when the parkland adjoining the Lake and Pleasure Gardens was full of the great and the good from the Welsh capital.

Indeed, it was here in Roath Park Lake, as well as later at the public baths in Guildford Place, that the young Irene first developed her talents that would win her a place in British Olympic history.

John Lawless. (Andrew Weltch)

JOHN LAWLESS

'The star coach of the Cardiff Devils'
by Andrew Weltch

At 5ft 6ins, Ontario-born John Lawless was hardly the textbook ice hockey star, yet his phenomenal on-ice skills and ambitious off-ice management took Cardiff Devils to the top of the sport.

Ice hockey was a late arrival in Cardiff. The sport has been played in Britain since the nineteenth century, and the national team won Olympic gold in 1936, but it was another half-century before it reached the Welsh capital – along with John Lawless. Considered too small to make it in big-time hockey in his native Canada, Lawless was lured to Britain by the 1980s rink-building boom, which took him initially to Peterborough – where his role as a fast-skating centreman helped the Pirates to promotion, at least for a season, to the Premier Division.

Three years later, at the age of twenty-five, he was offered the post of player-manager with a new club at a new rink in Cardiff, which was entering the bottom-level Second Division of the British League. Lawless put together a small but talented team, which swept through the division's Midlands section – notably starting their home campaign with a 32-0 win in front of a capacity crowd of almost 2,500. Lawless was top scorer that night with nine goals and six assists. They dropped just one point all season – a 3-3 tie with Welsh rivals Deeside Dragons – and although they lost a nail-biting play-off final, they were promoted to the First Division, thanks to a restructuring of the Heineken League.

He had contracted hepatitis mid-season, but returned from his sickbed against medical advice and ended the season as the club's top scorer, famously celebrating each goal by 'shooting' the scoreboard with his stick as a rifle. Two years later, he led the team to the Premier Division, and in front of live BBC *Grandstand* television cameras, they clinched the play-off final against Murrayfield at Wembley in a penalty shoot-out, after overtime had failed to split the teams. The win saw the completion of the league and championship double in their first top-flight season – defying pre-season odds of 100-1.

It marked the first of Cardiff's five Wembley visits in the next six years. Under Lawless, the Devils won the double again in 1992/93 and 1993/94, adding the Benson & Hedges Autumn Cup in 1992 to complete the grand slam. He was voted Coach of the Year in both seasons.

The Devils never finished outside the top three in the league under his management, and they achieved success overseas too, becoming the first British team to reach the semi-final stages of the European Cup, after they sensationally defeated the champions of Ukraine and Kazakhstan in the 1994 quarter-final tournament in Holland. Lawless left Cardiff in 1995 to become coach of newly-formed Manchester Storm in their 17,000 seat arena, and he took the English side to the First Division title and into the all-pro Superleague, before a difficult season as player-coach at Telford and a return to Canada in 1999.

During his decade in Cardiff, Lawless took UK citizenship and made twelve appearances for Great Britain, competing in the World Championship campaigns of 1990 and 1991, scoring five goals and ten assists. He was inducted into the British Ice Hockey Hall of Fame in 1997 in recognition of his achievements. John returned to Cardiff in April 2006 to play a final game, marking twenty years of the soon-to-be-demolished Wales National Ice Rink, alongside other former Devils stars against the current Elite League team.

THE HARLEQUINS GROUND
by Gwyn Prescott

The Harlequins Ground owes its name, and indeed its very existence, to the Cardiff Harlequins club which was a major force in Welsh rugby in the late nineteenth century. The Quins produced two Welsh internationals and a string of players who went on to win international honours with Cardiff RFC, the legendary Gwyn Nicholls amongst them. For a period, they were one of the eight senior Welsh clubs, recording victories over all the leading Welsh teams (except Cardiff who would rarely give them fixtures), as well as Leicester and Northampton.

Receiving notice to quit on their Penarth Road ground, the Quins moved to temporary playing accommodation at Corbett Road. However, this ambitious club desperately needed a permanent enclosed ground of their own. In 1892 they took a lease from the Tredegar Estate on a former brick field at Newport Road. The club then invested huge financial resources in developing an enclosed sports ground, with a grandstand and changing accommodation and a cycling track. It was this initiative which created a facility which has been used by generations of Cardiff sportsmen and women ever since.

Even though teams like Neath, Swansea, Llanelli, Bath and Bristol all played – and lost – at the new Harlequins Ground, the financial burden nevertheless proved too great for the Quins and, after an acrimonious dispute over yet another transfer of a player to Cardiff RFC, the club virtually disbanded within a few years. One attempt to improve finances involved an innovative partnership with the newly formed Cardiff AFC, who played at the ground in 1894/95. However, owing to poor gates, this was not a success and the association club moved to the Grangetown sports ground after a season and disbanded soon afterwards.

The Harlequins continued to be used for a variety of rugby events, including a Welsh trial in 1892, the WRU Challenge Cup final in 1893, the first ever Cardiff and District

The Harlequins Ground in 1899, as seen from the Taff Vale Railway embankment. (Stewart Williams)

Mallett Cup final in 1894, and a Glamorgan County match against Lancashire, who were defeated there in 1895.

In 1895, the Harlequins also played host to the British Ladies Football Club, when 3,000 watched the North defeat the South 7-2. The ladies had been refused permission to play at Stradey Park, prompting the *Western Mail* to comment that (unlike Cardiff) there was 'no room in Llanelly for the New Woman.'

For some years, the Quins had an athletics section initially known as Cardiff Harlequins Harriers. Since 1883, their regular athletics meetings, many held at Penarth Road, were a feature of Cardiff's sporting scene. The new Harlequins Ground proved to be ideal for athletics and consequently many events, including professional races, were held there around the turn of the century. It was also the venue for the Welsh Cross-Country Championships of 1896 and 1897.

When the lease expired in 1902, the Tredegar Estate allowed Cardiff High School – who had been renting the ground since 1898 – to take over the ground free of charge and eventually it passed into the ownership of the education authority. For the next sixty-eight years, it remained the High School's playing field, catering for soccer initially and then rugby, as well as hockey, cricket, lacrosse, tennis and cross-country.

In 1909/10, Cardiff City arranged a friendly there against Middlesbrough of the First Division, the winning goal being scored by Welsh amateur international Alan Boswell, who was, appropriately, an old boy of the school and presumably very familiar with the pitch.

International hockey, baseball and women's lacrosse matches were played at the ground which also became the home of the Cardiff High School Old Boys rugby, cricket and hockey clubs until 1962 when they purchased the Elyn Ground, Whitchurch and renamed their new home the Diamond Ground. The latest occupants of the Harlequins are St Peter's RFC, who have recently opened a splendid modern clubhouse at the ground on Minster Road.

Although it is many years now since the original Harlequins rugby club went out of existence, it is fitting that their memory lives on in the name of the versatile Cardiff sports ground that they created.

JOHN SCOTT

'The influential and successful captain of Cardiff RFC'
by Gwyn Prescott

Welsh birth has never been an essential requirement for the captaincy of Cardiff RFC. At least ten of the men who led the club before the First World War had been born in England, though, of the eight who became internationals, all played for Wales. So there was nothing particularly unusual, as is sometimes suggested, about John Scott's election as captain in 1980. He wasn't even the first English international to be so honoured, as Bristolian Barry Nelmes preceded him in 1978/79. However, those early captains had all come to Cardiff either as children, like Gwyn Nicholls, or to make a living in the booming 'coal metropolis', like Frank Hancock. John Scott's reasons for moving to Cardiff were rather different.

During the 1970s, Welsh club rugby was still regarded as by far the most competitive in Britain, and Cardiff in particular enjoyed one of the strongest fixture lists in the game. So in 1978, John determined to move from London to Cardiff in order to test himself at the highest level week-in, week-out. How much British club rugby has changed since the coming of professionalism!

John was born in Exeter in 1954. Showing much early promise, he played his first county match for Devon at only seventeen and then became the youngest ever English trialist at forward. He followed this with the captaincy of the 1977 England Under-23 tour to Canada. After studying at St Luke's Exeter, a teacher training college which was then one of Britain's leading rugby academies, he moved to London and joined Rosslyn Park. He made an immediate impact there and within a short time he was awarded his first English cap at no.8.

For the next seven seasons, he was an automatic choice for England, winning 34 caps and missing only two of their games during his international career between 1978 and 1984. This was not the most distinguished period in English rugby history, but there were some notable successes. John was a member of Bill Beaumont's 1980 side which won England's first Grand Slam for twenty-three years and their first outright Five Nations Championship since 1963. In his last international season, he helped England record only their third victory over the All Blacks in thirteen meetings by 15 points to 9. John led England on four occasions, including the 1984 tour to South Africa when an under-strength and weakened team were comfortably beaten in both the Test matches.

It was after playing one season of international rugby that John joined Cardiff and he subsequently won the remainder of his 30 English caps as a Blue and Black. In his very first game for England as a Cardiff player, he was accompanied in the pack against New Zealand by his club teammate Barry Nelmes.

'Scotty' proved to be a significant acquisition for Cardiff, as he was a powerful and rugged forward who would lead them through a period of remarkable success. During seven seasons in the 1980s, Cardiff reached six Welsh Cup finals and won five of them. Three of those victories came during his period of captaincy between 1980 and 1984. It is a measure of his leadership skills that no other player in the club's long and distinguished history had held the captaincy for four successive seasons.

He was captain in 1981 when Cardiff won their first ever Welsh cup and also when they repeated this success the following season. That year Cardiff recorded the double by winning the unofficial Welsh Championship for the first time since 1958. The third cup victory under John's leadership came in 1984. He then relinquished the captaincy, but that was not the end of his cup success, for he subsequently played in two more winning teams, those of 1986 and 1987. Injury almost prevented him from taking the field in the 1986 final but, despite this,

A cigarette card of Alf Sherwood.

he proved to be a key man in the line-out that day and his physical presence was crucial in subduing of the powerful Newport pack.

John had also performed a similar role when Cardiff overwhelmed the Australian forwards in October 1984 to record the club's sixth successive win over the Wallabies by 16 points to 12. For 'Scotty' and for the rest of the Cardiff pack, the highlight of that match was forcing the much-vaunted Australian scrum to concede a penalty try whilst trying to avoid the humiliation of a push-over try.

After his playing days were over, John remained in his adoptive city where he now runs a textile business but he continues to contribute to the sporting life of Cardiff with his regular and sometimes controversial rugby column in the *South Wales Echo*.

ALF SHERWOOD

'Cardiff City's finest full-back'
by Dennis Morgan

Alf Sherwood was born at Aberaman in November 1923 and will always be remembered as probably the finest full-back ever to play for Cardiff City. Cyril Spiers, the Cardiff manager, signed him after a wartime match in 1942 when Sherwood was playing for Aberaman against the City. During the war, football was a spare-time activity as Alf worked down the pits as a Bevin Boy. After the war, he enjoyed his greatest success as a key member of that splendid Cardiff City team that rose from the Third Division to the First in the space of six years.

Sherwood won his first full Welsh cap when he was selected to play against England in 1946. Over the next ten years he played 41 times for his country, captaining the side on many occasions. His duels with those two great England wingers, Stanley Mathews and Tom Finney, were legendary. It would be untrue to say that Alf always came out on top but both of them paid tribute to his skill.

Matthews said, 'he was a fair and fine tackler, one of the best I ever came up against. It was never going to be a good afternoon when you came up against Alf.' Buller Lever, his fellow full-back at Cardiff City, believed his 'tremendous power of recovery' was another asset. Many famous wingers thought they had gone past him only to discover that he was still blocking their path. Perhaps his greatest claim to fame was the fact that he was never booked and never sent off. This was despite Sherwood's use of the sliding tackle which, if it was mistimed, not only resulted in a foul but could be very dangerous. Alf's timing was perfect.

His value in today's transfer market would be enormous. In an age when the full-back was expected to concentrate on marking the opposing winger, Sherwood showed his versatility on more than one occasion. Playing against Doncaster Rovers at Ninian Park in January 1952, Alf had to leave the field after sustaining a head injury. City were already a goal down and substitutes were not allowed in those days. Just before half-time Alf returned with his head swathed in bandages. For the rest of the match he played at centre forward and scored two goals to give Cardiff a vital victory in their promotion race. 'City's bandaged hero' was the headline in the *South Wales Football Echo* that evening.

Sherwood was also a very able goalkeeper. When Jack Kelsey was forced to leave the field in an international at Wembley in 1956, Alf took over but could not prevent England from winning 3-1. He was more successful two years earlier when the Cardiff City goalkeeper, Ron Howells, was stretchered off at Anfield. Late in the game Liverpool were awarded a penalty. Sherwood saved Billy Liddell's spot kick and condemned the home side to Second Division football as City won 1-0.

It is rather sad that Alf never finished his football career with Cardiff City. After more than 370 appearances and fifteen successful years with the club, he was transferred to Newport County in 1956. He was still good enough to win two more Welsh caps and play more than 200 times for Newport.

Like so many footballers of that era, Sherwood never reaped the rewards his talent deserved. For a short time he was manager of Barry Town and in 1960 he became player-manager of the United States team in the North American International League. This was one of the early attempts to promote football in America. For his contribution to improving British–American understanding, Alf was given a silver tankard. Later he worked as a security officer with the National Coal Board but kept in touch with football by scouting for a number of League clubs.

Sherwood had always been an all-round sportsman. In his younger days he was a good club cricketer and later in life found another passion in golf. On 11 March 1990, he suffered a massive heart attack on the third tee at Llantrisant Golf Club. His son, Robert, said: 'It was the way he would have wanted to go, playing the other game he loved.' More than 100 mourners attended Alf's funeral at the Church of the Holy Cross in Cowbridge. Players, past and present, came to pay tribute to the man whom Stanley Matthews claimed was, 'one of soccer's finest gentlemen'. As the editorial in the *South Wales Echo* put it: 'he graced his sport and era without a blemish.'

GARETH DAVIES

'Record points scorer for Cardiff RFC'
by Gwyn Prescott

Over the years, Cardiff RFC have enjoyed many outstanding partnerships but one of the most enduring was the half-back pairing of Gareth Davies and Terry Holmes. For ten years, they played together over 200 times for Cardiff, Barbarians, Wales and the Lions, developing an almost telepathic rapport along the way.

The person responsible for bringing them together was Barry John who invited Gareth to join the club in 1974. He had played a few games for Llanelli but the nineteen-year-old from Tumble had just moved to Cardiff to study at UWIST. This was to lead to a long association with the club. Gareth quickly established himself as a fixture at outside half, playing over 300 times over the next eleven years.

He was a key contributor to the club's success, both as an astute tactician and a prolific match-winner. Elected captain in 1979/80, he was vice-captain to John Scott in each of his following four years of captaincy, playing in three WRU Cup-winning sides. In 1983/84, Gareth established a club record of 383 points in a season. He also smashed Percy Bush's seventy-year-old club record with his career-best 53 dropped goals. Gareth represented Cardiff against four major touring sides and twice played in club victories over Australia, dominating the scoring in both games.

After graduating from UWIST, where he helped win the 1975 UAU championship with a desperate last-minute dropped goal, Gareth went up to Oxford, and played in the 1977 varsity match when the Dark Blues recorded their first win for six years.

Had Brian McKechnie missed a highly controversial penalty in the dying moments of the game against the 1978 All Blacks, Gareth would have been immortalised alongside the Welsh victors over New Zealand of earlier generations. But it was not to be and Wales lost 12–13. Sport can be a cruel business.

Gareth was a stylish and elusive outside half who could kick with great precision. A fine exponent of the game, he was fated to be the successor to Barry John and Phil Bennett at a time when Welsh rugby was going into decline. Despite this, expectations remained unreasonably high and he was sometimes unfairly judged.

He won the first of his 21 caps in the summer of 1978 on the brutal tour to Australia, where he impressed. This was followed by a successful Five Nations campaign with a championship title and a fourth successive Triple Crown. But Welsh rugby lost its way thereafter.

After three seasons with Wales, he was deservedly selected for the 1980 Lions tour to South Africa but unfortunately injury restricted him to four matches with only one Test appearance. After being dropped in February 1981, he returned to captain Wales against Australia in December, when he orchestrated a brilliant 18–13 win, including a crucial dropped goal. However, after five games as captain he lost his place again and went into international wilderness for three years, despite playing some of the best rugby of his career for Cardiff. Eventually reinstated in 1985, he nevertheless announced his retirement before the final match against England, frustrated with his treatment by the selectors.

After working as assistant director with CBI Wales and as head of sport for BBC Wales, he made a remarkable return to the Arms Park in 1994 to become Cardiff RFC plc's first chief executive during the difficult early years of professionalism. He is now vice-president of International Business Wales for Australia and is based in Melbourne.

FRANK HANCOCK

'Cardiff's rugby revolutionary'
by Gwyn Prescott

Few men have contributed more to both the sporting and the business life of Cardiff than Frank Hancock. In the autumn of 1883, the twenty-four-year-old arrived in Cardiff to establish his family's brewing interests in the town. William Hancock & Co. would eventually grow into the largest brewery in Wales.

However, he is better remembered, and not just in Cardiff, for his contribution to rugby football. Already a successful player with Wiveliscombe and Somerset when he joined Cardiff RFC, it was his on-field organisational skills that were to leave the most lasting effects on the club and on the wider game.

In 1884, teams customarily lined up with nine forwards and only three three-quarters. The forwards spent much of their time in interminable scrums and mauls, whilst the backs, apart from an occasional individual run, played a largely defensive role of kicking and tackling (hence 'backs'). They rarely combined in passing movements. Hancock, however, was to change all this by handing the main attacking thrust, for the first time, to the backs.

How often in Britain does the weather influence sport! Suffering from a period of torrential rainfall in February 1884, Cardiff were struggling to raise a First XV for their match at Cheltenham College, so they drafted in Frank from the reserves. So well did he perform at centre on his debut that the selectors were reluctant to leave him out of the next match against Gloucester. Not wanting to drop any of the regular threes, they took an inspired decision to select four three-quarters and so a new system was born.

Hancock settled well into the team and Cardiff soon realised that they had discovered a very talented new recruit. Renowned for his 'dodging' and 'corkscrew runs', after a mere five games for the club and only six months in Wales, he won the first of his four Welsh caps in the victory over Ireland the following April.

Frank Hancock is often credited with 'inventing' the four three-quarter system but Cardiff had been experimenting with it for a good eighteen months before he was unanimously elected captain in 1885. However, it wasn't so much the placing of four men in the line-up which was revolutionary. In fact, several clubs had occasionally done this before Cardiff, though largely for defensive purposes. Rather, it was the way in which the new formation was used which was so radical and which was to have such a lasting impact. This is Hancock's – and indeed Cardiff RFC's – great legacy to the game.

With a reduced – and rather lightweight – pack of only eight, Hancock encouraged his forwards to release the ball quickly, rather than engaging in prolonged scrums and mauls. In 1885, this was a real innovation and, outside Wales, it was criticised and resisted by many die-hards for a long time. Instead of kicking or running with the ball, the half-backs were expected to move it out to the centres, whose role was now, by means of low and accurate passing, to transfer the ball swiftly to the wings. Since they were facing only three opponents, the wings invariably had a clear overlap, from which tries easily flowed. Hancock also stressed the importance of correct alignment in the backs and insisted they took their passes on the run.

Practice, of course, was essential. The level of combination and precision required by this new style of 'machine-like' or 'scientific' play (as it was often termed) could not have been achieved without it. Drawing on his strong leadership skills, Hancock therefore imposed a firm discipline both on the field and in training. Despite this, he was much admired and respected by his teammates as an outstanding captain and a highly gifted, yet unselfish and modest player.

The success of his new tactics was astonishing. The speed and accuracy of the passing confounded opponents and spectators alike: nothing had been seen like it before. Under Frank Hancock, the Cardiff club enjoyed one of their most successful seasons ever. Out of 27 fixtures only the last was narrowly lost, when nerves seemed to get the better of the players. A staggering 131 tries were scored with only a mere four conceded. It was the 1885/86 season, therefore, which established Cardiff RFC as one of the game's elite clubs, with a tradition of playing open and attractive rugby.

The 'Cardiff' game rapidly became the 'Welsh' game. There is no doubt that this new and exciting method of play contributed greatly to the enormous growth in rugby's popularity in late Victorian Wales. Within four years of Hancock's season, the number of teams playing in the immediate Cardiff area alone had risen from sixty to well over 200. With the arrival of the 'Rhondda forward', the superiority of the new system was finally proved at international level when it became the basis of Wales' great successes during the 'Golden Era' in the first decade of the twentieth century.

Frank Hancock retired from rugby at the end of his momentous season and he returned to Wiveliscombe a few years later, remaining there until his death in 1943. It is no exaggeration to argue, however, that the brief time this man of Somerset spent in Wales was of immense and lasting significance to the sporting life of Cardiff and to the game of rugby worldwide.

STEVE ROBINSON

'Another great featherweight from Cardiff'
by Gareth Jones

It became the most famous pie in Welsh sport. Some stories are destined to become legend, true or not. But this was true. Steve Robinson was tucking in to the aforementioned comestible when the phone rang. His trainer, Ronnie Rush, was on the line. Would Steve like to fight for a world title? The day after tomorrow?

Even in the unpredictable world of boxing this was a bizarre chain of events. Ruben Palacio, the Colombian World Boxing Organisation (WBO) featherweight champion, had been due to defend against Englishman John Davison, but had failed a pre-fight HIV test and had been stripped of his belt. Promoter Barry Hearn, desperate to save his ITV date, turned to the unranked Robinson and, despite a record showing nine defeats in 23 contests, the WBO – no doubt equally worried about missing out on a sanctioning fee – agreed.

That pie was the last for a while as Steve, who had recently given up his £52-a-week job as a storeman with Debenhams, set about shedding 6lbs to make the 9st limit, while a minibus was hastily organised to transport a handful of supporters to the Durham outpost of Washington, deep in Davison's intimidating heartland.

But the Welshman, with nothing to lose, blanked out the deafening choruses of 'Blaydon Races', gritted his teeth, dug deep and played his part in a torrid tussle. Somehow, despite his lack of preparation, he found the stamina to batter Davison around the ring for the final minute. It was enough for two of the three judges to give him the verdict by a single point.

That victory in April 1993 climaxed a journey which had started when the nine-year-old Ely boy, son of a West Indian father and Cardiffian mother, first went to Rush's Ely Star amateur club. There was a break as he represented Glyn Derw High School at rugby and soccer, but the smell of the gloves called him back to the gym. His amateur career was undistinguished, however, and few took much notice when he turned pro with Rhymney Valley manager Dai Gardiner. Six defeats in his first 11 bouts gave little reason for that situation to change.

Okay, Robinson outpointed Swansea redhead Peter Harris to win the Welsh featherweight title, but when he tried to add the super-feather belt he was edged out by Llanelli southpaw Neil Haddock. Even a twelve-round decision over Paul Harvey, himself half-Welsh, which brought the spurious Penta-Continental strap, meant little, especially when he lost in Paris next time out.

Then came that phone call. Suddenly, the London press wanted to know Steve and his 'Cinderella Man' story. Mind you, they considered him a temporary phenomenon enjoying his fifteen minutes of fame. His reign, they were sure, would end with his first defence. But when British champion Sean Murphy came to the National Ice Rink, Robinson demolished him in nine rounds. Yes, wrote the metropolitan media, but Murphy was nothing special. Wait till former champion Colin McMillan, who had only lost to Palacio because of a dislocated shoulder, had his chance.

Wrong again. McMillan was beaten on points. Ah well, Colin was never as good as Paul Hodkinson, the Liverpudlian who used to hold the prestigious World Boxing Council version. When Steve ended the Scouser's career with a twelfth-round stoppage, he finally earned acceptance as a worthy champion.

A vicious left to the ribs finished Duke McKenzie's dream of becoming Britain's first four-weight world titleholder, while Latin trio Freddy Cruz (Dominican Republic), Domingo Damigella (Argentina) and Pedro Ferradas (Spain) were all seen off in the cauldron of the ice rink.

But the Cardiffian had a stalker. For most of those fights, a small man with a large mouth was at ringside, invading Steve's post-fight television interviews. Prince Naseem Hamed left

A caricature of Steve Robinson.

few in doubt about his intentions. He planned to be a legend – and his antithesis, the modest, quietly spoken Robinson, was his chosen stepping stone.

Both sides accepted the inevitability of the showdown. But Robinson's camp showed a little naivety in assuming the purse would be negotiated outside the multi-bout deal he had with promoter Frank Warren. That contract included specific fees for facing a mandatory challenger. No problem, it appeared, as Hamed was ranked at super-bantam. But once Naz indicated he was stepping up to feather, the WBO, keen to have the charismatic Sheffielder wearing one of their belts, immediately listed him at no.1. Steve would get no extra cash. Then came the honeymoon saga: Robinson was due to marry long-term partner Angela Jason and wanted a fortnight away. Maybe the bout would be put back.

But 30 September was as late as could be risked for an outdoor show and there was no way it could change. So the champion took to the ring in the centre of the Cardiff RFC ground without his usual training period. Hamed, that rainy night in 1995, would have beaten anyone on the planet. Robinson, stung by Naz's appearance at a pre-fight press conference in an outfit already reading 'World Featherweight Champion', was as game as ever. But it was all over in eight painful rounds.

The deposed monarch took a year out, but returned to win more honours. He travelled to Spain to upset local Manuel Calvo and claim the European crown, defending it twice before losing to the brilliant Hungarian, Istvan Kovacs, in Budapest.

A bid for the minor World Boxing Union belt at Ebbw Vale saw Steve floor unbeaten South African Cassius Baloyi only to lose a wafer-thin decision. Another trip to Madrid saw Calvo, this time, get the nod. And Glasgow witnessed Scott Harrison stop a weary Robinson in his only attempt to win the British and Commonwealth titles.

The writing was on the wall. Angela was desperate for him to call it a day, but the fighter always needs to know for sure. A points defeat by the ordinary Steve Conway spelled it out for him and Steve hung up his gloves. Since then he has become a respected trainer, guiding Dazzo Williams to the Lonsdale Belt that eluded him, and introducing sons Luke and Jacob (he also has a daughter, Ebony) to the fistic arts. A humble man, he never sought the limelight. When it came to him, he never gloried in it. And his demeanour, as much as his achievements, meant that he occupies a special place in the hearts of all Cardiffians.

Terry Slocombe. (*Western Mail and Echo*)

TERRY 'SLOGGER' SLOCOMBE

'The big hitter of Cardiff baseball'
by Andrew Weltch

As his nickname suggests, 'Slogger 'was renowned for his big-hitting style – noted for a trademark shot over first base – but he is also remembered for his loyalty to one club, St Alban's, throughout a long and illustrious baseball career.

Born in Barry on 9 July 1934, he joined the club while still a pupil at St Alban's School in Tremorfa. He received his Wales call-up in 1955 and his respectable 11 in the match against England at New Brighton helped Wales to a comfortable win by an innings and 40 runs.

His most remarkable international appearance came in the 1959 game at Edinburgh Park, Liverpool, when his tremendous 43 helped Wales to a phenomenal 204 for 9 declared – a total which England could not get near in their two innings. Slocombe's score, which included seven fours, has been bettered only once in international play – Fred Hayes' 49 remains the record.

His performance was rewarded a year later, when he was made captain for the 1960 game at Maindy Stadium. A much-improved England put up a real fight in a game which Slocombe's team won narrowly and which is regarded by many as the best international for a decade. Further honour came in 1966, when he was named Welsh National Baseball League player of the year – an award presented by Olympic long jump star Lynn Davies.

Curiously, he was not selected for the Wales team that year, and he missed the whole of the following season because of an injury at work. In a second work accident, he lost the tops of two fingers, but went on to win his ninth cap in the 1968 international, when he received a huge ovation for taking his total of international runs to 100, becoming only the seventh Welshman to reach the landmark figure in the then sixty years of the Wales–England match.

His loyalty to St Alban's extended beyond his playing days, and he worked with the club's youth and women's teams into his sixties. But some thought his loyalty went too far – in the middle of the night he once repainted the house of Grange Albion's Don O'Leary in the black and amber of St Alban's!

CARDIFF PARKS
by Andrew Hignell

The Cardiff Parks – the venue for so many generations of amateur and semi-professional sport, the place where so many sporting careers began – and ended – and the location over the years for the blissful dreams of so many Cardiffians.

Unlike many cities of a similar size, Cardiff has been extremely well blessed over the years in the size and scope of its public recreation fields and open spaces. Thanks are largely due to the landowners in the city – and on its suburban fringes – for their foresight and benevolence in granting their land, especially in the nineteenth century, to the population of Cardiff, and to the City Corporation for maintaining these fields and encouraging their use by a wide variety of sporting organisations.

Foremost amongst these landowners – like so many aspects of Cardiff life – stand the Bute Estate, who in September 1947 gave the city fathers their entire, and extensive, areas of open space. This was the culmination of many years of generous patronage by the Marquess, who since the 1850s had provided land for healthy recreation. It was from this time that the use of Cooper's Field, the Arms Park and Sophia Gardens was encouraged, followed in the twentieth century by Blackweir and Pontcanna Fields which previously had been farms and market gardens producing food and fresh fare for the city's inhabitants.

The Butes were also instrumental in the design and creation of Roath Park, presented to the inhabitants by the Marquess in 1887, as well as the Roath Recreation Ground to the south of the lake which has been used for rugby, football, baseball and hockey.

Llandaff Fields were purchased in 1897 at a cost of £69,000 by the City Corporation, and aided by a generous gift from the Thompson family. The seventy-one acres of parkland have been used over time for football, cricket and rugby, whilst a bowling green, miniature golf course, tennis courts and open-air swimming pool were also provided. During the Empire Games in 1958, polo was also staged on the fields, with HRH The Duke of Edinburgh being amongst the participants.

On the western side of the city is Victoria Park – opened in 1897 – which was home to a bowling green and numerous tennis courts. To the east was Splott Park – presented to the Corporation in 1901 by Lord Tredegar – on which tennis courts and football pitches were laid out, together with an open-air pool and bowls green. Also on the eastern side of the city were Llanrumney Playing Fields in Ball Road, which have also been the base for the recreational activities by students from Cardiff University, as well as professional teams including Cardiff City.

To the north of the city were Heath Park – the site of the old racecourse and mansion house – where the fields have subsequently been used for football, rugby, hockey, baseball, cricket, cross-country, tennis and golf, as well as Parc Caedelyn, close to the suburbs of Whitchurch and Rhiwbina which were incorporated inside the city boundary from 1 April 1967, and where a similar range of team games have been staged during the summer and winter months.

Amongst the other public parks to have hosted sporting activities are Grange Gardens, Hailey Park, Waterloo Gardens, Jubilee Park, Leckwith Common, The Marl, Sevenoaks Park, Cyncoed Gardens, Llandaff Court Gardens, Fairwater Recreation Ground, Hill Snook Park, Llwynfedw Gardens, Rumney Recreation Ground, Trelai Park, Tremorfa Park, and Parc Cefn On, which included a golf course leased to the Llanishen Golf Club.

Terry Yorath (back left) promoting membership of Glamorgan cricket.

TERRY YORATH

'The hard man of Welsh football'
by Andrew Hignell

Triumph and tragedy: two facets of the life so far of Terry Yorath, the Cardiff-born footballer and father, who savoured heady days whilst a member of Don Revie's highly successful Leeds United side of the early 1970s – a stark contrast with the depths of despair he experienced when, in 1992, his teenage son Daniel died suddenly of a rare heart disease.

Born in Cardiff on 27 March 1950, Terry and his brother David attended Rhydypenau Junior School and Gabalfa Primary School, with both boys showing an aptitude for ball games, the pair one season scoring 56 goals between them for the Rhydypenau School. Terry went on to spend five years at Cathays High School, where he shone at many sports and represented Cardiff Schools at football, rugby, baseball and cricket. Aged fourteen he had to make a decision about which winter sport in particular to focus on and, after some advice from his brother and father, he opted for football rather than playing rugby, where he had been chosen at scrum-half in the Cardiff Schools team.

Rugby's loss was football's gain as he progressed to the Cardiff Schools side alongside John Toshack, and briefly followed 'Tosh' to Ninian Park where he trained twice a week with their junior staff. At the time, his parents were keeping the Cambridge pub in Tyndall Street, and one afternoon in December 1964, young Terry arrived home from school to be greeted by his mother, who asked, 'Would you like to spend a week of your Christmas holidays up at Leeds?' She then pointed in the direction of a man sitting at the bar, adding, 'Well that gentleman is a scout for Leeds United, and he wants to take you there.'

The man in question was Jack Pickard, the part-time scout for Leeds in South Wales who had 'discovered', amongst others, John Charles, Gary Sprake and Leighton Phillips. As it turned out, the trip up north was postponed because of snow, but over the Easter break, he went up to Elland Road and, after agreeing terms at the age of fifteen, he took his first steps towards becoming a professional footballer.

Initially, Terry played at right-back in the youth and reserve teams, before moving into midfield as he grew stronger and became able to handle the physicality of professional soccer. Leeds under Don Revie were certainly very rugged and robust – labelled 'dirty Leeds' in some quarters, but as Terry freely admitted, everyone had to be prepared to put their feet in where it hurt for the good of the team, as in order to succeed, a combination of ruthless determination and aggression were needed as well as ball skills.

Terry became a full-time professional in his second year at Elland Road, and in May 1968, aged eighteen, he made his first-team debut against Burnley. He put in some thumping tackles and showed that he had the nerve as well as the nous to hold his own in the First Division, but it was a measure of the strength of the Leeds squad that Terry did not become a first-team regular for several years. Despite playing in the Leeds reserve team, he was appointed captain of the Wales Under-23 team, and for several years, he heeded Don Revie's advice to bide his time and be patient for the chances to come.

It was not easy, though, especially when he had to sit in the stand at Wembley and watch his colleagues defeat Arsenal in the Centenary FA Cup final. By this time, he had also won the first of 59 caps for Wales, making his international debut in 1970 against Italy. But Revie was proved right as, from 1972/73, Terry got regular opportunities to play alongside the likes of Billy Bremner, Peter Lorimer, Johnny Giles and Jack Charlton. The following summer he became a member of the Leeds side that won the First Division Championship, including a lengthy spell out on the left-wing when Eddie Gray sustained a serious injury in an often brutal draw at home with Manchester United.

Despite a quite volatile six weeks in 1974 when Brian Clough ruled the roost at Elland Road, Terry continued to establish his reputation as a hard man, and under new manager Jimmy Armfield, he cemented a regular first-team place. It was also in the Armfield era that Terry achieved his boyhood dream of playing in the 1975 European Cup final against Bayern Munich at Parc des Princes in Paris. But as he later recounted in his autobiography, it was a match he remembered for all the wrong reasons, as he shattered Bjorn Andersson's knee in a ferocious tackle after four minutes:

> It was the most high-profile of a certain number of tackles in my career which I'm deeply ashamed of. At the start of the game, my job was clear – I was just going to get in there and try to win every ball for Johnny and Bill to make use of. That was the only thought in my head. There was a loose ball, and it was a case of me going in as hard as I possibly could to win it. I just went in, and in the process 'did' Bjorn. There was no response at all from any of my teammates, but I became ashamed of what I'd done pretty soon afterwards. It remains the one big regret of my playing career. To play in a European Cup final and be remembered for that one incident sours the memory of the achievement.

He remained a first-team regular the following year, but at the end of 1975/76, with many of the team assembled by Revie now having their best years behind them, Yorath realised that it was time to move on, and went to see Jimmy Armfield to ask for a transfer. The manager agreed, and shortly afterwards he moved on to Coventry City, before a spell with Tottenham Hotspur, and then Vancouver Whitecaps in Canada. Terry maintained a regular presence in the Welsh side until 1981, before embarking on a new career with Swansea City in 1986, initially as player-coach, then concentrating on management and helping them secure promotion in 1988 to the Third Division. He later joined Bradford City, before returning to South Wales where he has also managed Cardiff City, in addition to fulfilling a similar role with Sheffield Wednesday.

But Terry would have willingly changed all of this in return for not having to go through the ultimate nightmare for any parent – the death of his son, which happened, totally without warning, whilst the two were playing football in the back garden of their home. Terry later recalled:

The moment I saw Daniel's eyes, I knew he was dead. We were playing football when the ball rolled to the bottom of our garden. Daniel went to fetch it and on his way back, fell flat on his face. It was a hot day and I thought he was playing a joke on me – he was that kind of boy, full of fun. When he didn't move for about a minute, I went to see him. As I turned him over, his eyes were completely blank. He was gone.

At the time, Terry had become manager of Wales, but over the next few months the national side had no fixtures, and over the summer months there were no games, and life became difficult as he had no way of filling the void in his life. These were very low times for Terry, as within a couple of years, a contract dispute saw him being replaced as Wales manager by John Toshack, despite having taken the side to the brink of qualifying for the 1994 World Cup. In 1995 he left the UK and spent two years in Beirut coaching the Lebanese national team, before returning and helping Huddersfield win promotion in 2004.

TERRY HOLMES

'The bone-crunching scrum-half for Cardiff and Wales'
by John Billot

Holmes and Moriarty on the same side? Surely not! Arthur Conan Doyle's legendary super-sleuth Sherlock Holmes repeatedly locked horns with his arch-enemy, evil master-criminal Professor Moriarty. But here we are talking about Terry Holmes, the Cardiff scrum-half and fellow Welsh international Richard Moriarty of Swansea, who appeared together for Wales on nine occasions in the late 1970s and early 1980s.

There must also have been many a time in club clashes against the Arms Park men when Moriarty's Swansea side wished they could have finished off Holmes as did Conan Doyle, although hardly as spectacularly as plunging over the Reichenbach Falls while grappling with the murderous professor!

Born in Cardiff on 10 March 1957 – the day after Wales had toppled Ireland 6-5 at the Arms Park – Terry developed his rugby skills first at Bishop Hannon School, where he went on to play for Cardiff and Welsh Schoolboys. He then progressed to Cardiff's youth team and the Welsh Youth side, for whom he played for three seasons. He made his debut for Cardiff against Newport at just eighteen, while still a youth player. When he moved up to senior ranks, Cardiff already had two Lions scrum-halves in the legendary Gareth Edwards and his stylish understudy Brynmor Williams. Terry was to duly follow them into Lions' ranks on the tours to South Africa in 1980 and New Zealand in 1983, although serious injuries affected him on both tours and restricted him to only one Test appearance.

With his bone-shattering tackling, it was surprising that Terry did not suffer more from the physical contact. One Holmes big hit is remembered above all others when he hurled giant Scotland lock Bill Cuthbertson flat on his back in the 19-15 victory at Murrayfield in 1983.

Tough as teak Terry captained Wales on five of his 25 appearances, and he was on the winning side more often than his country lost. After winning his first cap against Australia in June 1978, Terry played in all four matches of the successful 1979 Triple Crown and Championship season, the highlight of which was the humiliating 27-3 defeat of England. He snapped up eight tries for Wales in full-cap fixtures, and not many players either can claim three tries in matches against France: Terry and Gareth Edwards both enjoyed that experience. Terry's scores helped Wales win in Cardiff in 1980 and 1982. His was the only try in 1982, but victory was secured 22-12 with six penalty goals by Maesteg full-back Gwyn Evans – the first time such a feat had been recorded in what then was the Five Nations tourney.

Terry Holmes in action as the Welsh scrum-half. (*Western Mail and Echo*)

From ten metres out, there were few defences capable of preventing Terry from scoring. His physical presence was awesome and, although pound for pound Gareth Edwards was the more explosive, Terry could take on big forwards fearlessly and this frequently proved a decisive factor in desperate defensive situations. Lord Macaulay in his epic poem 'Horatius' had Spurius Lartius volunteering 'Lo, I will stand at thy right hand and keep the bridge with thee' to help save Rome from Lars Porsena's hordes. The man to stand at your right hand in any crisis was Terry Holmes.

With his long, sweeping service to Gareth Davies, Terry kept his fly-half safe for both Cardiff and Wales. Intensely proud of being a Blue and Black, Terry played in 195 games for his club, scoring 123 tries and leading them in the 1984/85 season. He returned as their coaching supremo, after having briefly appeared in rugby league's Bradford Northern colours from December 1985. Injury dogged him there and he retired from playing in October 1987. Sherlock Holmes will never be displaced amongst the most famous characters of literature. Equally, the other Holmes will always be remembered as a luminary in the history of Cardiff and Welsh rugby.

HARRY CULLUM

'The first Cardiff athlete to win a world title'
by Clive Williams

Who are the four Cardiff athletes to have won world athletics titles? Well there's Tanni Grey-Thompson and Colin Jackson of course... and Jamie Baulch... and there's Harry Cullum! Born in 1874, Cullum was one of the finest pedestrians – as professional athletes were called at the time – in Britain in the late 1890s and early 1900s and he won the world professional

880 yards championship at Rochdale in 1899. In his amateur days, he twice won the Welsh cross-country title, three Welsh mile titles and the 440 yards twice. During his career, he won 'hundreds of races from 100 yards to 10 miles,' he said in a letter to his grandson.

He turned professional in 1899 after a successful amateur career with Roath (Cardiff) Harriers and, in his finest race, he won the world professional half-mile championship in Rochdale on 4 November 1899, defeating the holder, Edgar Bredin, in two minutes flat for a prize of £200. Describing the race forty years later, Harry said: 'It was a very bad day and blowing a gale… I had run 1:55 and 1:56.2 in time trials at Bradford and Leeds, so if the race had have been held in July or August, I would have smashed the record for I was flying at the time!' Bearing in mind in his amateur days Bredin had won the AAA 880 yards title for three successive years between 1893 and 1895, clocking 1:55.3 to win in 1893, Harry's times were entirely believable. The Welsh amateur record at the time was 2:02 secs set by A.D. Williams of Usk when taking the Welsh title in 1899, and the long-standing professional record of 2:00.25 set in 1866 by William Richards.

Cullum had also beaten Bredin by twelve yards at the Cardiff Harlequins Ground on 3 September 1899 over 1,000 yards. Bredin was reported to be very upset at Cullum's win in Rochdale, and demanded a rematch, which Cullum (apparently) refused. In all, Cullum is reported to have won more than £3,000 in his professional career, a sum that is worth nearer £100,000 today.

Before turning professional, he won the second Welsh cross-county title as a member of Roath Harriers on a course from the Cardiff Harlequins Ground, beating teammate Egbert Fairlamb. The next year he was a prime mover in the formation of a new club in Cardiff, Cardiff Harriers, and it was in their colours that he retained his title, beating the 1894 winner Hugh Fairlamb of Roath by the wide margin of 1 minute 39 seconds. He could only finish sixth in the 1897 championship, but had the satisfaction of being part of the Cardiff team that won the team race.

There is no doubt that Cullum was one of the finest athletes produced by Wales, and one of the leading British athletes of his time. He worked for many years in the Co-operative Wholesale Society in Cardiff, and died at his Llandaff North home in 1953 aged seventy-nine.

GUS RISMAN

'The rugby league star from Tiger Bay'
by Huw Richards

Under a decade on from Jim Sullivan, another teenage prodigy excited the attention of sporting talent scouts, and not just in the rugby codes. Augustus 'Gus' Risman, the son of Latvian-born parents who settled in the Tiger Bay melting pot, educated at South Church Street and Barry County schools, was wanted by Cardiff RFC; Tottenham Hotspur were also keenly interested, but he chose to sign for Salford Rugby League Club.

This was in 1929, when Risman was only eighteen. His signature was worth £52 to Salford, who added a further £25 when told that his father was unwell. It secured his services for league at a rate that would turn out to be just over £3 per year. His final game was not until 1954, when he was forty-three, completing an unmatched quarter of a century in senior league. His 873 matches are second only to Jim Sullivan and might well have run into four figures but for the war.

Salford were an undistinguished club, deep in the shadow of neighbours Swinton – a single championship in 1914 the sum total of their trophies. They were to enjoy the greatest period in their history in the 1930s, winning thirteen trophies – more than any other club. These included championships in 1933, 1937 and 1939 and their only ever Challenge Cup victory in

A cigarette card of Gus Risman.

1938. In addition, their missionary visits to France, where league began in 1934, earned them the 'Diables Rouges' Red Devils nickname subsequently misappropriated by near-neighbours Manchester United.

No great team relies solely on one player. Risman was surrounded by the talent, artifice and power essential to any successful rugby team. It is clear, though, that he was the indispensable element in the mix credited, within a few months of his debut in 1929, with transforming Salford's back play from his position of full-back – he was equally adept at centre or outside half.

He was an outstanding tactician and leader. One teammate wrote: 'He could read a game the way other men read a newspaper.' Towards the end of his career, one critic hailed him as perhaps the most gifted all-round footballer to have played league: 'a big, strong man, who used his physical attributes when he found strength and weight necessary, but more generally he preferred to charm us with the sly dummy, the scintillating side-step, the acceleration through the half-opening... his defence was like a stone wall.'

As the same critic noted, he relied on guile and timing, rather than sheer pace: 'His long raking stride made him appear deceptively slow, but once away he was not often caught and he had a curious little jink, part side-step and part dummy, which created the gaps.'

He was similarly successful at international level, winning 18 caps for Wales, one for England, and 17 for Great Britain, spread over a record fourteen-year span. He played in five Ashes series against Australia, including three tours (all victorious), and in 12 games against them was on the losing side only once. He received the Ashes trophy as the winning captain, deputising for Jim Brough, after victory in the final Test of the 1936 series in Australia and as captain in his own right at home in 1937.

The wartime amnesty on league players allowed him to play international union for Wales, although it was St Helens, Swansea rather than the bomb-damaged Arms Park that saw his home matches. Among his colleagues was the young Bleddyn Williams, who to this day remembers gratefully lessons learnt from him, particularly about the game's attacking possibilities.

If he had retired in 1945, he would have been remembered as one of league's greatest players. Instead he continued for almost a decade, at thirty-five leading the 1946 Great Britain team known as the 'Indomitables' after the converted aircraft carrier that took them to another Ashes victory in Australia; then as player-coach leading the new Workington Town club to the heights of the game, winning both a championship and a Challenge Cup within seven years of joining the league. He was forty-one when he led them to their cup win over Featherstone Rovers at Wembley. Nor was there any falling off in the quality of his play – his last full season, 1953/54, saw him record his highest ever season's tally, 294 points.

Tony Lewis.

He resigned at the end of that season after a dispute over selection, played his final few matches for Batley and subsequently coached Salford, Bradford Northern and Oldham. He also founded a rugby dynasty. His son Bev played outside half for England and the 1959 British Lions before turning to league where he captained both Leeds and Great Britain, making them so far the only father and son to lead tours of Australia, while his grandson John won Blues in both rugby codes at Oxford University. In spite of leaving Workington, Gus Risman remained in Cumbria for the rest of his life, dying in 1994.

TONY LEWIS

'Captain of Glamorgan, the MCC and England'
by Andrew Hignell

The summer of '69 – a wonderful time for Wales with HRH Prince Charles invested as the Prince of Wales, and Glamorgan becoming county champions for the second time in their history. They clinched the championship title by beating Worcestershire at Sophia Gardens, their new home in Cardiff, and at the helm was another adopted son of the city – Tony Lewis, for whom 1969 was also the year when his second daughter, Anabel Sophia, was born.

Born in Swansea, and educated at Neath Grammar School and Christ's College, Cambridge, Tony Lewis had made his Glamorgan debut in 1955 as a callow youth. Right from the outset, he was groomed for the county captaincy by Wilf Wooller – the legendary leader of post-war Glamorgan. In 1967 'AR' duly succeeded Ossie Wheatley and, in the glorious summer of 1969, Glamorgan were unbeaten, winning 11 matches – one more than Gloucestershire, who were second – to lift the Championship crown for the first time in twenty-one years.

After a nail-biting victory over Essex in the final over of their match at Swansea, Tony and his Glamorgan team arrived at Sophia Gardens for their final home match of the 1969 season knowing that a win over Worcestershire would clinch the title. The Cardiff wicket at the time was a spiteful one, making batting at times a lottery in the face of some uneven and unerring bounce. But Tony had a trump card up his sleeve in the form of Majid Jahangir Khan, the gifted Pakistani batsman, who played a majestic and astonishing innings of 156, and all on a wicket where the next highest individual score was 71.

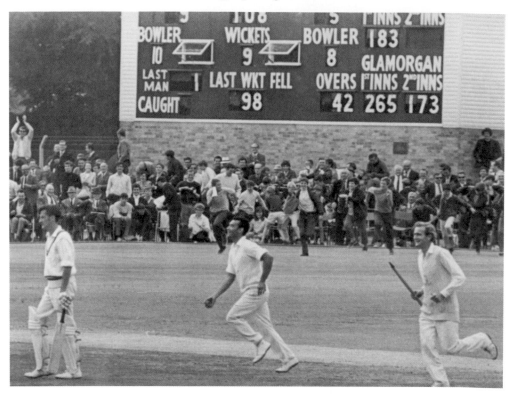

Glamorgan take the final wicket against Worcestershire at Sophia Gardens to win the 1969 County Championship.

None of the Worcestershire batsmen were comfortable against the Glamorgan seam bowlers, with left-armer Malcolm Nash and Tony Cordle – the Bajan fast bowler who was another adopted Cardiffian – both fully exploiting the conditions. Don Shepherd, the wily off-spinner, also drew on his vast experience to stifle the visiting batsmen as the ball got older. The task of making 256 was way beyond the Worcestershire men on the final afternoon and, when Nash claimed the final wicket with their total on a mere 108, the delirious spectators swarmed across the Sophia Gardens outfield, and then gathered in front of the pavilion, opened in 1967 following the county's move from the Arms Park.

Above them on the balcony, the champagne corks were flying as the celebrations got into full swing, whilst in their tiny dressing room, Tony and his colleagues read the many telegrams of congratulations that had been sent to the Cardiff ground – one was from Balmoral Castle which read, 'I am delighted by your splendid win, especially in this particular year. Many congratulations. Do it again next year. CHARLES.'

The royal request, though, was disobeyed as Glamorgan came second in 1970, but 'AR' remained highly regarded by the MCC's mandarins and, in 1972/73, he was appointed to lead the MCC on their winter tour to India and Pakistan. The first leg of the tour saw Tony become the first Glamorgan player to lead England in a Test, as well as recording his maiden Test century – with 125 against India in the fourth Test at Kanpur – before the second leg saw Tony and his England team in action in three Tests against Pakistan who were led by Majid Khan – a rare occasion in Test history when two sides have been led by Glamorgan men.

A knee injury – a legacy from his rugby playing days with Cambridge, Neath, Pontypool and Gloucester – hastened his retirement from cricket in 1974, with a tally of 20,495 first-class runs and 30 centuries to his name. He subsequently became a distinguished broadcaster and journalist, writing for, amongst others, *The Sunday Telegraph*, as well as commentating on BBC radio's *Test Match Special* and acting as BBC TV's anchorman in their coverage of Test and county cricket.

Tony has also had other business interests – in the 1960s, his wife opened the first ever boutique in Cardiff in the northern suburb of Rhiwbina – and in recent years, he has been involved with both the Wales Tourist Board, and the consortium that has brought the 2010 Ryder Cup to The Celtic Manor Resort. In 1998/99 Tony served as president of the MCC, and it was fitting that, during his year in office, Sophia Gardens staged its first international cricket match – between Australia and New Zealand – thirty years after Tony had won the Championship title with his Glamorgan teammates at the Cardiff ground.

JANET ACKLAND

'World champion bowler'
by Andrew Hignell

Janet Ackland – a retired schoolteacher from Llandough – is widely regarded to have been one of Wales' finest lady bowlers, representing Wales and the Penarth Belle Vue club with distinction for over three decades.

Amongst her many honours have been captain of the Welsh team, two British Isles titles, and four Welsh crowns. But, undoubtedly, the greatest moment of Janet's illustrious career came in 1988 when she won the world outdoor singles titles in Auckland.

Janet began bowling in 1959, and in the 1960s she won her first national title at Llandrindod Wells. In 1973, Janet won her first cap for Wales, and she has since won over a hundred indoor and outdoor caps. In 1977 she won the bronze medal in both the pairs and fours in the World Championships, before appearing in four successive Commonwealth Games. Her first appearance was at the Brisbane Games in 1982, before twelve years later winning, with Ann Dainton, the bronze in the women's pairs competition in the Games at Victoria, British Colombia.

BOWLS IN CARDIFF
by Andrew Hignell

Cardiff Bowls Club is the oldest in Wales, having been formed in 1878, and like so many aspects of Cardiff sport, there is a close link with the Marquess of Bute. The club initially played in Cooper's Fields, adjacent to the Castle Grounds, before moving the following year to a specially created green in the north-eastern corner of the Sophia Gardens Pleasure Grounds, having been kindly given the land by the Marquess.

In 1891 the Mackintosh Bowling Club was formed in the Roath area, adjacent to the Mackintosh Institute – known as Roath Castle because of its castellated roof – and in 1903 the two clubs became the founder members of the Welsh Bowling Association.

In 1909 a third bowls club was formed in the City as a 'splinter' group of players who used the public green at Roath Park, formed their own private club on land rented to them at Penylan by Lord Tredegar.

Many international competitions have been held at these various clubs, and in 1958 the three clubs – Mackintosh, Penylan and Cardiff – all hosted the lawn bowls events in the Empire Games.

Lynn Davies addresses the crowd who had gathered outside Cardiff General Station to welcome him home after his Olympic gold medal in the Tokyo Games of 1964. (Clive Williams)

LYNN DAVIES

'Lynn the Leap!'
by Clive Williams

Remarkably, after almost forty years, Lynn Davies' long-jump best of 8.23m, set in Berne in June 1968, is still the third best long jump of all time by a British athlete – despite the improved facilities of today, where all-weather run-ups have replaced the soggy loose cinders that Lynn mostly competed on. The nearest any Welsh athlete has got to Lynn's extraordinary feat is the 7.75m leap by Ken Cocks in 1978. Almost unbelievably, Lynn's performances four decades ago will still place him amongst the world's elite today. Put in a nutshell, he was a brilliant and extraordinary athlete. He was like Barry John, JPR, Gareth and John Charles all rolled into one.

It is a well-known fact that he became Wales' first and still only individual Olympic athletics Champion when he won in Tokyo in 1964, but also consider these statistics:

He jumped over eight metres 21 times. In 2006 only three British athletes exceeded eight metres.

He became the first athlete to hold Olympic, European and Commonwealth titles at the same time.

His 43 senior international appearances for Britain included a remarkable tally of 28 victories in 100 metres, long jump and relays.

He set 17 British and Commonwealth records.

But where did it all start for the UWIC lecturer, who has lived in Cardiff since being a student at Cardiff Training College (now UWIC), apart from a three-year stint as technical director of the Track & Field Association of Canada in the mid 1970s?

Well, the Nantymoel-born superstar was an outstanding sportsman at Ogmore Grammar School and naturally enough played on the wing for his school rugby team and also had a soccer trial for Cardiff City. But all that was to change when the then national coach for Wales, the late Ron Pickering, attending his very first athletics meeting in Wales since his appointment, noticed Lynn's 'fantastic' potential. Said Ron, who died in 1991, 'I asked him if he wanted to be the greatest athlete Wales had ever produced and whether he was prepared to work harder than any other athlete had ever worked.' Ron continued, 'Although quiet and shy, he was quite firm in saying that he wanted exactly that.'

Lynn, an ambassador for Welsh sport, with Sir Terry Matthews, the owner of the Celtic Manor Resort.

Lynn remembers that occasion in 1961 well: 'I had played in a seven-a-side rugby tournament the previous week and thought that that would stand me in good stead for the Welsh championships – such was my naivety.' He continued: 'I won the triple jump in a new Welsh record and came second in the long jump to the late Bryan Woolley, the reigning champion. By absolute coincidence Ron was there and that was how it all started.'

Still only twenty years old, his first major championships were the Commonwealth Games in Perth the following year, where he just missed the bronze medal by a tantalising one centimetre, setting a new Commonwealth and British record of 7.72m to beat Peter O'Connor's British best set sixty-one years previously. Remarkably, all three medallists' performances were wind assisted, but Lynn's jump was wind free, so a puff of wind could have given him a medal. Just imagine, a year earlier, he was second in the Welsh Championships long jump at Maindy, and in Perth he is setting a new Commonwealth and British record just missing-out on a Commonwealth medal!

Not many people predicted a medal in Tokyo, let alone a gold. He went into the competition the fifth best in the world with 8.04m, with Ralph Boston of the USA leading the list with his world record 8.34m. As we now know, Lynn won in a rain-swept stadium jumping 8.07m, with the reigning champion Boston second four centimetres behind, and Russia's Igor Ter-Ovanesyan third another four centimetres back.

The whole of Wales went mad. On his arrival back in Cardiff, it seemed as though everyone had turned up at Cardiff station to meet him. All of the buses and trains out of the city stopped, and traffic around the Central Bus Station came to a halt.

However, Boston had his revenge in Lynn's back yard the following year. Maindy Stadium on North Road, Cardiff was then the Mecca for Welsh athletics. The Welsh Games, started in 1959 to keep alive the spirit of the 1958 Cardiff Empire Games, had been held there each year, and was one of the major events in the British calendar. Cardiff City Council and the Welsh Games Council decided to bring the still world record-holder Boston over from the United States to jump against Lynn to give his adoring Welsh fans a first-hand view of their Welsh idol.

At great expense, Cardiff City Council dug a special long-jump pit in front of the main grandstand to give the event maximum exposure. For a whole hour there were no other events on the programme so that the crowd had no distractions, and Ron Pickering gave a commentary on the event over the public address system. Boston won with a leap of 8.18m which still stands as a Welsh all-comers' record to this day. Lynn says of that day in his autobiography *Lynn Davies: Winner Stakes All*: 'He slaughtered me in front of 10,000 Welshmen... It was so quiet when I jumped... I could hear my own footsteps on the cinders... Everybody was shouting for me as I jumped... But I was absolutely humiliated.'

Bob Beamon put paid to Lynn defending his Olympic title in 1968 with a jump that startled the world. The American soared to 8.90m in the rarefied atmosphere of Mexico City for a world record that was to stand for almost a quarter of a century until beaten in 1991 by another American, Mike Powell with 8.95, which still stands as the world record today. Beamon's jump not only bettered 28ft for the first time, it also breached the 29ft barrier in

Lynn and his wife Meriel
welcome Ralph Boston
to Cardiff for the special
long-jump event at Maindy
Stadium. (Clive Williams)

one go. At the time Lynn said that the mark will stand for 'a thousand years', such was his admiration for the leap.

Lynn's European title came in Budapest in 1966 when he beat his friend and great rival Igor Ter-Ovanesyan by ten centimetres with his last jump. He took the first of his two Commonwealth titles in Jamaica in 1966 and defended the title in Edinburgh in 1970.

As well as his long-jumping exploits, he was an outstanding sprinter being a regular in Britain's sprint relay team. As he said recently following the untimely death of Berwyn Jones: 'I looked up to Berwyn, and when he went north to play rugby league, just before the 1964 Olympics, I took his place in the British relay sprint squad.'

His last major championships were the Munich Olympics – his third appearance in the Games – in 1972 where he was Britain's team captain, narrowly failing to reach the final round.

His last competition before retirement came in the colours of Cardiff AAC, fittingly enough at their 'home' British League fixture in Cwmbran in 1973. By then, the once-proud Maindy Stadium had fallen below international standards, and Cardiff had to use Cwmbran for their British League matches. He ran the last leg of the sprint relay to seal Cardiff's win and lay the foundation for Cardiff's eventual retention of the British League title that year.

After retirement, he was appointed Canada's technical director for athletics in July 1973 and was responsible for their teams at the 1974 Commonwealth Games in Christchurch, New Zealand, the 1975 Pan American Games in Mexico City and the 1976 Montreal Olympics. At the time he said that he didn't know what to expect from the Welsh team and their supporters in New Zealand. He said, 'At least I wore a red blazer, but with a maple leaf and not the three feathers!'

But, along with his wife Meriel, he was feeling homesick, so he returned to Cardiff soon after to a new appointment as technical officer for the Sports Council for Wales. He was soon into his stride, so to speak, back on home soil, and was later appointed British athletics team manager to follow in the footsteps of Cardiff colleague Ted Hopkins who held the position at the 1960 Rome Olympics.

He received a well-deserved CBE for his services to athletics in 2006 to add to his MBE. To this day he is still in the forefront of British athletics as the well-respected president of UK Athletics.

Serious sport always has a funny side, as Mike Walters recalls in *The History of Welsh Athletics*. In an interview, Lynn described an embarrassing incident at the Sports Personality of the Year Awards which he had to miss because of illness. He chuckles, recalling the incident as the person announcing the awards said, 'and the runner-up is that great Welsh long jumper Lynn Davies. Unfortunately she can't be with us tonight because she has got the 'flu.'

In an international career spanning eleven years, he competed in 13 major games, winning seven long-jump medals, setting 17 British and Commonwealth records, 25 Welsh records, winning six AAA (British) and eight Welsh titles. The only Welsh athlete to come anywhere close to this remarkable record is former 110-metre hurdles world record holder Colin Jackson, who still holds the world record for 60-metre hurdles indoors, but never won an Olympic title. Lynn's UK record stood for a phenomenal thirty-three years until beaten by Chris Tomlinson with 8.27m, which still stands today. Superstars like Lynn Davies are a very rare breed.

UWIC
by Russell Holden

Cardiff's rich sporting tradition has been strengthened over the past fifty-five years by its School of Sport based at the University of Wales Institute (UWIC) in Cyncoed. Today it is recognised as a centre of sporting excellence within the United Kingdom, equivalent to that located at the University of Loughborough. Although its name has frequently altered (from Cardiff College of Education, to South Glamorgan Institute of Higher Education, to Cardiff Institute and ultimately to UWIC), the School of Sport's pedigree has remained constant. Over the years, it has developed a national and international reputation for the quality of its sporting, academic and professional consultancy work.

In its early days, the emphasis was on training specialist physical education teachers. Today, there are over seventy academic specialists in sports science and physical education, coupled with a clutch of academics who examine sporting issues in the context of social science, most notably in politics, history and sociology and who teach students at undergraduate and graduate level. They are based in both the School of Sport and the Centre for Humanities located in UWIC's School of Education.

Amongst the many famous figures in post-war Welsh sport, who have either come through the ranks of UWIC or have used the facilities on offer, arguably the best known in the Principality is Lynn Davies. The former 1964 Olympic gold medallist (now president of UK Athletics) has long been associated with the UWIC sporting tradition and remains a key member of staff. He continues to play an important liaison role between UWIC and the Sports Council for Wales.

Amongst its alumni, UWIC boasts six captains of the Welsh rugby team, fourteen British Lions and seven National Rugby Coaches. It has also produced national coaches for athletics, basketball and weight training and technical directors for British gymnastics, English swimming and the England and Wales Cricket Board (ECB). Numerous internationals in football and rugby have emerged, along with international players in minority sports such as squash and netball.

It was during the last fifteen years that the most dramatic expansion took place. An initial £15 million investment in sports facilities helped to treble student numbers and extend the range of courses on offer. In 1996 the Wales Sports Centre for the Disabled opened, providing specialist training facilities for Wales' elite disabled athletes such as Chris Hallam, John Harris and Tanni Grey-Thompson. Three years later, UWIC was approved as an ECB centre of excellence for cricket, joining forces with the universities of Glamorgan and Cardiff to field the Cardiff University Cricket Centre of Excellent team, or Cardiff UCCE.

Since its inception, the Cardiff UCCE has produced several individuals who have played domestic county cricket , most notably Ian Thomas of Glamorgan and Mark Pettini of Essex, whilst opening batsman Stephen Outerbridge has represented his native Bermuda, including several appearances in the 2007 ICC World Cup.

The crowning achievement, however, was the opening of the National Indoor Athletics Centre incorporating a 200-metre track and specialist field event facilities. This has since been utilised for national athletics meetings and as a training facility by elite Welsh athletes including Colin Jackson, Jamie Baulch, Christian Malcolm and Darren Campbell.

For those not destined to compete at the highest level, UWIC's School of Sport has provided varied career opportunities for its graduates in the spheres of teaching, recreational management, commercial leisure promotion, sports management and development, professional coaching, outdoor pursuits, exercise and health promotion and the media.

Finally, as the United Kingdom looks towards the 2012 Olympics, UWIC is playing its part preparing young athletes and their coaching staff through the equipment housed in the Centre for Performance Analysis, which provides access to one of the best videos archives available. This is a far cry from the school's origins at an army barracks in Heath Park with three physical education staff and thirty students.

RONNIE BOON

'Sprinter, cricketer and international rugby player'
by Andrew Hignell

Ronnie Boon was a sportsman for all seasons, excelling in team games as well as individual events in both summer and winter. During his illustrious career, the Barry-born athlete was a Welsh champion sprinter, a county cricketer with Glamorgan, and a Welsh rugby international. Indeed, it was in the red rugby jersey that Ronnie's finest sporting moment came, as in January 1933 the winger helped to lay to rest the Twickenham 'bogey' by scoring all of Wales' points – with a try and a drop goal – in their first ever victory in a rugby international at England's headquarters.

He opened his account shortly after half-time as he picked up a fly-hack from an English boot, and then, from about twenty yards out, he deftly slotted the ball over the crossbar with a sweetly-struck drop kick. Then, later in the half, he was on the receiving end of a pass, after a midfield manoeuvre by the centres Wilf Wooller and Claude Davey, that put Ronnie in the clear, and enough space to score under the posts.

The dapper Boon had a fine record for Cardiff RFC, scoring 76 tries in 98 games, playing mainly on the wing, but he had such outstanding ball-handling abilities and running skills that he could play anywhere in the three-quarter line, or even at stand-off, as he did in the late 1930s for New Brighton. He was also a strong tackler and allied to his whippet-like speed were good kicking skills – as he displayed at Twickenham in 1933. Indeed, Ronnie could punt or drop kick with unerring accuracy, and these all-round talents, allied to his shrewd rugby brain, meant that he was a most dangerous opponent when on the attack, having both the running and kicking skills to convert pressure into points.

Ronnie was a keen student of the game, and recognised that displaying a confident manner was an invaluable psychological weapon. Some interpreted this as arrogance – hence his nickname of 'Cocky' Boon, which probably stemmed from his habit of swanning into the changing room shortly before the kick-off and saying, 'Have no fear, Boon is here!' He was never afraid to try something unorthodox or outrageous, as at Swansea in 1930, when he intercepted on his try line, before running the length of the field to score a try, whilst on another occasion, at Richmond, his fine reading of the game, and the opposition's moves, led to him making three interceptions, and three tries.

Ronnie Boon (seated, third left) with the rest of the Welsh rugby team that defeated England at Twickenham in 1933 (Tim Auty)

Educated at Barry Grammar School, his sporting prowess was evident from an early age, and he progressed from the school team to honours at both rugby and cricket for the Welsh Secondary Schools. His excellence on the athletics track also saw him win junior honours for both the school and Roath Harriers, before in 1929 he won the 220 yards in the Welsh AAA championships.

Ronnie was also a capable cricketer, playing some important innings for both Barry and Cardiff, but it was his lightning-fast speed over the ground, and good ball-handling skills, as much as his capabilities as a batsman, that were responsible for his selection by Glamorgan in the early 1930s. At the time, the county fielded several portly amateurs who, whilst worth their place as strong-armed batsmen, were something of a liability in the field. To compensate for their limitations, Maurice Turnbull, the Glamorgan captain, called up Ronnie, knowing that the aged amateurs could be 'hidden' close to the wicket, whilst the fleet-of-foot youngster patrolled the covers and outfield.

Indeed, even after Ronnie had trained as a games teacher and moved to Scotland, Turnbull remained in touch with the gifted runner, and persuaded him to play for Glamorgan during his school holidays. The rugby selectors from Cardiff and Wales also persuaded Ronnie to travel south from his base in Dunfermline to turn out for club and country and, after events at Twickenham in January 1933, Welsh rugby fans were eternally grateful for his willingness to regularly return home. In all, he played for Cardiff RFC over eleven seasons.

Ronnie continued to teach in Scotland until 1938, before moving to work in London and North Wales. He became an inspector of schools, and also secretary of London Welsh RFC between 1961 and 1969, before returning to his native South Wales, where he was chairman of the South Glamorgan Education Committee.

Ronnie, sitting at a piano, leads a sing-song after a Welsh victory.

THE NATIONAL STADIUM
by Andrew Hignell

The Commonwealth Games in 1958 were one of the most important sporting events ever to take place in Cardiff, but they drew attention to some of the problems with the Arms Park as a modern sporting venue and they therefore heralded the formation of a National Stadium for Wales.

From the 1860s, the Arms Park had simply evolved as a sporting location, and by the 1950s there were too many eggs being forced into one quite small and tight basket in the heart of the Welsh capital. The difficulties were highlighted by the Commonwealth Games, in particular the provision of a running track around the rugby pitch which was used for both the opening and closing ceremonies, and the athletics events. Initially, the athletics events were allocated to Maindy Stadium, but concerns over its size and suitability meant that they were transferred to the Arms Park where, with the agreement of the Cardiff Athletic Club, a running track was laid on top of the greyhound track.

After the Games ended, the arena had to be quickly restored to its normal state, with the greyhound track being reinstated. But in their haste, the workmen forgot to fork and break up the sub-soil which had been intensively packed and rolled so that the athletes could run on a level and firm surface. Other areas had also been compacted, and the net result was that the turf never recovered from the pounding it took. To make matters worse, the early 1960s saw a series of wet winters, with the Taff spilling over and covering the pitch with over two feet of flood water in December 1960, the day after South Africa had beaten Wales 3-0 there.

With the First and Second XVs of Cardiff RFC, plus Cardiff Schools, the Barbarians and Wales all playing a plethora of games and training sessions at the Arms Park, it meant that the ground frequently resembled a muddy quagmire. This caused quite a lot of embarrassment to the Welsh Rugby Union who had long treasured the thought of a stadium of their own to match those at Twickenham and Murrayfield. WRU officials therefore started to think about creating a National Stadium at other locations – two other sites in Cardiff were considered, as well as the ninety acres at Island Farm, near Bridgend. The owners of the latter, Dunraven Estates, offered to sell their land to the

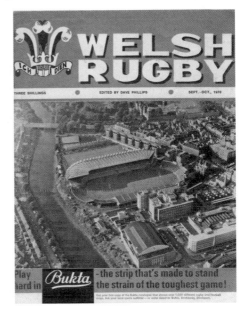

Right: The new National Stadium as seen on the cover of the September/October 1970 issue of *Welsh Rugby.*

Below: The National Stadium, as seen in 1978.

WRU for £19,250 and, with plans for the sale progressing, the city councillors in Cardiff started to ask why the union were thinking of taking international rugby, and the National Stadium, away from the capital city.

The upshot was that an alternative to Island Farm was put forward, with Hubert Johnson, later to be chairman and president of the Athletic Club, and Ken Harris masterminding a scheme whereby the existing Arms Park would be enlarged to a 60,000-seat complex for major games, with a smaller rugby ground for club and junior matches being created on the site of the cricket ground, and the cricket, tennis and hockey sections of the Athletic Club moving to Sophia Gardens.

Difficulties also started to arise over the Island Farm plan with the Ministry of Transport lodging their protest to the scheme as a result of fears of traffic jams on the A48. With the city council supporting the Arms Park redevelopment, and the Athletic Club and Glamorgan CCC agreeing to move, the plans over Island Farm were dropped in 1964, and the creation of the National Stadium was set in motion.

Left: The British Steel Corporation advertises the creation of a National Stadium built entirely from British steel.

Opposite: The hard-working ground staff uncovering the pitch at the National Stadium before a Five Nations match in February 1978. (*Western Mail and Echo*)

On 17 September 1966, Cardiff Cricket Club staged their last fixture on the Arms Park, and the following day, the historic wicket was ploughed up and work began on developing the new stadium for Cardiff RFC. In 1968 the freehold of the Arms Park was bought by the Welsh Rugby Union, and the National Stadium, with its new North Stand – built at a cost of over £1 million – was formally opened on 17 October 1970 by a match between a Welsh XV and a WRU President's XV.

In 1977 the West Stand and West Terrace, costing a further £1 million, were opened, whilst in 1980 the East Terrace, and the Centenary Suite beneath, were completed as the union celebrated its centenary with a special match, watched by Her Majesty The Queen and the Duke of Edinburgh on 29 November between England and Wales against Scotland and Ireland. Four years later, the final parts of the redevelopment scheme were completed – at a cost of £9 million – as the South Stand and enclosure were completed.

On 31 May 1989 the first major soccer match was staged at the National Stadium, as Wales drew 0-0 with West Germany. It followed an agreement between the WRU and the FAW to allow up to six matches per annum to be played at the stadium for the next fifteen years. In 1991 a set of modern floodlights – costing half a million pounds – were installed at the ground, and two years later, the Arms Park played host to the first all-British heavyweight world boxing title contest as Frank Bruno fought Lennox Lewis. The bout – watched by a television audience estimated at two billion – ended in the sixth round as Lewis was declared the winner.

However, the National Stadium will probably be best remembered by sports fans as the ground in Cardiff where Gareth, 'King Barry', Gerald and J.P.R. proudly strutted their stuff in Wales' legendary rugby side of the 1970s – a world-class side worthy of, at long last, a world-class stadium.

DAVID JACOBS

'The first Welsh athlete to win an Olympic gold'
by Clive Williams

David Jacobs is not a name that modern Cardiffians will readily recall. But he was the first Welshman to win an Olympic gold medal in athletics. Born in Cardiff on 30 April 1888, he ran as part of the British 4 x 100-metre relay team in Stockholm in 1912 in a world record 42.4 seconds. Jacobs was also part of the same team (Applegarth, Macintosh, and D'Arcy) which set a new world record for 4 x 110 yards in London in 1913.

He captained the British team in those Stockholm Olympics and also took part in the individual sprints winning both of his heats in the 100 and 200 metres in 10.8 seconds and 23.2 seconds respectively, but was eliminated in the next round of both events. His 10.8 equalled the Olympic record, but several athletes subsequently beat this time later in the Games, though it remained the Welsh record for the next thirty-four years. In the 4 x 100-metre relay, he ran on the third leg and handed over to anchor man Vic D'Arcy five yards in the lead.

A member of the London club Herne Hill Harriers, he was a prolific winner at the Welsh Championships, taking twelve titles in all between 1910 and 1914, and uniquely taking the 100/220/440 yards treble in 1911 at Barry and in 1913 at Newport.

Jacobs placed second in the AAA (British) Championships on two occasions. Firstly in 1912, when he was runner-up in the 220 yards to the legendary Willie Applegarth, who won in 22.0 seconds, and the following year when George Nicol beat him over 440 yards winning in 49.4. Unfortunately, there is no record of the times he recorded in both races, but in 1913, he almost certainly bettered his own Welsh 440 yards record, which at the time stood at 50.4 seconds. His best 220 yards time of 22.0 seconds set in the heats of the 1912 AAA Championships stood as the fastest Welsh 220 yards/200 metres time until equalled by Kenneth Jenkins in the 1938 Paris European Championships

During the Second World War, his parents' house in Denmark Hill, London was severely damaged by German bombs, and he lost virtually all of his medals and trophies, including that Stockholm gold. Although he left Cardiff at the age of eleven, he never forgot his roots and returned to Cardiff whenever possible. He also studied at Cardiff University. Jacobs returned to Wales to live in later life and died in Llandudno in 1976, aged eighty-eight.

Right: Ossie Wheatley.

Opposite: Ossie Wheatley celebrates with Matthew Maynard, the captain of Glamorgan, in 1996 as work starts on the creation of the National Cricket Centre – funded with support from the Sports Council – at the Sophia Gardens cricket ground in 1996.

OSSIE WHEATLEY

'Cricketer, Cardiff businessman and sports administrator'
by Andrew Hignell

An adopted son of the Cardiff area, Ossie Wheatley was Wilf Wooller's successor as captain of Glamorgan between 1961 and 1966, and the Cambridge Blue led the Welsh county in their final ever Championship game at the Arms Park, against Somerset in mid-August 1966. It was not a winning finale for Wheatley and his men, as Somerset won the contest on 16 August by 71 runs. But three years later – at their new home at Sophia Gardens – Ossie was a member of the Glamorgan side, and their opening bowler, which won the Championship crown by beating Worcestershire.

The 1969 season was Ossie's thirteenth and final one as a county cricketer, having started his career in 1957 with Warwickshire. Educated at King Edward's, Birmingham and Caius College, Cambridge, Ossie played for the West Midlands county until 1960, before moving to South Wales at twenty-five to step into Wilf Wooller's shoes. Given Wilf's most distinguished career on the field with Glamorgan, whoever took over from Wooller was always going to have a hard act to follow. But Ossie proved to be a more-than-capable replacement, leading the county with a mix of good humour and debonair authority, and proudly captained them to victory over the 1964 Australians at Swansea.

Ossie's fast medium bowling also added an extra dimension to Glamorgan's attack and, during the early and mid-1960s, he developed a most effective partnership with Jeff Jones, the left-arm pace bowler who went on to win a place in the England attack. A measure of Ossie's success as a new ball bowler can be gauged from the fact that he took over 100 wickets in both of his first two seasons with Glamorgan, whilst in 1968 he took 9-60 against Sussex, and finished on top of the county's averages with 82 victims at 12 apiece – a feat which also saw him become nominated as one of *Wisden*'s Cricketers of the Year.

By this time, Ossie had stepped down as captain – handing over the baton to Tony Lewis – and had started his successful career in advertising, hotel management and the media in South

Wales. Even though he was in semi-retirement when the county won the Championship in 1969 – and hampered by trouble with his Achilles tendon – Ossie played a key role in the county's success. None more so than in the last-ball victory against Essex at Swansea, where his nimble fielding and throw from the third-man boundary led to Essex's last batsman being run out as Glamorgan clinched a nail-biting victory which put them in a virtually unassailable position at the top of the Championship table.

Ossie's final game for the Welsh county came during their celebratory tour of the Caribbean in April 1970, but he has since remained very closely involved with cricket, acting as an England Test selector in 1973 and 1974 and, between 1977 and 1983, serving as chairman of Glamorgan CCC, in addition to chairing the Test and County Cricket Board's cricket committee. Ossie has also served as the chairman of the Sports Council of Wales, and has helped to put back into sport many long hours of work, and successfully shaping the sporting lives of so many people in his adoptive city and country.

TIM ROONEY

'The legendary point-to-point rider'
by Brian Lee

Tim Rooney had his first ride in a point-to-point in 1971, aged fourteen, in a twenty-six-runner race on a five-year-old called Craigeous which was also having its first run. Quite a daunting introduction for both horse and rider and, needless to say, they didn't get very far. Tim, though, was not disheartened, and two years later, he notched up his first win on Roughan Again in the maiden event at the Curre Hunt races – one of 144 winners between the flags, plus a dozen or so under Rules in hunter chases at Cheltenham, Ludlow, Leicester, Hereford and Worcester.

Tim Rooney aboard Devil's Walk. (Brian Lee)

Tim's family had strong connections with the development of sport in Cardiff around the turn of the century. Various family members had close associations with rugby and cricket at the Arms Park. But, as far as Tim was concerned, racing became his life – his uncle was the legendary Irish trainer Willie Rooney, who hailed from the Vale of Glamorgan, who rode over 400 winners in the Emerald Isle, whilst two cousins – Rosemary Stewart and Anne Ferris – were leading riders in Ireland. Two other cousins, Gerry Rooney (sadly killed in a riding accident) and Steve 'Buster' Rooney were both highly successful jockeys, whilst Tim's father, Gus, rode seventy winners himself. Indeed, it was his father who first taught Tim to ride and also impressed upon him the need to have a trade – with his love of horses, it was not surprising that Tim became a farrier.

Tim won the Welsh riders' championship several times and on half a dozen occasions he rode a hat-trick of winners at meetings on horses which a few hours earlier he had plated. In 1979 he also rode a brilliant four-timer at the Gelligaer Farmers point-to-point on Quiz Master, Fitz, Crosstown and Saucy Kiss. The highlight of his career, though, came in 1977 when he won the 1977 Horse and Hound Cup at Stratford, riding Devil's Walk – owned and trained by wholesale fruiterer, Mike Bishop from Caerphilly.

Devil's Walk beat Byzantium, trained by top professional trainer Arthur Stephenson and, as Tim later reflected, 'he never really got going until he had gone three miles and then he would change gear." Not only was he the first Welsh-trained horse to win this prestigious event but, at 50-1, he was also the longest-priced winner in the history of the race and amazingly, earlier that same season, Tim and Devil's Walk had scored at Ludlow at the same odds! The following year, Tim proved that their win had not been a fluke, as Devil's Walk finished a close second, beaten by a neck in a photo finish by the red-hot favourite, Rolls Rambler, saddled by another professional trainer, the immortal Fred Winter.

Another favourite of Tim's was Bill Evans' exuberant front-running Timber Tool, who took his fences fast and low at breakneck speed, and who fought back tenaciously when challenged. Tim teamed up with him to win fifteen races and this son of Wolver Hollow won the 1990

The grandstand at Ely Racecourse, 1898. (Local Studies Department, Cardiff Central Library)

Daily Telegraph Trophy. However, 5 May 1990 saw Tim have the misfortune of badly breaking an ankle and being sidelined for the rest of the season – at the time, he had ridden seventeen winners and besides going great guns in the national men's title, he seemed on course to beat the legendary Cowbridge farmer John Llewellyn's then seasonal Welsh record of twenty wins set in 1988.

A sympathetic horseman, who was never hard on his mounts, Tim had the knack of putting a horse in the right place at the right time in a race. And, if it hadn't been for all the broken collarbones, cracked shoulders, broken fingers and ankle injuries, he would have ridden well over 150 winners. He is still in great demand today at point-to-points as an official and, whereas he used to wear a jockey's skullcap, he now wears a steward's bowler hat!

CARDIFF'S VANISHED RACECOURSES
by Brian Lee

Cardiff's Ely Racecourse, which was the home of the Welsh Grand National from 1895 until 1939, opened in 1855, and was in direct line of descent from the old racecourse at the Great Heath. On the Yates map of 1799, the Heath racecourse shown is almost as big as the two parishes that together made up Cardiff. A local newspaper dated 16 March 1840 informed readers:

Cardiff Racecourse, commonly known as The Great Heath, presented a most animated and very interesting scene, dotted with groups of spectators of various grades... As early as 11 o'clock, the different roads leading from Cardiff to the Heath, and those from

Llandaff and places adjacent, sent forth a bustling spectacle, both of pedestrians and equestrians as well as those fortunate to have gigs and similar vehicles.

One Cardiff rider who had much success over both racecourses was Joseph Butler Jones, of Crwys Farm, now the site of Maindy Barracks, and who was known on the racecourse as 'Joe the Crwys'. He once went through the four-race card at the old Oakgrove Chepstow Racecourse and it was on his grey Cabin Boy that he won the Cardiff Open Hunters Steeplechase, a race from which the Welsh Grand National is derived. During his esteemed race riding career he collected a magnificent array of valuable trophies and he died in Woodville Road, Cardiff, in January 1924 at the age of eighty.

Of all the Welsh racecourses in those days, Ely was the most important, attracting better-class horses and larger attendances. Crowds of 40,000 were not unknown and Aintree Grand National winners such as Emblem, Emblematic, Father O' Flynn, Cloister, Glenside and the immortal Golden Miller all raced there. The famed Anthony and Rees brothers from West Wales and other leading jockeys who graced the Ely turf included Jack Fawcus, Wrexham-born Fulke Walwyn, Bruce Hobbs, Fred Rimell, Danny Morgan and many other top jockeys.

Sadly, however, on 27 April 1939, after Keith Piggott – the father of Lester – had won the Cardiff Club Juvenile Handicap Hurdle on a horse called Grasshopper, Ely Racecourse closed its gates for ever. In 1953 the defunct racecourse was officially opened as Cardiff's biggest recreation centre with facilities for playing rugby, soccer, hockey, cricket and baseball. The old grandstand, which had served as a constant reminder of the great days of Ely racecourse, was pulled down in 1961.

Unfortunately for the capital city of Wales, the plans drawn up by the Jockey Club to lay out a new racecourse across the Sophia Gardens Recreation Field and Pontcanna Field in 1953 were turned down by the city fathers.

JOE ERSKINE

'Cardiff's champion boxer'
by Gareth Jones

Lightning may not strike twice in the same place, but genius does. That's the only explanation for the events in Angelina Street, in the heart of Tiger Bay, in 1934. Within six months, two legends – and Cardiff sporting greats – were born: at no.11 Joseph William Richard Erskine came into this world; six months later, at no.7, rugby league's incomparable Billy Boston arrived.

Erskine was always destined to hit the heights. After all, his father, Johnny, a noted booth fighter, took one look at him and cried, 'It's a boy – and he's going to be British champion!' Boxing was in the blood – even great-aunt Ann Moore was a feared bare-knuckle brawler – and Nana Erskine bought young Joe his first gloves when he was four. At eleven, and weighing just 5st 6lbs, the lad was taken to the Victoria Park club and the trophies began to accumulate. Not just for boxing: Joe picked up a Boys Clubs of Wales cap and played for Cardiff Youth at rugby and he also shone at cricket and swimming. But a broken arm on the rugby field prompted him to concentrate on the ring. The decision was rewarded with a profusion of junior titles, leading to the ABA heavyweight crown in 1953 and an inevitable professional career.

His first nineteen months as a pro brought 25 contests, with a single draw the only blemish, and Erskine was being talked of as championship material. He was matched in a British title eliminator at Harringay with the day's other leading prospect, a tram-driver's son from London, Henry Cooper. The Bellingham boy led 2-1 from their three amateur meetings, but was never in serious contention and the Welshman's hand was raised at the bell. For the first time Joe had to box with the distraction of a cut eyebrow. It was far from the last.

Next up was the 'Macsglas Marciano', Dick Richardson, with 35,000 enraptured fans at Maindy Stadium watching a titanic tussle before Joe emerged with the verdict – but only after the Newport milkman had floored him for the first time in his life. The victor was back at the same arena three months later, in August 1956, to face former holder Johnny Williams for the vacant British title. Barmouth-born Williams was game, but could not overcome the seven-year age difference, and a points decision brought Joe the Lonsdale Belt. The BBC Wales Sports Personality of the Year title for 1956 soon followed. But there was a dark shadow looming, in the shape of Nino Valdes, the Cuban who had already stopped both Cockell and Richardson. Erskine, giving away height and reach, was down twice and beaten after just two minutes and three seconds.

After one rehabilitation win, Joe was ready for his first challenger: that man Cooper. Erskine did just enough to secure a verdict, greeted with some disapproval among the Harringay faithful. In November 1957, a slimmer Joe added the Empire championship with a points win over dangerous Jamaican Joe Bygraves at Leicester's Granby Halls, and the boys from the Bay chanted 'Erskine! Erskine! Erskine!' throughout the last round – 'in foreign fashion', as a contemporary report put it.

Three months later, the Welshman tried for a third title, challenging Ingemar Johansson for the European honour in Gothenburg. Hampered by a lack of sparring and a feud between his father and his manager, Erskine had no answer to the Swede's wrecking-ball power and his face was grotesquely swollen by the time his handlers rescued him after thirteen rounds.

A further painful encounter awaited Erskine back in Britain. Brian London, son of a British and Empire champion, was out to regain the titles for the family. At London's White City, in June 1958, his dream came true – but its fulfilment depended on a clash of heads in the seventh round. The collision split Joe's left eyebrow and he had to protect the wound, ceding the initiative to the challenger. He was decked twice and counted out in the eighth, a champion no more.

Erskine, after plastic surgery to combat the cuts, fought his way back with points wins against Willie Pastrano, a consummate ring artist from New Orleans, and Richardson, seen off in front of 12,000 rain-drenched Welshmen at Porthcawl. It was time for another shot at 'Enery, who had dethroned London. But the tide in their rivalry was on the turn. Badly hurt by a punch after the bell to end the fifth, the Cardiffian was eventually knocked out in the twelfth, arched across the bottom rope, his heels on the canvas inside the ring, his head and arms on the apron.

Official protests brought a rematch, but it was an anti-climax. Erskine suffered an eye injury in the third, it closed dramatically in the fifth, when Cooper compassionately held back the right Joe would never have seen, and the Welshman retired at the end of the round.

The old antagonists were to meet just once more. A below-par champion was booed when facial damage yet again halted Erskine in nine rounds at Nottingham Ice Stadium. The Cardiffian had been dominant until his left eye was split, and he was insistent that he would win next time.

There was no next time. Joe never again boxed for a title. In October 1964, he faced the 'Blond Bomber', Billy Walker, a popular Londoner of no great ability but a sustained aggression that convinced referee Bill Williams in a close contest. Before the bout, the Welshman had vowed, 'If I can't beat Walker, I'll feel so bad I'll retire.' He kept his word. At his best, Erskine was unsurpassed for skill, subtlety and sleight of fist; one observer described an opponent as 'like a man trying to catch a moonbeam with tweezers'. It's not a bad epitaph.

Rhys Gabe.

RHYS GABE

'The Welshman who prevented that try!'
by Gwyn Prescott

To have – in Bleddyn Williams and Jack Matthews – one of the greatest centre partnerships ever to have graced the game would be enough to satisfy any rugby club. But Cardiff RFC can lay claim to another equally gifted world-class centre pairing, from an earlier era, in Gwyn Nicholls and Rhys Gabe.

Unlike Nicholls, however, Gabe was not a product of local club rugby. He was born in Carmarthenshire in 1880 and it was with his village team, Llangennech, that he came to the attention of rugby's elite, making his debut at centre for Llanelli at a youthful seventeen. Within three years, he had won the first of his 24 caps, playing on the wing in the victory over Ireland in March 1901.

A few months later, Rhys moved to London to begin a teacher training course at Borough Road College and there he joined London Welsh. The 'Exiles' already possessed two fine wings in Willie Llewellyn and Teddy Morgan, so he was persuaded to play at centre. This move proved so successful that he was partnered with Gwyn Nicholls for the 1902 match against England. With Llewellyn and Morgan also selected on the wings, this combination became arguably the most brilliant three-quarter line ever to represent Wales. Gabe made a significant contribution to that 1901/02 Triple Crown team, scoring vital tries against England and Scotland and displaying unyielding defence against Ireland.

Writing in 1948 about the 'superlative' players he had seen in his sixty years as a rugby correspondent, W.J. Townsend Collins argued that Nicholls and Gabe were the best centre combination ever to play for Wales. Of Rhys Gabe, he tells us that he ran very straight in attack and possessed a quick deceptive swerve. A sound tackler, he himself was difficult to stop, presenting 'an undue proportion of elbows and knees' to his opponents. In his later career, his passing skills were honed to perfection. Collins was clearly a great admirer of Gabe whom he summed up as 'one of the greatest exponents of centre play'.

Rhys Gabe's connection with Cardiff began during 1902/03, when he took up a teaching appointment at Howard Gardens School. He was to remain a resident of the city for the rest of his life. In that first season, he played for the club only when not required by Llanelli, but from 1903/04 onwards he turned out regularly for the Blue and Blacks. Rhys won the majority of his Welsh caps – 17 – as a Cardiff player and represented the club in the Welsh Triple Crown teams of 1904/05 and 1907/08. In all, he played 115 times for Cardiff over eight seasons. He scored a try in the astonishing 17-0 victory over the Springboks in January 1907 and he also captained the club successfully in 1907/08, when only four matches ended in defeat.

During the summer of 1904, he was selected, along with teammate Percy Bush, for the British Lions' tour to Australasia. A member of a highly praised, predominantly Welsh three-quarter line, Rhys played in all three victories over Australia and in the defeat in the single Test with New Zealand.

Rhys Gabe is probably best remembered today, however, for his contribution to the historic Welsh victory over New Zealand in 1905, for he was crucially involved in the two most important incidents in the game. With one of his characteristic perfectly judged passes, it was he who put Teddy Morgan clear to score the only try of the game. Then later, displaying the all-round skills for which he was famous, it was also Gabe who, with Morgan, tackled Deans just short of the Welsh goal line. When Deans then tried (illegally) to struggle out of the Cardiff centre's tackle, in an attempt to ground the ball across the line, Gabe became aware that the All Black could not have scored. He remained firmly convinced about this for the rest of his life. Despite later claims to the contrary, Gabe's account is now the generally accepted version of what happened in perhaps the most controversial incident in the history of international rugby.

Rhys Gabe was also a fine club cricketer who occasionally turned out for Glamorgan. He captained Radyr Golf Club and later joined Cardiff Golf Club where he still played well into his eighties. One of the last two survivors of the 1905 match, he died in 1967, acclaimed throughout the rugby world as one of the game's all-time greats.

JOHN TOSHACK

'Star striker with the Bluebirds and a favourite with the Kop'
Andrew Hignell

Lexicographers currently define the word 'tosh' as 'complete rubbish' and 'utterly worthless'. Quite the opposite of the feelings that so many gleeful schoolboys in Cardiff had back in the late 1960s when chattering away about 'Tosh', the Bluebirds' centre forward, or trying to emulate in the city's playgrounds the goal-scoring ability of the giant striker who, at the age of twenty-one, was transferred from Cardiff City to Liverpool in November 1970 for the small matter of £110,000.

By the time he swapped Ninian Park for Anfield, Tosh had scored 100 goals in over 200 League appearances for Cardiff City, with the 6ft striker from Canton combining consummate technique with devastating power. He had become a football nut right from his earliest days at Radnor Road Junior School, avidly following the fortunes of Cardiff City, as well as Manchester United – so much so that the tragic events in Munich in 1958 prompted the nine-year-old to write to manager Matt Busby wishing him a speedy recovery after the air crash.

However, Tosh's heart at the time lay with the Bluebirds and, as he wrote in his autobiography, published in 1982:

> I had decided that one day I would play for Cardiff City, and as I stood behind the goal down at the Grange End, I began to feel a special affinity for my home town club. I remember being among 55,000 people and watching Graham Moore score the goal that took Cardiff up to the First Division in 1960.

From Radnor Road, he then passed his exams and went to Canton High School, where rugby was the major winter sport rather than football. For the next few years, he duly spent his Saturday mornings playing fly-half for the Canton school team, before playing at centre forward for a side called Pegasus in the afternoons in the local leagues. His outstanding goal-scoring record for Pegasus led to his selection for the Cardiff Schools team, and then the Welsh Schoolboys, for whom he struck a hat-trick in their 3-0 victory over Ireland at the Vetch Field

John Toshack.

His abilities in front of goal also attracted the attention of several Football League scouts, and in 1965/66 he went up to White Hart Lane for a short trial with Tottenham Hotspur. Offers also came from Leeds United and Wolverhampton Wanderers, but Tosh decided to sign amateur forms with Cardiff City whilst completing his school exams, before signing on as an apprentice professional in June 1965.

His first appearance, and his first goal, came on his debut in November 1965, as the sixteen-year-old came off the substitutes' bench and scored the final goal in the 3-1 home victory over Leyton Orient. At the time, he was the youngest ever player to appear for the City, and his appearance resulted from a knee injury to Graham Coldrick just twenty minutes into the game.

A week later, the Welsh Schoolboy international was on the scoresheet again as he scored twice in the 4-3 win at Middlesbrough and, in the course of the next five seasons, the tall youngster showed that he possessed both the strength and the skill needed in regularly finding the net. In January 1968 he recorded his first hat-trick for the Bluebirds as they beat Ebbw Vale 8-0 in the Welsh Cup, followed two seasons later by his first League hat-trick in the 4-2 home win over Queen's Park Rangers. Together with Brian Clark, he formed a potent strike force that saw Tosh score no less than 31 goals in the 1968/69 season.

By this time, he had also won the first of 40 Welsh caps, and his good showing on the international stage, allied to his outstanding record as a goal scorer for Cardiff City, made him one of the hottest properties outside the First Division. Some leading English clubs showed an interest in signing Tosh, with Fulham – managed then by Bobby Robson – making an offer of £70,000 for his services in 1969. Tosh turned down the offer feeling that he was not then ready for the First Division or a life in London. But the following November, Liverpool made a successful approach to Toshack and, with the approval of Jimmy Scoular, the City manager, the striker swapped a blue shirt for a red one, just a week after having scored his 100th goal for the City during their European Cup tie with Nantes.

As Tosh later recalled:

At the time there were a lot of rumours going around that Liverpool were interested in me. I knew that Geoff Twentyman had been to watch me play a few times and I think Liverpool were suffering a bit of an injury crisis at the time, with strikers Alun Evans and Bobby Graham both out injured. I played for Cardiff at QPR on the Saturday and the following morning Jimmy Scoular came up to my house in Wenvoe to explain that Cardiff had accepted a big offer from Liverpool for me… I felt that the time was right for me to move on. I was grateful to Cardiff City for giving me the chance in the game, and to Jimmy Scoular who always treated me fairly... It was a lot of money in those days, and I remember getting off the train at Lime Street station with my wife, Sue, to meet Bill Shankly. The reception we received was fantastic and he took us off for a meal at his favourite restaurant. It was all done and dusted very quickly. I didn't need much persuading and I signed almost straight away.

Three days later, Toshack made his Liverpool debut in their goalless draw with Coventry City and a week later, at Anfield, he displayed his goal-scoring abilities in a thrilling Merseyside derby against Everton, which saw Liverpool come back from a 2-0 deficit early in the second half. Steve Heighway started the fightback with a goal in the sixty-ninth minute, and then seven minutes later Tosh slotted one into the back of the net to the delight of the Kop, who then nearly lifted the roof off the grandstand, as Chris Lawler prodded home the winner in the eighty-fourth minute.

Shankly's signing in August 1971 of Kevin Keegan, then a little-known centre forward with Scunthorpe United, was another major milestone in Toshack's career, as the curly-haired striker teamed up with the 6ft Welshman to form as effective a partnership as any other pair of strikers playing in the League at that time. Their understanding was almost telepathic, with Tosh winning almost everything in the air, and Keegan deftly finishing off these knock downs. Remarkably, the pair never spent hours on the training ground working at their combined skills. Tosh later confessed:

> We just hit it off. We just complemented each other. I think defenders knew what we were trying to do, but they couldn't stop it. When a ball was in flight I would see Kevin out of the corner of my eye, and knew exactly where he would be. For his part, he knew where I would put it, and we had six great years together.

In the minds of the Anfield faithful, Toshack and Keegan were as successful a partnership as comedians Morecambe and Wise, or TV cops Starsky and Hutch, and *Shoot* magazine even went as far as likening them to comic book heroes Batman and Robin, and got Liverpool's 'Deadly Duo' to dress up as the pair of crimebusters!

During his time at Anfield, Toshack scored 75 goals in 162 League appearances and helped Liverpool to win the Football Championship in 1972/73, 1975/76 and 1976/77, as well as lifting the FA Cup in 1973/74 and the UEFA Cup in both 1972/73 and 1975/76. It was a purple patch in the history of the famous Merseyside club, which owed much to the power and aerial mastery of Toshack, the fast and skilful talents of Keegan, and the managerial skills of the immortal Shankly. Their collective abilities were amply demonstrated in the first leg of the UEFA Cup final in 1972/73, as Liverpool defeated Borussia Moenchengladbach at Anfield, with Tosh's strength and dominance in the air proving too much for the highly respected West German defence. Two of the Welshman's headers set up Keegan for a brace of goals as Liverpool won 3-0. Although they lost the second leg 2-0 in the away leg, it was enough for a 3-2 win on aggregate and Liverpool's first ever European title.

The following season, Liverpool failed to secure back-to-back championship titles, as they finished as runners-up to Leeds United. It was a season when Tosh was hampered by injuries and a loss of form but, as the Merseyside club progressed to the final of the FA Cup, he regained form and got the nod, ahead of Phil Boersma, to line up in the final at Wembley against Newcastle United. He justified his selection as he helped to set up their second goal, heading on for Steve Heighway, as Liverpool went on to win 3-0 and lift the famous trophy for only the second time in their eighty-two-year history.

The following year he lost his place in the team, as he was bedevilled again by a thigh injury as well as poor form. With his place no longer guaranteed in the Liverpool line-up, Tosh began to think about the future. He agreed a move to Leicester, but nothing happened as he failed the medical. But, as it turned out, his struggles with these ailments proved to be another important stage in the Cardiffian's career. As he later recalled:

'Tosh' celebrates another goal at Ninian Park. (Richard Shepherd)

> My chronic thigh injury meant that I couldn't get about the pitch like I had done previously. It meant that I had to look at the game in a more tactical way, and this helped me enormously the following season, and when I made my move into management later on.

Indeed, 1975/76 was his most productive season with Liverpool as, free from injury, he scored 16 times in 35 League appearances, including hat-tricks against both Aston Villa and West Ham United. He also scored in the vital last match of the season, as a 3-1 victory at Wolves clinched the First Division title. The following year, the Reds chased an historic treble, as they sought to win the Championship again, and lift both the FA and UEFA Cups. To their credit, they achieved two of these goals, with Manchester United ending their dreams of the treble winning 2-1 at Wembley.

The 1976/77 season was bittersweet for Toshack, as he limped off in the second half of the European Cup quarter-final against French Champions St Etienne. The injury to his Achilles tendon meant that he missed the rest of the season, and a third championship medal in five seasons was small comfort as others started to cement their place in the Liverpool line-up. It was the beginning of the end for both Tosh and his goal-scoring partner who had so thrilled the Kop and terrorised so many defences across England and Europe. During the summer, Keegan was sold to SV Hamburg, and with Tosh well down the pecking order to play alongside the new striker, Kenny Dalglish, he embarked on his new career in football management, hoping to follow in the footsteps of his mentors Bill Shankly and Bob Paisley.

Tosh met with immediate success in his new role as, after being granted a free transfer to join Swansea City as their player-manager in 1978, he oversaw a meteoric rise for the Vetch Field club as they rose up from the Fourth Division to the First, and, for a few games into the 1981/82 season, they were top of the table. After hanging up his boots in 1983, Toshack left Swansea the following season, and then spent time managing clubs in Portugal, Spain, France and Turkey. Amongst his greatest achievements was steering Real Madrid to the La Liga title in 1990, as well as successful spells with Real Sociedad, including a period when the Basque side won the Spanish Cup.

After this success in the super-charged atmosphere of European club football, he was appointed manager of Wales in 1994 in the aftermath of the departure of Terry Yorath, another

John Toshack, scoring against Coventry in 1967. (Richard Shepherd)

Cardiff sporting great. Tosh had intended to combine the work with his duties as manager of Real Sociedad, but he only spent forty-one days in the post, resigning after a 3-1 defeat to Norway. Ten years later, things had improved, especially off the field, and Tosh returned to the post in November 2004, helping to mastermind the emergence of a new generation of Welsh soccer talent.

TIM BENJAMIN

'The emerging star of Welsh athletics'
by Clive Williams

It was great news for Welsh athletics fans when Tim announced in 2006 that he was returning to Cardiff to live and train with Colin Jackson's Leckwith Stadium group. This news came fresh from his silver medal (along with Cardiff clubmate Rhys Williams) in the 4 x 400 metres at the European Championships in Gothenburg.

Born in Cardiff in May 1982, and a former pupil at Radyr Comprehensive School, Tim is a product of Cardiff AAC and has won Welsh titles in virtually all of the junior age groups of Welsh athletics, as well as at UK level.

Initially he was a 100-metre runner, but progressed first to 200 metres and then 400 metres when he found that he was not as fast as he thought at the shorter sprint. He first realised that he could run quickly when playing football for Peterston-Super-Ely Primary School, Cardiff. When he got his first pair of spikes as an eleven-year-old, there was no turning back, although he was a high-quality roller-hockey player before finally deciding on athletics.

Prior to the 2007 summer season, Tim had amassed a total of eleven medals at international championships, but injuries have so far prevented him from achieving his full potential. He met with severe problems when an injection to alleviate back and groin pain went wrong in April 2005, and he has suffered many other ailments, mostly hamstring injuries, but now happily these are all behind him as he looks forward to the Beijing Olympics in 2008.

He first burst onto the international scene in 1999, when he won the inaugural World Youth 200-metre title in Bydgoscz, Poland, in a UK Under-17 record of 20.72, a time that ranked him the ninth fastest in Britain – a remarkable performance for a seventeen-year-old. Later in the year, he took the silver in the 200 metres in the European Junior Championships in Latvia, in a wind-assisted 20.60 seconds. His only other individual gold medal so far has come in the European Junior Championships in Grosseto, Italy, in 2001 when he won the 400 metres in a personal-best 46.43. He improved this time to 46.10 in the Edinburgh International Games some weeks later to end his first season as a 400-metre runner as fifth fastest Briton, just five hundredths of a second ahead of Cardiff clubmate Jamie Baulch.

Tim will be the first to admit that he has so far failed to deliver in the major senior championships, with injuries getting in the way of success. His first major senior championship was the 2002 Commonwealth Games in Manchester, where he ran a magnificent first leg to help set up the 4 x 400-metre silver medal for Wales. But in the individual event he went out in the semi-finals. Earlier in the year he won the first of his four senior AAA (British) titles, producing a powerful finish to win in a personal best time of 45.73.

He took a bronze medal with the British 4 x 400-metre team at the 2003 World Indoor Championships in Birmingham, but had keyhole surgery to remove a tendon in his knee at the end of the year. This seemed to work as he returned to establish himself as Britain's top 400-metre runner in 2004, winning the European Cup in 45.37, the AAA title in 45.58 and setting a personal best of 45.04 for third at the London Grand Prix before making the Olympic semi-final in Athens.

In 2005, everything came together, and in a brilliant race in the London Grand Prix meeting at Crystal Palace, he beat the 2004 Olympic champion Jeremy Wariner and a multi-talented field to shatter his personal best with 44.75 secs. He clipped this by a further hundredth when finishing second to Jamaica's Brandon Simpson at the Brussels Grand Prix a month later, effectively making him the top European of the year. At the Helsinki World Championships in August, he came an excellent fifth for the highest placing of a British male at the Championships and then ran the first leg for the British 4 x 400-metre team which just missed out on the bronze medals by three-quarters of a second.

He then ended the 2005 season in brilliant style further reducing his best to 44.56 – the sixth fastest time ever recorded by a UK athlete – to finish second in the World Athletics final in Monaco behind Tyree Washington of the USA.

Following a winter frustrated by further injury, he was bitterly disappointed to have to withdraw from the Welsh 2006 Commonwealth Games team in Melbourne. But he returned to form to run an outstanding final leg to secure the silver medals for Britain in Gothenburg, after finishing sixth in the individual event. Earlier in the season he took the AAA title for the third successive year.

There is no doubt that Tim's best is still to come, and his return to Wales to train with a group including fellow European 4 x 400 medallist and teammate Rhys Williams will be the shot in the arm he requires to fulfil his true potential.

REX WILLIS

'Cliff Morgan's better half'
by Gwyn Prescott

To be described by one of the greatest ever exponents of outside half play as an 'ideal partner – brave, resourceful and unselfish' is praise indeed. But this is how Cliff Morgan wrote of the Cardiff and Wales scrum-half Rex Willis, whom he always refers to as his 'better half'. Cliff

Rex Willis and Cliff Morgan.

was well placed to know, as they played at half-back together for Wales on 14 occasions – a record at the time.

A courageous and rugged scrum-half, Rex knew precisely when to pass and when to retain the ball, even if it meant taking the punishment himself. He never shirked from this – Cliff confirmed that he always protected his outside half and wouldn't pass just to get himself out of trouble – particularly when confronted with bad ball from his forwards. When Rex did release the ball, his lengthy passes were immaculate and their accuracy enabled his partners to run on to the ball at full speed. Also superb in defence, he was fearless in falling on the ball.

Rex Willis was born in Ystrad Rhondda in 1924 and privately educated at Llandaff Cathedral School and Pangbourne College in Berkshire. After serving in the Royal Navy, when he commanded an invasion landing craft, he returned to Wales and joined Llandaff RFC. Unable to win a place as a centre, he switched to scrum-half and, from then on, he never looked back. He joined Cardiff in 1947, where he understudied Haydn Tanner for two seasons. It was whilst playing for the reserve XV that he first teamed up with Cliff Morgan and this would eventually blossom into one of the classic Welsh half-back partnerships. To Cliff, this public-school-educated businessman and cinema proprietor was an exciting personality. In his autobiography he writes: 'He was posh, drove fast cars and had long hair, and looked an unlikely scrum-half.'

After Tanner retired, Cardiff were in the extremely fortunate position of having a replacement who was of a similar calibre: there were even some who dared to suggest that Rex Willis was the better all-round player. During his first full season with Cardiff, Rex's partner was the brilliant Billy Cleaver. The Welsh selectors failed to include Rex in any of the three trials but when they chose Cleaver at outside half for the England international in 1950, they decided to opt for a club partnership and so Willis was capped before taking part in a trial. His international debut was a memorable one, as Wales won at Twickenham for only the second time since 1910. They went on to win the first Triple Crown and first Grand Slam since 1911 and Willis was a prominent member of the side, protecting his outside half well from the attentions of the powerful Scottish and Irish back rows. After merely one season of

Rex Willis (front row, centre with the ball) leads the Barbarians against New Zealand at the Arms Park in 1954. Also in the Barbarians squad were Sid Judd (standing behind Willis) and Cliff Morgan (sitting on the ground, second from the right). (John Billot)

international rugby, Rex was then selected for the 1950 British Lions tour to New Zealand and Australia. It had been a meteoric rise from struggling to get into the Llandaff midfield only four years earlier.

It would be no easy task for Rex to challenge for a Test place, however, as the Lions took three scrum-halves. The more experienced Gus Black and Gordon Rimmer were tried in the first three Tests but eventually Rex established himself as the first choice and he was selected for the last three internationals and he completed the tour by playing in more matches than either of his two teammates. The final New Zealand Test was lost 8-11, but the two Tests against Australia ended in comfortable victories. Rex's partner in these matches was Ireland's Jackie Kyle, regarded as the finest fly-half of the era.

In 1951/52, Wales again achieved the Grand Slam but Rex only played in the first two games. Early in the second half against Scotland, he fractured his jaw in two places but, even though scrum-half is hardly a hiding place, he displayed the courageousness for which he was renowned by refusing to leave he field. This, of course, was in those far-off days before substitutions were allowed.

After a season plagued by injuries, when he took part in only 12 matches in his year as club captain, Willis returned in 1953/54 to contribute heroically to the historic victories by both Cardiff and Wales over the All Blacks and he was rewarded with the captaincy of the Barbarians against the tourists. The following season, he captained Wales and was then invited to tour with the Lions again, this time to South Africa. It was rumoured that, had he been able to accept, he might have been appointed tour captain, an honour which, up to then, had never been offered to a Welshman.

He gave up the game in 1956 but, having played for Cardiff against South Africa and New Zealand, he decided to make a comeback in 1957/58 to play for his club against Australia. He celebrated his final season with another victory over a major touring side and, when he retired, this bravest of scrum-halves had played in over 200 matches for his club and in 21 internationals for Wales.

Don Skene. (Brinley Matthews)

DON SKENE

'Cardiff's cycling legend'
by Gwyn Prescott

Little did the spectators realise, at the very first cycling race ever held at the new Maindy Stadium in 1951, that there was a Cardiff youngster in the field who would take an Empire and Commonwealth Games medal on the very same track only seven years later.

Don Skene was born in Splott in 1936 and, at fifteen, he was first introduced to the sport which was to change his life when he joined the Tigers Cycling Club and began participating in time trials and races at Maindy. Showing great promise, he was soon competing successfully throughout Wales and England. But Don was more than a promising young cyclist: he was also a budding entrepreneur. For, when aged only sixteen years, he opened a small business selling and repairing cycles and, since 1952, his shop in Newport Road, Rumney has been a Cardiff landmark. He ran Don Skene Cycles for over fifty years before eventually handing it over in 2004 to his daughter and son.

In 1954 he was selected to represent Wales in the Empire and Commonwealth Games in Vancouver when he took the bronze in the ten-mile track event. At just eighteen, he became the Games' youngest ever cycling medallist. Four years later, the Games came to Cardiff and, on his home track, Don won bronze again, over the same distance. The significance to Welsh sport of this double achievement should not be underestimated. Not only had no Welshman ever previously won a Commonwealth Games cycling medal, but it would be another forty-four years before Wales would win a medal again in a men's individual cycling event.

During the 1950s and early 1960s, Don – as a member of the Cardiff Byways Club – was one of Britain's most successful cyclists. He won many Welsh championships and raced on numerous occasions for Great Britain in both long and short tours to Europe, South Africa and South America. He won the British Ten Mile Championship and was awarded British

J.H. Edwards, J.C. Luke, R.T. Luke and D.C. Edwards competing in the coxless fours at the 1962 Empire Games in Perth. (Brinley Matthews)

cycling's most prestigious trophy as the Best All Rounder on the track. He broke many track records both here and abroad and, remarkably, he held the Maindy flying one-lap amateur record for forty-four years until it was eventually beaten in 2002.

His last appearance in the Commonwealth Games was in 1962 at Perth, Australia, where he realistically hoped to improve on his previous medal performances but, unfortunately, when poised to take the gold, he was knocked off his bike. After eleven highly successful years in the sport, Don then decided to retire to concentrate on running his business. An active cyclist in his seventies, Don now spends most of the year living in central Florida, where he still devotes time to promoting the sport he loves by helping local youngsters into cycling.

ROWING ON THE TAFF
by Andrew Hignell

The thought that sporting contests would one day take place on the River Taff must have been a million miles away from the minds of the many boatmen and sailors who journeyed up and down the river in the early nineteenth century. To them, the Taff was just the best route south from the valleys, to the growing docks at Cardiff, the Severn Estuary, and to fame and fortune beyond.

Everything changed following the creation of railway lines throughout the valleys from the mid-nineteenth century onwards. With a faster and alternative means of transporting goods and minerals, the volume of traffic using the river decreased sharply and, with the construction of several weirs, the stretch of the Taff adjacent to Llandaff Bridge became increasingly used for rowing.

The Taff Rowing Club was formed in 1879, followed five years later by the Cardiff Rowing Club and, by the turn of the century, each club had flourishing boathouses at Llandaff. But disaster struck after the Second World War when the returning members of the two clubs found their boathouses burnt out and in disrepair. But out of the ashes rose a phoenix in the shape of an amalgam between the two clubs, with the newly constituted Llandaff Rowing Club rebuilding the clubhouses and restoring the boats which had been washed up on the estuary mud flats.

A measure of the success of the new club's endeavours was that they were able to hold their first regatta in 1947 and, when Cardiff hosted the Empire Games in 1958, several of Llandaff's senior members officiated at the rowing events. It was not long either before some of the club's members excelled in major events, with the Luke twins reaching the trials for the paired oared events in the 1960 Olympics and, together with the Edwards brothers, winning the silver medal in the coxless fours at the 1962 Empire Games in Perth, Western Australia.

Further honours have been won by Charlie Wiggin, most notably in the 1980 Moscow Olympics when he won a bronze medal in the coxless pairs. Whilst in recent years, David and Robert Luke have won events at the Henley Regatta, in addition to representing Great Britain at the World Championships.

BERNIE PLAIN

'The stalwart Cardiff athlete'
by Brian Lee

Bernie Plain had a long and successful athletics career. As well as representing Wales on the track, cross-country and road he ran for Great Britain for nine years, competing in one European and two Commonwealth Games. At the peak of his career he was one of the top three British distance runners and was highly thought of by his fellow athletes for being able to run 5,000 metres, 10,000 metres and the marathon at international standard.

A runners' runner, Bernie first represented his country in the 1965 World Cross-Country Championships and won his first senior Welsh title in the 5,000 metres in 1968. The following year he won both the 5,000-metre and 10,000-metre national titles, with the 10,000-metre crown coming his way again in 1970. In 1973 he finished fourth in the Boston Marathon and nineteenth in the New York Marathon and, on a rain-soaked Bristol track that year, set a British record of 1:40:34.6 for 20 miles, beating Jim Alder's record by 15.4 seconds, and was not far off the world mark.

In 1973 he was third in the AAA 10,000-metre championship behind Dave Bedford's world record run. 'I will never forget taking part in that race – it was a wonderful occasion,' he remarked. He ran his best marathon time of 2:14:56, setting a Welsh record when finishing seventh in the 1974 Christchurch Commonwealth Games and it should be noted that the winner Ian Thompson set a UK record in this race. Later that year, in the European Championships marathon, held on a sweltering hot day in Rome and not enjoying one of his better days, Bernie was just beaten for the bronze medal by the great Belgian runner Gaston Roelands. The race was won by the then unbeatable Ian Thompson from the German Eckhard Lesse, whom Bernie had defeated previously. 'I went through a bad patch, but when I got going again I finished much faster than the second and third runners,' Bernie recalled.

Bernie, who had been the first British runner home – he finished second to Akio Usami – in the famous Polytechnic Marathon, which doubled as the European trial race in 1974, went on to win this prestigious event in 1976 and again in 1981 when he was aged forty-two. His Welsh record for 10,000 metres stood for twenty years and, strangely enough, he is still the holder of the AAA 10-mile track championship. How come, when he won the event back in 1973, clocking 48:25.8? Well, the reason is that the event hasn't been held since!

Unlike many of today's international athletes, Bernie held a full-time job as sports officer at Cardiff's Maindy Stadium and he sacrificed a professional career for the honour of competing

Bernie Plain. (*Western Mail and Echo*)

for his country. Bernie is quick to point out that, if it hadn't been for the support of his wife Thelma, a physical education teacher, he would not have been able to fulfil his dreams.

A member of Birchgrove Harriers, before the club amalgamated with Roath Harriers to become Cardiff AAC in 1968, Bernie made seven appearances for Wales in the Senior International Cross-Country Championship between 1969 and 1977. He became the first Cardiff AAC runner to win the Welsh Senior Cross-Country Championship in 1976 and his athletics career took him around the world representing Great Britain in Europe, America and Africa.

In 1975, he captained his country in the World Cross-Country Championships in Rabat and the same year was awarded the AAA's gold medal for outstanding performances in the 10,000-metre event. Despite work and running commitments, he helped organise the first *Western Mail* Cardiff Marathon in 1981 and won the event on the first three occasions it was held. His passion for running – he still runs five or six days a week – still continues and in 1986 he won the British National Veterans 10,000-metre title. A life member of Cardiff AAC, Bernie has been president of the club, a vice-president of both the Welsh Vets Association and the Welsh Masters Committee, and a member of the Welsh Cross-Country Committee. He has coached athletes at junior and senior level and is not too proud to act as a marshal at cross-country events.

One of the few international athletes who have put something back into the sport he loves, and for no financial gain, he has certainly earned his inclusion as a Cardiff sporting great.

Grand Charity Football Match

IN AID OF THE SID JUDD MEMORIAL FUND

The late Sid Judd (centre) seen after passing the ball

THE FABULOUS

SHOWBIZ XI

V.

CELEBRITIES XI

CARDIFF ARMS PARK   Thursday, May 7th 1959
Kick-off 6.30 p.m.

Souvenir Programme . . . 6d.

Programme from the 1959 charity football match arranged to raise money for the Sid Judd Memorial Fund.

SID JUDD

'The try-scorer for both Cardiff and Wales against the 1953 All Blacks'
by Gwyn Prescott

On a dull November day in 1953, a Cardiff back-row forward seized a Gwyn Rowlands cross-kick near the All Blacks' goal-posts and crashed over for an early try. Four weeks later, the same player, now wearing a Welsh jersey, pounced on a loose New Zealand pass several metres out and again burst over the line to score in exactly the same place. Thereafter, 'Sid's spot' marked the position where Sid Judd scored both his crucial tries in the historic victories by Cardiff and Wales over the 1953/54 All Blacks.

A robust, aggressive and yet skilful forward, Sid was always particularly dangerous with the ball near the goal line. He was a prolific scorer of tries for a forward, grabbing 45 in his career for Cardiff, and he was also a very useful goal-kicker. A big man with a big personality, he was the life and soul of the club. To his teammates he seemed indestructible.

Sid Judd was born in Adamsdown in 1928 and learned his rugby just down the road at Cardiff High School. After playing for the Welsh Secondary Schools, he joined Cardiff and he made his First XV debut in December 1946 when aged only eighteen. He went on to represent the club another 183 times. Like many other local footballers, during the summer months Sid kept himself fit by playing baseball, and he became a familiar figure on the city's public parks with Roath Labour

For several years, his appearances for Cardiff were restricted while he was taking a teacher training course at Trinity College, Carmarthen. However, from 1949/50 onwards, he became a Cardiff regular and was a member of the XV who were narrowly robbed of victory over the 1950/51 Springboks by poor refereeing.

Sid quickly evolved into one of the most promising forwards of his era. Cliff Morgan described him as 'majestic' and a 'phenomenal worker', whilst Bleddyn Williams wrote that Cardiff would not have defeated New Zealand without his 'magnificent effort' as vice-captain and pack-leader.

He was first capped against England in 1953 and was virtually an automatic choice until the Scottish match of 1955, after which his health began to deteriorate. During that time, he won ten caps and was on the winning side on seven occasions. It was widely believed that, had it not been for his illness, Sid would have gone on to win many more caps and would have become one of the all-time great forwards of Welsh rugby. Regarded by the 1953/54 All Blacks as the best no.8 they had faced, he was expected to gain selection for the British Lions tour to South Africa in the summer of 1955.

His illness that year came as a great shock. He was captain of Cardiff in 1954/55 and under his leadership the club made a wonderful start, remaining unbeaten in their first 22 matches. Sid made 24 appearances, during which time he scored seven tries and kicked 23 goals, but his condition prevented him from continuing in the second half of the season.

Sid Judd tragically died of leukaemia aged only thirty in 1959. Such was the measure of the enormous regard and affection in which he was held that several special events were staged at the Arms Park in his memory, including a Showbiz *v.* Celebrities soccer match, and a game between Cardiff Past and Present. His untimely death robbed Cardiff and Wales of an outstanding player.

NIGEL WALKER

'Athlete and rugby winger for Cardiff and Wales'
by John Billot

What an outrageously inappropriate surname, as Nigel Walker seemed as swift as any gazelle and just as graceful. But not just as a speedster on the athletics track, since Nigel showed in playing rugby for Cardiff and Wales that he possessed the elusive qualities of the classic wing. It was not his style to leap about like Jackie Chan – not for Nigel either the wild farrago of stuttering steps, but instead the gliding stride of the trained athlete. Indeed, in his heyday as an athlete he worked out with fellow Cardiff sporting great and Welsh superstar of the track Colin Jackson, with Nigel competing in the semi-final of the 110-metre hurdles at the 1984 Olympics in Los Angeles.

Indeed, Cardiff-born Nigel was one of Britain's leading high hurdlers, representing Great Britain on 32 occasions between 1983 and 1992. Besides being an Olympian, he also participated in World and European Championships, placing fourth in the final of the 1986 Europeans. In 1987, he took the 60-metre hurdles bronze medal in both the European and World Indoor Championships. Nigel was UK high hurdles champion in 1983, and won the Welsh title three times. He also won 16 Welsh international vests, reaching the final in both the 1986 and 1990 Commonwealth Games. But in 1992 he decided to retire from athletics and take up a second sporting career by joining Cardiff RFC. This move proved so successful that within two years, he was helping the club win the Welsh National League title for 1993/94.

Nigel made his debut in a Welsh rugby shirt at the age of twenty-nine against Ireland at the Arms Park in 1993 – a game that the visitors won 19-14. The selectors had worried over

Nigel Walker safely gathers the ball. (*Western Mail and Echo*)

their choices for more than seven hours following the 20-0 defeat by Scotland at Murrayfield, and eventually they made just one change – opting for Nigel on the wing, where he joined a three-quarter line comprising sleekly sinister Ieuan Evans on the right wing, plus Mike Hall and Scott Gibbs in the centre.

The former Rumney schoolboy flashed at breakneck pace across the rugby scene for five years, figuring in all in 17 games for Wales and scoring 12 tries – four of them in one game. But his most memorable try was the one that helped Cardiff win the Swalec Cup 33-26 against Swansea in 1997. He had to cover some fifty yards with only a mousehole in front of him. To score a try, a miracle was needed, but Nigel made it, and all with covering defenders hurtling towards him – no-one has scored a more thrilling solo try in cup finals.

At the time, I wrote in the *Rugby Annual for Wales*:

It was the great goodbye try in the final match at the much-loved and historic Cardiff Arms Park before the demolition squads moved in to their deadly work and destroy a great sporting venue. One day, those responsible will have to answer to the ghosts of the famous players who paraded their skills there! Those same ghosts one day will embrace Nigel Walker with delight because his try will be talked about for a hundred, or even two hundred, years in heaven and earth!

Nigel was tagged 'the fastest wing in the world' when Wales first chose him, and he displayed his running qualities in his second appearance as he scored a splendid try – the first by a Welshman in Paris for ten years – but the season ended with Ieuan Evans' team winning the wooden spoon, with their only success coming in the opening fixture against England – before Nigel had caught the selectors' eyes – when Ieuan chased a wide chip from the perceptive Emyr Lewis and whizzed past the sleepy Rory Underwood to score a shock try and seal events 10-9.

Injury forced Nigel to withdraw from the summer tour to Zimbabwe and Namibia, but the Cardiff-born sprinter was back on the left wing in October 1993 as Wales overwhelmed Japan 55-5 with no less than nine tries, with the first just forty-five seconds after kick-off as Ieuan

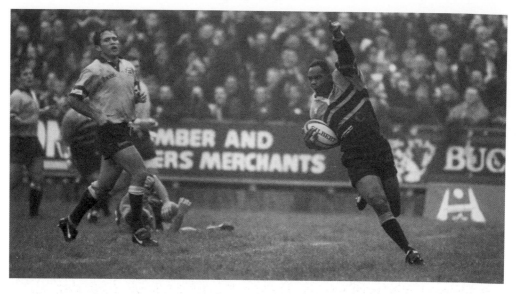

Nigel Walker celebrates scoring another try for Cardiff. (*Western Mail and Echo*)

swooped over the line again. The following month, Nigel was in the side that went down to a shock 26-24 defeat to Canada, but after Christmas, the selectors kept faith with the Cardiff winger for the Five Nations opener against Scotland – a game in which Wales triumphed 29-6. Nigel had to depart for repairs and the replacement Mike Rayer – his Cardiff clubmate – normally a steadfast full-back, snapped up two tries on the wing.

Nigel returned for the visit by France and he celebrated with a try, thanks to a smart pass from Scott Quinnell, as Wales won 24-15 to set up a Grand Slam chance at Twickenham. However, Ieuan's men failed 15-8 as England won the contest. Nevertheless, Nigel's try still clinched the Championship for Wales, as this was the first season when it was decided by match points.

Then it was on to Lisbon for a World Cup qualifier against Portugal, and a match in which Nigel stormed away to score four of the 16 tries as Wales won by the record margin of 102-11. His feat equalled those of four other Welsh internationals, including Reggie Gibbs in 1908 and Maurice Richards in 1969, both fellow Cardiff players, and Willie Llewellyn in 1899 and Ieuan Evans in 1987. Four days later, Nigel was on the scoresheet once again as he skipped across the line in Wales' 54-0 victory over Spain in Madrid in the second qualifying match for the World Cup.

But as well as featuring in some comprehensive victories whilst proudly wearing the scarlet jersey, Nigel also took part in some nail-biting victories, including a couple of scary moments in the summer of 1997 during Wales' visit to North America. The flying winger added to his tally of tries in the opening 30-20 victory over the United States in North Carolina, but the other internationals were a lot closer, with Wales gaining a narrow 28-23 win over the Eagles in the second Test, followed by a 28-25 success over Canada in Toronto.

Nigel was on the scoresheet again in August 1997 as Wales visited North Wales to play against Romania at Wrexham's football ground – a game that saw Nigel come on as a replacement for Llanelli's Wayne Procter, and score a try as Wales won 70-21. He was restored to the starting line-up for Wales' first full cap match at Swansea for forty-three years, as Wales beat Tonga 46-12 at St Helen's with the Cardiff man scoring another good try. Thirteen days later he pounced once again for Wales' only try against New Zealand at Wembley Stadium – a game that saw the All Blacks continue their fine run against Wales by running out victors 42-7, and their winning margin would have been greater had it not been for two try-saving tackles by Nigel on the speedy Jeff Wilson.

Nigel's illustrious sporting career was abruptly and cruelly ended at Twickenham in 1998 as he dislocated his right shoulder after only four minutes of the match against England – a contest that ended in a heavy defeat for his Welsh colleagues as England ran in eight tries to win 60-26. It was an injury that ended his rugby career, but it did not mark an end to his involvement in sport, as Nigel soon became immersed in his new career as an administrator at the Sports Council for Wales and then becoming BBC Wales' Head of Sport in 2001. He has also recently been appointed to the board of UK Sport.

Nigel will always be remembered as one of the quickest wingers to ever wear a Welsh rugby jersey. He certainly was fast – so was legendary quick-draw gunfighter 'Wild Bill' Hickock, and like 'Wild Bill', Nigel regularly left a trail of opponents for dead on the rugby fields of Cardiff and Wales.

THE MILLENNIUM STADIUM
by Gwyn Prescott

When a group of young blades began playing 'football' on a piece of open ground near the centre of Cardiff in the late 1860s, they could not possibly have imagined that they were beginning a process which would eventually lead to that frequently waterlogged pasture becoming, 130 years later, the focus of worldwide media attention. But, with the arrival of the 1999 Rugby World Cup and in 2001 the FA Cup final, this little piece of Wales has become familiar to millions around the globe.

In 1995 the WRU, who by then owned the site, won the right to host the Rugby World Cup. The National Stadium, however, had been built for an earlier era. It was showing its age and could only accommodate 53,000. The bold decision was taken, therefore, to replace it with a modern, multi-purpose, state-of-the-art building. The scheme cost £126 million and this was funded by the National Lottery, ticket debentures and loans, the latter leaving the WRU in substantial debt.

Demolition work began immediately after the last game in the old stadium on 26 April 1997. Appropriately, this occasion saw Cardiff RFC lift the WRU Cup for the seventh time with a 33-26 victory over Swansea, whom they had first played (and defeated) in their then guise of Glamorgan FC, on the very same pitch in January 1875. The plans for the new stadium involved the complete realignment of the playing area so, as well as the National Stadium, the famous old pitch would also disappear.

Since the site is in the heart of a busy city centre, the developers had to contend with severe access and operating restrictions in both the demolition and the construction phases. There was also the added difficulty of incorporating Britain's first retractable roof in a sports stadium. Nevertheless, just over two years later, the first match at the new sporting venue took place on 26 June 1999, when Wales recorded their first ever victory over South Africa, in a partially completed stadium. By October 1999, the Millennium Stadium was ready in time for the launch of the Rugby World Cup. This remarkable achievement is regularly ignored by many in the media who criticise Britain's seeming inability to complete sports development projects on time.

With a capacity of 74,500, the new stadium was the largest sporting venue in Britain until eventually overtaken by Old Trafford in 2006. It is now a popular venue for the promotion of many sports besides rugby. The first Welsh football international was played there in March 2000, when Finland were the opponents and when a record attendance for a home Welsh soccer match was recorded. The redevelopment of Wembley has also enabled the Millennium Stadium to play host to many major football finals, including the most important of them all, of course, the FA Cup final. Amongst other major sporting events to have visited the stadium are the Rugby League Challenge Cup final, Grand Prix speedway, World Rally Championships, World Championship boxing and indoor cricket. Since 1999, such events, together with a variety of musical concerts, have brought huge

numbers of new visitors to the city who cannot have failed to have been impressed by what Cardiff has to offer.

The Millennium Stadium, situated in the middle of a thriving city centre, is a highly visible statement about the importance of sport in the life of Cardiff and Wales. Besides acting as a tangible barometer for the state of the nation, it is a building in which all sportsmen and women in Cardiff can take pride. Perhaps, therefore, we should offer up a little thanks to those Victorian sports enthusiasts who long ago set the whole thing rolling.

MATTHEW MAYNARD

'Glamorgan's batting legend who led them to the 1997 county title'
by Andrew Hignell

Born in Lancashire and raised in North Wales, Matthew Maynard has lived in Cardiff since the mid-1980s, during which time he became one of the greatest and most entertaining batsmen in Glamorgan's history, scoring more hundreds for the county than any other player.

After a brief spell on the staff of Kent, Matthew burst onto the world of cricket in 1985 with a remarkable debut hundred against Yorkshire at Swansea, with the nineteen-year-old reaching his century with three successive straight sixes. This was the first of 54 first-class hundreds he scored for Glamorgan between 1985 and 2005 and, in the course of his glittering career, the right-handed batsman broke the club record, previously held by Alan Jones and Hugh Morris.

Right: Matthew Maynard displays his batting talents for a special photo shoot at Cardiff in 1991.

Opposite: Welsh heartbeats are set racing in the Millennium Stadium as Max Boyce, Charlotte Church and Kathryn Jenkins sing the national anthem.

Matthew achieved this with a century against Leicestershire in 2004 at Sophia Gardens and, by a strange quirk of fate, the umpire standing at the bowler's end was Peter Hartley who had been playing for Yorkshire at Swansea when Matthew had made his glorious debut.

Initially headstrong and impetuous, Matthew learnt to mix his attacking flair with more measured strokeplay and, amongst others on the Glamorgan staff, he greatly benefited from the presence of West Indian batting maestro Viv Richards in the Welsh county's batting line-up in the early 1990s. The sorcerer and his apprentice shared several partnerships when they put opposing bowlers to the sword and, after Viv retired in 1993 – with a Sunday League champions medal in his pocket – Matthew tormented county sides the length and breadth of England with some withering assaults on their bowling in both Championship and limited-overs cricket. This brought a total of 24,799 runs in all first-class cricket, plus a tally of 13,506 runs in major one-day games.

There were many highlights during his twenty-one-year career, but head and shoulders above these was leading Glamorgan to the county title in 1997, with Matthew scoring a match-winning century against Somerset at Taunton which clinched the title for his team. It was a display of vintage batting, with the Glamorgan captain reaching his hundred without scoring any singles, treating the Somerset attack with complete disdain, and all in quite murky conditions. Commentators described it as one of the finest innings that they had ever seen him play and, a week or so later, Matthew led his team on an open-top bus tour around the city centre, proudly showing off the county title.

As far as one-day cricket was concerned, the undoubted highlight of Matthew's career was leading the side out in June 2000 at Lord's in the final of the Benson and Hedges Cup – Glamorgan's first appearance in a knock-out cup final since 1977. Although they lost to Gloucestershire, it was a red letter day for Matthew as he won the Man of the Match Award for a magnificent hundred, in which he displayed his class and finesse as a batsman and against an attack that was regarded as the finest at the time in one-day cricket.

Matthew proudly displays the 1997 County Championship Trophy.

He also created a unique record by becoming the first batsman in the history of one-day cricket to have scored a century in both the final and the semi-final of the competition as, a few weeks earlier at Cardiff, Matthew had led from the front and had clinched a place in the final for his side, with a typically destructive 109 against Surrey, as well as showing great tactical acumen as the visitors attempted to chase 245 against the Glamorgan attack.

He was also a member of the Glamorgan side that won the one-day league titles in 1993, 2002 and 2004, and his outstanding batting and astute captaincy played a major part in what many people believe to have been the greatest era in the Welsh county's history. His efforts were also recognised, albeit a little belatedly, by the England selectors, with Matthew winning four Test caps and appearing in 14 one-day internationals.

Matthew is now England's batting coach – working alongside head coach Duncan Fletcher, with whom he formed a close bond whilst leading Glamorgan to the county title in 1997 – and it was in this coaching capacity that Matthew was at the England–Pakistan one-day international in August 2006 at Sophia Gardens – the scene of so many of his thrilling and brilliant innings.

JOHNNY WILLIAMS

'Arms Park favourite and Mametz Wood hero'
by Gwyn Prescott

Of all the rugby players celebrated in this book, John Lewis Williams is probably one of the least well known. Yet in his day, he was a highly-regarded member of one of the most successful Welsh teams of all time. As the *South Wales Daily News* put it, he was 'a great footballer… and a universal favourite with the crowd'. That his story is worthy of being retold to a modern audience was confirmed by a recent HTV documentary, *The First XV*, which included an account of his life.

Born in Whitchurch in 1882, he was discovered by Newport officials when playing on the wing for his village team and thus he became one of the surprisingly large number of men who have worn both black and amber as well as blue and black. Aged only seventeen when he joined Newport in 1899/1900, his first-class career was to span fifteen seasons. After four years at Newport, Johnny (or Johnnie – the spelling varies) began to find the travelling irksome so, in 1903/04, he transferred to his home-town club. It was to be a long and happy association, involving eleven seasons and 199 games, as well as the captaincy in 1909/10. His total of 150 tries for Cardiff was not surpassed for nearly forty years and it took a player of Bleddyn Williams' calibre to do it.

In 1905/06, Cardiff enjoyed perhaps their greatest ever season – they lost only once to the All Blacks – and their winger Johnny Williams was in fine form, heading the list of try-scorers with 35 touchdowns. He played in numerous spectacular club victories, none more so than in those over the 1906/07 South Africans and the 1908/09 Australians. Johnny was famous for his inward swerve from the touch line and also for his clever sidestep which he used to great effect in the 17-0 defeat of the Springboks when he left their full-back for dead and scored wide out.

He played on the wing for Wales 17 times between 1906/07 and 1910/11. Such was the strength of Welsh rugby at the time, Johnny was only ever on the losing side twice and he played in three Grand Slam seasons. His strike rate for Wales was quite exceptional, averaging a try a match. Only one man has ever bettered this and that was his Cardiff contemporary, Reggie Gibbs, who scored 17 tries in 16 internationals. Johnny also went on the 1908 Lions (Anglo-Welsh) tour to Australasia, where he played in two of the three Test matches and finished the tour as the leading try-scorer.

His last game for Cardiff was in 1913/14 but he was to appear at the Arms Park just once more, a little over a year later. Johnny enlisted as soon as the First World War broke out and in late 1914 he was commissioned in the 16th Battalion Welsh Regiment. This was the renowned Cardiff City Battalion in which many local sportsmen served, including five rugby internationals. Sport contributed in other ways too and both Cardiff RFC and Cardiff City FC donated full sets of kit to the battalion for inter-platoon matches. Just before going overseas in 1915, the 16th Welsh returned to their home city for one last time to visit loved ones. There was only one suitable place for the thousand-strong battalion to parade before a large and admiring audience of relatives and friends, and that was the field on which Captain J.L. Williams had in the past performed so frequently in front of his adoring fans. It is doubtful whether even the Arms Park has ever witnessed a more emotional scene as the battalion was given its send-off.

Not many months later, the City Battalion was on the Somme, and there it spearheaded the attack on Mametz Wood, which was eventually captured by the 38th (Welsh) Division after several days of desperate fighting. On the morning of 7 July 1916, attacking down a slope, they were met by withering machine-gun fire from the menacing wood which was heavily defended by the Germans. The City Battalion were also caught by machine-guns located in another wood on their right flank. The covering smoke which was promised had not materialised. The attacking troops stood little chance. With around 150 killed and twice as many wounded, approximately half of the battalion became casualties. Amongst these was Captain J.L. Williams who, when leading his company towards the wood, was severely wounded. Taken to a casualty clearing station, his left leg had to be amputated. A few days later, his wife of just eighteen months received the fateful telegram informing her that he had succumbed to his wounds.

Sportsmen and women of all persuasions and abilities dominate the lists of the thousands of Cardiffians who have lost their lives in war over the last century. Even the most cursory examination of the casualty lists in the local press during both the First and Second World

Wars will confirm this: footballers, cricketers, baseballers, athletes, cyclists, golfers, tennis players, boxers, oarsmen, hockey players and swimmers, they are all found there.

This should cause us to wonder, then, how many potential Cardiff greats have been lost to us because they gave their lives in war. Johnny Williams' story reminds us just how much later generations of sportsmen and sportswomen owe to their sacrifice.

GARETH BALE

'The next sporting great from Cardiff'
by Andrew Hignell

Born in Cardiff on 16 July 1989, Gareth Bale has been hailed as 'Welsh football's wonderkid' after becoming the country's youngest ever international, pulling on the Welsh jersey for the first time when just sixteen years and 315 days old.

Educated at Eglwys Newydd Junior School, and Whitchurch High School, Gareth showed outstanding prowess at a number of sports. Whilst at Whitchurch, he began training with Southampton's satellite academy in Bath, and was so good with his left foot that at school, his PE master had to write special rules for the youngster, allowing him to only play one-touch football and not use his deadly left foot.

On 17 April 2006 Gareth made his first-team debut for Southampton, and soon developed a growing reputation as a free-kick specialist. Within a few weeks, he was awarded his first cap for Wales against Trinidad and Tobago, and later in the year, was the winner of the BBC Wales Young Sports Personality of the Year.

Who knows what further honours lie ahead for the gifted left-back recently valued at £10 million and the subject of transfer speculation involving Tottenham Hotspur and Manchester United?

LECKWITH STADIUM: THE NEW SPORTING BASE FOR THE CITY
by Andrew Hignell

During the 1980s there were calls for a new purpose-built athletics stadium in Cardiff, and with the continued demise of Maindy Stadium, Cardiff AAC moved in 1989 to the more modern complex at Leckwith Stadium on the south-western outskirts of the city.

The new stadium was a fitting host for the Welsh Games and other major events during the 1990s, but a new chapter in the sporting history of Cardiff now begins with the move by Cardiff AAC to a new athletics complex on the opposite side of the road to the old site, with the Leckwith stadium being completely redeveloped as the new base for both Cardiff City FC and the Cardiff Blues regional rugby team.

It will be the first major sporting complex in the city not to have a direct link – in either name or location – to the Bute Estate and it is here, at the state-of-the-art complex, along with the sports village planned in Cardiff Bay, where some of the next generation of Cardiff sporting greats will hone their talents.

CONTRIBUTORS

John Billot – the former Sports Editor of the *Western Mail* and a well-known author on Welsh rugby.

Andrew Hignell – the archivist and historian of Glamorgan Cricket, and the author of several books on the county's history and players.

Russell Holden – a lecturer from the Humanities Department at UWIC, and the author of several papers on sports politics.

Steve James – the former Glamorgan batsman and captain, who is now a journalist covering cricket and rugby for *The Guardian* and *The Sunday Telegraph*.

Gareth Jones – the Cardiff based journalist who is a leading authority on the world of boxing.

Brian Lee – an expert on the local history of Cardiff, and the author of several books on both the city and horse racing.

Grahame Lloyd – the football writer and broadcaster, whose works have included *C'mon City! A Hundred Years of the Bluebirds*.

Dennis Morgan – the well-known author of many books on the history of Cardiff, and an enthusiastic supporter of Cardiff City and Glamorgan Cricket.

David Parry-Jones – the distinguished rugby writer and broadcaster who wrote *Taffs Acre: History and Celebration of Cardiff Arms Park* and *Prince Gwyn: Gwyn Nicholls and the First Golden Era of Welsh Rugby*.

Gwyn Prescott – university lecturer and a historian of rugby in Cardiff.

Huw Richards – the rugby correspondent of *The Financial Times* and a leading authority on the history of rugby.

Don Shepherd – the former Glamorgan bowler who took over 2,000 wickets for the county, and who is now a writer and broadcaster on the game.

Richard Shepherd – the writer and broadcaster who is Cardiff City's distinguished historian.

Peter Walker – the former England and Glamorgan cricketer who is a well-known broadcaster and writer.

Andrew Weltch – the Cardiff-based writer whose interests include speedway, ice hockey and baseball.

Clive Williams – the historian of Welsh athletics, and a leading authority on track and field events.

Gareth Williams – the professor of Welsh History at the University of Glamorgan, whose many works include the highly acclaimed *Fields of Praise: The Official History of the Welsh Rugby Union 1881-1981*.

Alun Wyn Bevan – the well-known writer and broadcaster on Welsh sport, and former rugby referee.

SIGNIFICANT DATES IN CARDIFF'S HISTORY

by Dennis Morgan

Approximately AD 55: The first of the four Roman forts was built by the River Taff.

1090s: Following his conquest of the region, Robert Fitzhamon established Cardiff as the administrative centre of Glamorgan.

1404: Owain Glyndwr ransacked the town of Cardiff, laying parts of it to waste for more than 100 years.

6 September 1538: After serving Cardiff for nearly 300 years, the Greyfriars and the Blackfriars were abolished on the orders of Henry VIII.

8 May 1648: The Battle of St Fagans ended in defeat for the Royalists and brought the Civil War to an end in Wales.

10 February 1794: The Glamorganshire Canal was opened to link Cardiff with Merthyr, the iron capital of the world.

1801: The first official census revealed that the population of Cardiff was 1,870.

8 October 1839: The Bute West Dock was opened, paving the way for Cardiff to become the greatest coal exporting port in the world.

1850: While building the South Wales Railway, Brunel altered the course of the Taff to end centuries of catastrophic flooding.

1850: T.W. Rammell's report revealed the appalling state of Cardiff's public health and led to widespread reforms in creating a healthier town.

1875: Cardiff's boundaries were extended to include Roath, Splott, Cathays, Canton and Grangetown.

21 October 1883: University College Cardiff was officially opened on the site of the former infirmary in Newport Road.

20 June 1894: Roath Park was opened by the third Marquess of Bute and his son, the Earl of Dumfries.

23 October 1905: Cardiff became a city by royal decree.

13 July 1907: The Queen Alexandra Dock was opened by Edward VII and Queen Alexandra.

15 June 1910: Captain Scott sailed from Cardiff on his fateful journey to the Antarctic.

12 June 1928: The Prince of Wales unveiled the Welsh National War Memorial in Queen Alexandra Gardens, Cathays Park.

2 January 1941: Llandaff Cathedral was severely damaged during the worst air raid of the war on Cardiff.

20 December 1955: Cardiff became the capital of Wales.

September 1988: The County Hall opened in Cardiff Bay – the first step in the rejuvenation of this historic district of Cardiff.

1 March 2006: On St David's Day, the Queen officially opened the Senedd, the award-winning Welsh National Assembly building.

SIGNIFICANT DATES IN CARDIFF'S SPORTING HISTORY

by Dennis Morgan

July 1819: The *Carmarthen Journal* reports the formation of a cricket club in Cardiff.

5 May 1845: Cardiff Cricket Club was reformed.

6 May 1848: The first record of a cricket match being played on Cardiff Arms Park.

22 September 1876: The Cardiff Football Club, later Cardiff RFC, was formed by a merger between the Cardiff Wanderers and Glamorgan (rugby) football clubs.

21-22 June 1889: Glamorgan CCC played their first official match, losing to Warwickshire at the Cardiff Arms Park by eight wickets.

7 October 1899: Riverside AFC, the future Cardiff City, lost their opening game against Barry West End at Sophia Gardens 9-1.

16 December 1905: Wales defeated the All Blacks 3-0 in a thrilling match at the Arms Park.

1 January 1907: Cardiff recorded a stunning victory over South Africa by 17 points to nil.

4 August 1908: Wales won by a comfortable margin in the first baseball international between England and Wales at the Harlequins Ground, Cardiff.

10 February 1909: 'Peerless' Jim Driscoll outclassed Abe Atell, the featherweight champion of the world, in New York but a 'no decision' verdict meant he was never officially world champion.

1 September 1910: Cardiff City played their opening match at Ninian Park, losing 2-1 to the Football League champions, Aston Villa.

18-20 May 1921: Glamorgan entered the County Championship with a victory over Sussex by 23 runs at Cardiff Arms Park.

3 May 1924: Cardiff City failed to win the First Division Championship by 0.024 of a goal after missing a penalty at Birmingham in their final match.

3 February 1925: More than 100,000 people followed the funeral procession of Jim Driscoll as he was laid to rest in Cathays Cemetery.

23 April 1927: Cardiff City became the first club to take the FA Cup out of England after defeating Arsenal 1-0 at Wembley.

27 April 1939: Horse racing ended at Ely Racecourse after more than eighty years, as Keith Piggott on Grasshopper won the final race.

21 November 1953: Cardiff defeated New Zealand 8-3 with a fine display of attacking rugby.

18-26 July 1958: Cardiff played host to the world as it staged the Empire and Commonwealth Games.

13-16 August 1966: Glamorgan play their final County Championship match at the Arms Park prior to the creation of the National Stadium.

5 September 1969: In their third season at Sophia Gardens, Glamorgan won their second County Championship after defeating Worcestershire by 147 runs.

24 October 1984: By recording their sixth successive victory over the Wallabies by 16 points to 12, Cardiff maintained their unbeaten record against Australia.

1990: The Cardiff Devils Ice Hockey team won both the Heineken Premier League and the Heineken Championship – only the second team to achieve this double.

20 August 1993: Colin Jackson's world record of 12.92 seconds in the 110-metre hurdles at the World Championships at Stuttgart was to stand for nearly thirteen years.

6 January 1996: Cardiff lost 18-21 in extra time in the final of the Heineken European Cup.

26 June 1999: As a preliminary to the World Cup, Wales beat South Africa by 29 points to 19 in the first match held at the Millennium Stadium.

12 May 2001: Liverpool defeated Arsenal 2-1 in the first FA Cup final to be staged at the Millennium Stadium.

6 June 2003: Following the reorganisation of Welsh rugby, Cardiff Blues were officially launched.

30 August 2006: England played Pakistan in a floodlight one-day international at Sophia Gardens – the first major one-day international in the Welsh capital city.

2009 and beyond: England play Australia in an Ashes Test at Glamorgan's redeveloped headquarters in Cardiff in July 2009; Cardiff City FC and the Cardiff Blues play for the first time at their new ground in Leckwith; and in 2012 Cardiff hosts teams and stages events for the London Olympics.

INDEX

CREU CYNNWYS
CONTENT CREATION

As a Cardiff based company, we have taken great delight in the sporting successes of our city over the years, many of which are featured in this book.

We are very pleased to be able to continue our support of sporting excellence in Cardiff.

·rning Resources
Centre

Multimedia Production

North Chambers Castle Arcade Cardiff CF10 1BX
email. info@cc4.co.uk **Tel.** 02920 664485

www.cc4.co.uk